Cars, Energy,
Nuclear Diplomacy,
and the Law

For Bob Lonergan —
Friend + colleague,
With admiration + regard,

J.T.

7/16

Cars, Energy, Nuclear Diplomacy, and the Law

A Reflective Memoir of Three Generations

JOHN THOMAS SMITH II

ROWMAN & LITTLEFIELD PUBLISHERS, INC.

Lanham • Boulder • New York • Toronto • Plymouth, UK

Published by Rowman & Littlefield Publishers, Inc.
A wholly owned subsidiary of The Rowman & Littlefield Publishing Group, Inc.
4501 Forbes Boulevard, Suite 200, Lanham, Maryland 20706
www.rowman.com

10 Thornbury Road, Plymouth PL6 7PP, United Kingdom

British Library Cataloguing in Publication Information Available

Library of Congress Cataloging-in-Publication Data

Smith, John Thomas, 1943–
   Cars, energy, nuclear diplomacy, and the law : a reflective memoir of three generations / John
Thomas Smith II.
      p. cm.
   ISBN 978-1-4422-2011-9 (cloth : alk. paper) — ISBN 978-1-4422-2012-6 (ebook)
   1. Smith, John Thomas, 1943– 2. Smith, Gerard C. 3. Smith, John Thomas, 1879–1947.
   4. Lawyers—United States—Biography. 5. Businessmen—United States—Biography. I. Title.
   KF373.S5697S65 2012
   340.092'273—dc23
                                                                          2012020656

∞™ The paper used in this publication meets the minimum requirements of
American National Standard for Information Sciences—Permanence of Paper for
Printed Library Materials, ANSI/NISO Z39.48-1992.

Printed in the United States of America

For Connor and Abigail

Contents

Preface

I began this short book for my three sons: John Thomas Smith III, William Gerard Smith, and Benjamin Tydings Smith, with the purpose of capturing the historical footprints and the personalities of certain of their progenitors including John Thomas Smith, William George Maguire, and especially my father, Gerard C. Smith. As a secondary matter, I planned to include some personal reflections and autobiographical materials. It was my hope that my three sons—and perhaps their children or grandchildren—would benefit from knowledgeable reflection upon the "lives" sketched in this small volume. As I progressed, friends suggested that my writings might benefit a somewhat broader audience, and that I should include rather more autobiography than I originally intended.

At the outset, I must note that all three of my sons have other, highly distinguished "ancestors" on the side of their respective mothers. In John and Will's case, there is a great-great-grandfather, Levi Mayer, a lawyer in Chicago and founder, in 1881, of one of the nation's preeminent law firms, now known as Mayer & Brown. John and Will knew his extraordinary daughter, Hortense Hirsh, who lived a rich and long life, extending beyond a century. Similarly, Ben's great-great-grandfather, Joseph Davies, as a young lawyer helped elect Woodrow Wilson and served on the Federal Trade Commission, and later was U.S. Ambassador to the Soviet Union and to Belgium. Ben knew well his great-grandmother, Eleanor Davies Tydings Ditzen, who died at the age of 102, when Ben was 19. Both Ben's great-grandfather, Millard Tydings, and his grandfather, Joseph Tydings, were U.S. Senators. These distinguished relatives on my sons' mothers' sides probably could provide a more colorful record than the Smith relatives chronicled in this book. Nevertheless, I have left it to others to profile these exceptional individuals,[1] and I stick closely to the side of the family that I know the best.

This book is not a conventional biography or memoir. It does not contain extensive detail of the remarkable careers of my father and grandfathers. The former wrote three books, and each of the latter is the principal subject of a book. I direct my sons and heirs to these volumes by drawing upon them in broadest outline. Instead, this book strives to combine biographical perceptions with reflections on the issues and events in their careers sketched herein.

This book is a "reflective memoir" in two respects. The first and obvious one is reflective opinion of the author on the significance of the characters, careers and events described in the book. The second and more important type of reflections are the ways in which the attributes and accomplishments of each generation may be mirrored by subsequent and still future generations.

I wish my sons, as well as their children and grandchildren, the opportunity to live good productive and even "virtuous" lives. Their prospects are good. They are part of a family of considerable accomplishment. They are, or will be, citizens of a powerful, free, and wealthy country. Nonetheless, consideration of the examples described in the book may further stimulate them in pursuit of fulfilling lives—in a world not without its terrors.

This book could not have been completed without superb help from Von Maddox and Judy Curtis, two of Covington & Burling's finest office assistants, who patiently and expertly transcribed my dictation and drafts. Similarly, I owe a great debt to my friend Mary Carpenter, an accomplished author in her own right, who took the time to comment on an early draft text and furnished me invaluable organizational guidance. Finally, I must thank my "Irish twin" sister, Sheila, who diligently read the entire manuscript and furnished welcome insights on tone and content.

J. T. Smith II
Easton, Maryland, 2012

Introduction

The world faces several, closely interrelated global challenges, with which the lives sketched in this book have been closely intertwined. The first arises from the growing awareness that we must take major measures to reduce emissions of carbon dioxide and other so-called greenhouse gases to mitigate potential worldwide climate change. This challenge is daunting in light of our "automotive" economy and our reliance on burning coal for a major portion of our electric needs. Second is the grave danger that accompanies the continued proliferation of the capacity to make and potentially to deploy and use nuclear weapons. This second danger is related to the first since nuclear power generation may be the most practical means to reduce emission of gases that may cause global climate change; but the nuclear power generation "fuel cycle" can enable proliferation of nuclear weapons. These dangers are amplified by a clash of values and interests between the so-called Judeo-Christian West and those of the broad arc of Islam extending from Africa through the Middle East, South Asia, and into the Far East. Islamic states control a significant portion of the world's hydrocarbons on which our society presently depends. One Islamic country (Pakistan) already has nuclear weapons and another (Iran) appears to be developing such capabilities.

As will be shown, both of my grandfathers unwittingly contributed to the problem of climate change. Both were active and successful participants in the vast industrial growth of the United States in the first half of the 20th century. My father's father, John Thomas Smith, after whom I am named, was a brilliant lawyer who helped create and nurture the General Motors Corporation, the predominant automotive manufacturer on the planet in

1

the 20th century. My mother's father, William George Maguire, was a pioneer in bringing a fossil fuel—natural gas—from Texas and Oklahoma to the industrial centers of the Midwest.

Due to the considerable success of his father, my father, Gerard Smith, was able to dedicate most of his professional life to public service pertaining to the interrelations of nuclear power and nuclear weapons. In a short memoir, completed in 1994, he concluded, "the risk of nuclear proliferation is the most serious danger facing the planet."[2] Although my grandfathers had nothing to do with the emerging clash of Islam and the West, their contributions to industrialization and to an automotively based economy increased our national dependence on hydrocarbons, which in turn intensifies the significance of the present cultural collision. And acquisition of nuclear weapons by Islamic terrorists would realize my father's worst fears. In considerable measure an unhealthy dependence on petroleum may be mitigated by expanded use of natural gas and increased reliance on nuclear power.

The "privileges of birth" accorded me by these distinguished progenitors allowed me to pursue exceptional public service opportunities in five cabinet departments and the Central Intelligence Agency before settling down to a law career in private practice at Covington & Burling, a very fine firm used by both my father and my grandfather. My public and private career touched upon many of the matters central to my father's and grandfathers' lives, including international negotiations, nuclear weapons, nuclear energy matters, the European Union, as well as national and international energy and environmental policies. Throughout my personal and professional life, I have benefited from the examples of my father and grandfathers.

This book does not simply highlight career milestones. It tries to capture the personalities, habits, and values of the individuals it describes. In aid of this purpose it contains a number of short reflections, or digressions, on such topics as religion, sex, nuclear weapons, alcohol, and reading.

Although much of this book focuses on my life and that of my father, I begin by introducing my two grandfathers, for their respective careers and personalities underpin the generational reflections that follow. John Thomas Smith and William George Maguire were dissimilar in education, temperament, manners, and outlook. Yet, on one occasion my mother commented to me that the reason she and my father were so compatible in a life-long marriage was that they both came from remarkably similar roots. Her comment is cause for reflection before I turn to a description of their respective careers.

Indeed, both my grandfathers were descendants of Irish refugees from the potato famine in the middle of the 19th century. Both were imbued with a strong drive for personal and financial success. As a result, both played important roles, and gained substantial fortunes, in the emergence of industries crucial to the growth of the United States in the first half of the 20th century.

More strikingly, both achieved initial success through friendship and collaboration with highly colorful financial speculators. Both survived and even flourished after the downfall of these creative, financially reckless individuals. The success of both was materially aided by members of the duPont family. As an avocation, both were extensive readers. Finally, both men came to reside in luxurious circumstances in Manhattan and on the South Shore of Long Island, John Thomas Smith in Southampton and Will Maguire in East Hampton.

There were, nonetheless, serious differences between the two men. John Thomas Smith was deeply educated and highly intellectual. Will Maguire had little formal education. John Thomas Smith was a life-long practicing Catholic, while Will Maguire had scant interest in religion. My Smith grandfather remained married to the same woman, a childhood sweetheart, friend and cousin, from 1910 until her death in 1943. Will Maguire divorced my grandmother (when divorce was more scandalous than it is today) and married his secretary. John Thomas Smith was somewhat shy, unfailingly polite, and disciplined in manner and practice. Will Maguire was of rougher demeanor. In 1949 he earned notice in *Fortune* magazine as a "fighting, feuding, litigious Irishman."[3] Family and colleagues feared the former's intellect but not his manner. In Will Maguire's case, family and colleagues respected his acumen, but had reason to fear his temper. The former ran a collegial legal office and delegated large responsibilities to subordinates. The latter ran a substantial business enterprise on autocratic and hierarchical lines.

There is scant record of the relationship of these two fathers-in-law in the period between my parents' marriage in August 1941 and my Smith grandfather's death six years later in September 1947. Smith lived in Manhattan and Maguire in Chicago during World War II, and both were fully occupied by their respective corporate responsibilities at General Motors and Panhandle Eastern. For most of this period, my parents lived in Washington, D.C. Nevertheless, I surmise that these two "titans" would not have gravitated to each other. Notwithstanding the similarities of their backgrounds and careers, they probably were mutually aware of their very different characters. An entry in my father's diary adverts, without elaboration, to the "huge difference between the two men," and mentions a luncheon meeting of my two grandfathers in 1941, implying but not stating that the event was not a success. (Here and elsewhere throughout this book, I rely on a highly candid, unpublished journal that my father created in late 1986 and early 1987, while he kept company with my mother during her fatal struggle with abdominal cancer. This stream-of-conscious diary has no chronological or other organization. When handing it to me, shortly before he died, my father commented, "Here is the full story." It has proved a valuable resource in preparation of this book.)

My father's diary also suggests that, as a young man, he found little delight in Will Maguire's company, characterizing him as a "robber baron"—I suppose in contrast to John Thomas Smith, a more "civilized" character who nonetheless achieved substantial wealth. One entry takes uncharitable satisfaction in his father-in-law's apparent trepidation during a trip on my father's sailing yacht in 1947, as the boat "heeled over" in a fresh breeze. It is likely that my father's wariness of the rough Will Maguire personality would have been shared by John Thomas Smith, although, the latter encountered many rough, self-made men in his career.

John Thomas Smith's example deeply influenced my father, and the former's wealth enabled my father to pursue a career of exceptional public service. Both their examples, in turn, have inspired me during a career in public service and the practice of law. Yet, I remain conscious of the significant influence of my mother and of Will Maguire, her father, on him and his siblings.

William George Maguire

Reversing birth order, I start with my mother's father, born seven years after John Thomas Smith. He died in 1965 when I was 21, and I have extensive memories of him. In contrast, my father's father died before my fourth birthday, and, though proud to bear his name, I have no conscious memory of him.

My vivid memories of Will Maguire reflect the fact already noted that he was a strong and colorful character. He was born in 1886 in rural Franklin Grove, Illinois, the son of Lawrence and Effie Bernice Maguire. His grandfather, William McGuire, and grandmother, Jane Myles, emigrated from Ireland in 1853. William McGuire apparently settled in Franklin Grove and worked as a blacksmith. Lawrence, who gentrified "McGuire" to "Maguire," was a lumber merchant. Will Maguire never attended college after graduation from Lewis Institute in Chicago in 1903.[4] Apparently drawn to St. Louis, Missouri, by the St. Louis World's Fair in 1904, Will Maguire determined to use his intellect and gumption to achieve the "American dream" of personal and financial success. He began as an office boy for the Burlington Railroad, where he applied a remarkable memory to learning the freight tables of all the railroads in the Midwest. In his early 20s he became a manufacturers' representative for coke, coal, steel, and pig iron companies. In this position he was able to outshine competitors by reciting freight rates from memory.

In 1908 he married Jessie Johnson, a devout Christian Scientist and talented amateur painter. Jessie, or "Ballo" as we knew her, was related collaterally to Benjamin Henry Latrobe, architect of the Capitol and other landmarks. She gave my mother the middle name "Latrobe." The young couple promptly produced four daughters: Jessie, Elizabeth, Bernice Latrobe (my mother, named after her grandmother without the "Effie"), and Zaida (named for Will Maguire's sister). Will Maguire gave his daughters the distinct impression that he had hoped for one or more sons, but it was not to be. Indeed, after divorce and remarriage in 1939 to his 29-year-old office assistant, Marian Lum, "Grandpa Maguire" in his mid-50s produced yet another daughter, my contemporary and half-aunt, Mary Anne.

In 1915, at the age of 29, "Mac" as he became known to business colleagues, helped form a company to develop a process to convert poor quality coal into coke for steel manufacture. In 1923 he became President of the St. Louis Coke and Iron Companies. In 1928 he moved from St. Louis to Chicago and incorporated his own company, W.G. Maguire and Company, to broker and develop utility properties in the Midwest. From his business endeavors in St. Louis, he had developed a good understanding of commercial and industrial activity in the Midwest. He was committed to the idea that natural gas, found in abundance in southwest Kansas, Oklahoma, and Texas, could be an efficient and cost-effective fuel for large-scale industrial plants in the Midwest, many of which were operating on "manufactured" or "coal" gas and other less desirable fuels. In early 1930, he focused on the Missouri-Kansas pipeline, which had been formed in Kansas City in 1928. The promoters of this "Mo-Kan" venture aspired to build a pipeline from southwest Kansas to Minneapolis-St. Paul and/or Chicago. The story of Will Maguire's involvement with Mo-Kan and its corporate affiliate, Panhandle Eastern Pipeline Company, is amply detailed by Christopher Castaneda and Clarance Smith in their history of Panhandle Eastern, entitled *Gas Pipelines and the Emergence of America's Regulatory State.*[5]

He was retained as a "utility consultant" in early 1930 by Frank P. Parish, who had helped organize Mo-Kan. Parish was nearly a decade younger than Maguire. A school dropout who had worked variously as a farm laborer, teamster, store clerk, machinist, and equipment broker, Parish had been in and out of personal bankruptcy before becoming, in 1927, a salesman for a pipe manufacturing firm. In this position he gained insight into natural gas supply and transport by pipeline. With more experienced partners, he began to seek financing for acquisition of natural gas distribution systems and construction of new transmission lines. In 1928–1929 he was able to raise significant capital by issuing and promoting equity at the height of the roaring 20s stock market boom. An adept stock salesman and manipulator, operating in Chicago's financial district, Parish earned the sobriquet "the boy wizard of LaSalle Street."[6]

Notwithstanding his skills in stock promotion, Parish and his partners faced formidable practical obstacles, erected by the existing Midwestern power utilities that wanted to remain in control of their sources of supply and transport of natural gas. Among his opponents were several figures who appear in American history books, including Henry Doherty, Chairman of Cities Service Company, which was then the sole supplier of natural gas to Kansas City. Also active in opposition to new sources of supply was the notorious Samuel Insull, whose empire embraced nearly 250 gas, coal, and electric companies serving nearly 5,000 communities in 50 states.[7] Other powerful opponents included Philip Gossler, Chairman of Columbia Gas & Electric Company, which controlled gas distribution in Ohio and Michigan;[8] and Christy Payne, in charge of Standard Oil's gas business. With the exception of Cities Service, these interests relied, not on natural gas, but on synthetic gas manufactured from coal gas. In aggregate these firms were the core of what became known as "the Power Trust." (In the period 1928–1935, the Federal Trade Commission, joined by the House Commerce Committee, undertook an exhaustive investigation of the activities of the Power Trust and its public utility holding companies. The resulting 97 volume report in 1935 details the early struggles of Mo-Kan and Panhandle.[9, 10]

On first meeting Frank Parish in early 1930, Will Maguire was intrigued by his proposal to build a pipeline to carry gas from the Texas Panhandle to the Midwest—initially to Minneapolis, St. Paul.[11] Parish focused on the Twin Cities, due to the interest of a significant early investor in Mo-Kan stock, Francis duPont, who had been attempting unsuccessfully to negotiate gas purchase contracts with Twin Cities Utilities. Parish placed duPont on the Mo-Kan Board in January 1930 in hopes that his illustrious name would give a good impression to the public and to financiers. (Francis duPont subsequently served on the initial Board of the Panhandle Pipeline.)

At the time, major oil companies that owned most of the gas reserves, and major utilities in industrial areas were interested in long-distance delivery of natural gas by pipeline, but aspired to conduct or control such business themselves. Nevertheless, Will Maguire, in the period March to June of 1930, obtained purchase contracts with major utilities in Illinois and Missouri and began the process of raising the then-substantial sum of $50 million with which to build a thousand-mile pipeline.[12] (A note about the changing value of money is in order. Many of the sums mentioned in this book will appear relatively modest in an era of billionaires, trillion-dollar deficits, and so forth. Historians in search of comparability look both to simple inflation adjustments, using the consumer price index [CPI] through time and to more meaningful gauges of "purchasing power" such as the relative percentage of gross domestic product [GDP] represented by certain sums. Using the CPI approach, $50 million in 1930 is the equivalent of approximately $650 million today. Using the relative percentage of GDP approach, this amount would be equivalent to $8 billion.)[13]

The Power Trust reacted harshly to these developments, organizing a series of "bear raids" on Mo-Kan stock, driving down its value. Parish in turn sought to buy shares to support its value and fell more and more deeply in debt. As construction costs mounted and revenues shrank, and with Parish deeply in debt due to market manipulations, the fledgling venture sought additional financing from a competitor, Philip Gossler of Columbia Gas & Electric. The result was that Columbia Gas obtained a controlling interest in what was to become Panhandle Eastern Pipeline Company. Columbia's interest in control was to keep the new company from success. There ensued a turbulent period involving industrial espionage against Mo-Kan and Panhandle by both Gossler and Henry Dougherty, with Columbia managing to push Mo-Kan into receivership.

Multiple lawsuits ensued, and Parish and others were indicted by a federal grand jury for mail fraud and misrepresenting the financial condition of Mo-Kan in materials sent to investors. Will Maguire, in turn, sued Parish claiming misuse of funds. At one point, Parish and a companion confronted Will Maguire at the Palmer House in Chicago and began to "pummel" him. Parish was subsequently arrested for assault.[14] Parish was ultimately acquitted in 1935 of stock fraud charges, but not prosecuted— the jury finding that he was a victim of corrupt competition by the Power Trust.[15] Nonetheless, by this time he had been removed from significant voting rights with respect to Mo-Kan. He eventually became a dairy farmer in Maryland.[16]

Throughout the 1930s, Will Maguire battled to regain control of Mo-Kan and Panhandle, on his own behalf and that of other original investors. The result was a multiyear tangle of litigation involving the Federal Trade Commission, the Securities and Exchange Commission, and the U.S. Department of Justice. During this New Deal era, Will Maguire proved himself adept at leveraging new regulations and political standards to defeat the economic strength of larger rivals.[17] His effort to wrest control of Panhandle Eastern Pipeline from Columbia Gas & Electric was significantly aided by antitrust actions brought by the U.S. Department of Justice and a parallel action brought against Columbia by Mo Kan's receivers in bankruptcy. The history of this decade-long legal and political battle is detailed in *Castaneda and Smith* in a chapter nicely titled "The Triumph of Will Maguire" and needs no repetition here.[18]

Once victory was at hand, Will Maguire confronted the further indignity of claims by dissident shareholders (including Frank Parish) that he had unduly enriched himself at these stockholders' expense. He was able to defeat this effort by showing that the leaders of the dissident group had previously stated their support for Maguire's efforts and remuneration.[19]

Panhandle did not achieve full independence until 1943—with Maguire as Chairman of its Board, a position in which he served for 22 years until his death in 1965. In the meantime, the original pipeline had been completed in the early 1930s. At the time, it was the world's longest natural gas pipeline, and Panhandle's order for steel pipe with which to construct the line was, up to that date, the largest single purchase ever made from the American steel industry. During the period 1930 until 1946, Panhandle was headquartered in Chicago. In 1946, my grandfather moved Panhandle's executive offices from Chicago to New York to be close to financial markets needed to secure capital for further expansion.[20]

Maguire spearheaded the construction of a second pipeline by a Panhandle subsidiary, the Trunkline Gas Company, to tap into the developing reserves in Louisiana and the Gulf of Mexico. This line was completed and connected with Panhandle in central Illinois in 1950. He started other new ventures. They included a joint venture with National Distillers to extract heavy hydrocarbons from the Panhandle gas stream for manufacture of petrochemicals; the establishment of the National Helium Corporation to extract helium from natural gas to supply the nation's space, defense, and scientific needs; and, notably, the creation of Anadarko Production Company in Kansas. (The latter has grown prodigiously and in 2006 acquired the Kerr-McGee Corporation for which I did extensive environmental law work in the final decade of my private practice career.)

Will Maguire's ironfisted management style was centralized and controlling. He did not delegate authority and he readily fired complaining subordinates. He remained an autocratic chief executive until he became ill and died in September of 1965 at the age of 79. According to his *New York Times* obituary, by this time Panhandle and its subsidiaries owned or controlled natural gas resources totaling 14 trillion cubic feet in Texas, Oklahoma, Kansas, Colorado, Nebraska, and Arkansas. Its 11,000 miles of pipelines supplied utilities, municipalities, and industrial users throughout the Midwest as well as in Ontario.[21]

"Grandpa Maguire"

Although a Midwesterner from birth until age 60, Will Maguire ended up living in Manhattan starting in 1946. It is in his New York incarnation that I knew him. Although housed in splendor in the River House overlooking the East River—and in the summer on the dunes of East Hampton, Long Island—"Grandpa Maguire" retained a gruff, and sometimes profane, exterior, appropriate for a self-made, Midwestern entrepreneur. Indeed, he could be somewhat intimidating to his daughters and to grandchildren. Although not a large man, he was a large presence. Not atypical for a man of his generation, he was a heavy smoker and was seldom seen without a cigar or cigarette in his hand. Indeed, it's remarkable given the now well-understood risks of smoking that Grandpa Maguire lived to the relatively ripe old age of 79. (Home movies of my parents' wedding reveal him, true to form, with a lit cigarette inside the vestibule of the church.)

His divorce of my grandmother and his remarriage to a woman who had worked in his office was somewhat scandalous in these earlier, simpler times. His command of the vernacular was also atypical for well-to-do Manhattanites and Hamptonites. For any number of reasons, as children, we did not see a great deal of Grandpa Maguire. As already noted, my father found him somewhat uncouth. In a diary entry my father remarks that he learned "to bite his tongue" when being criticized by his new father-in-law. He observes that this practice served him well when, in later life, he had to endure scathing comments of Soviet counterparts in Strategic Arms Limitation negotiations. Grandpa Maguire's relationships with his daughters were uneven. His nickname for my mother extending through childhood was "Tubby" and, if memory serves, he continued to use this endearment in later years. It was a practice that my mother surely thought at best a mixed blessing.

He compensated for his lack of formal education by voracious reading. He was a self-taught expert on the Civil War and British history. In these pursuits he was aided by a prodigious memory—the same attribute that allowed him to memorize freight tables as a young man. (Corporate colleagues stated that, on occasion, he would detail discussions and even the seating arrangements at meetings that had transpired 20 years earlier.) But business was both his vocation and avocation. He made fun of his wife's efforts to make him more of a gentleman. I remember, in particular, a visit to his apartment in the River House, the day after Christmas in the early 1960s; Marian had given him a royal purple "smoking jacket." He was wearing it, a cigarette in one hand and a stiff drink in the other. In his wife's presence, he announced to his daughter and grandchildren, "Look what the damn woman has bought me and is making me wear!"

After my sophomore year in college in 1962, I was given a job by Panhandle Eastern Corporation working on a pipeline survey crew in Kansas and Missouri. Any illusions I had that, as "John Smith," I would be anonymous were fast dispelled by a not terribly friendly colleague who, during my first week of work said in a resentful tone, "So you're Mr. Maguire's grandson." I set out to prove myself by working hard, drinking innumerable beers with coworkers at day's end and displaying modest prowess in arm wrestling. Accordingly, when Grandpa Maguire inquired down the chain of command as to how I was doing, he received the report that I was a "real son of a bitch," which, in the pipeline argot of the time was, I believe, intended as a compliment. Grandpa mischievously reported this good news to my mother, who was left to wonder whether the supposed compliment to me served as any compliment to her.

Once, later in my college career, my grandfather extended to me and a "date" the privilege of staying at his River House apartment while he and his wife were away for the weekend. Consistent with the sterner morals of the times, my date and I slept in separate rooms. My grandfather returned on Sunday in time to say hello to both of us. Briefed by the resident maid on the rooming arrangements, he expressed to me and my date his shock that his grandson had not availed himself of opportunity to bunk in splendor with a beautiful redhead.

In short, Grandpa Maguire was a bit of a terror. When I worked in the summer of 1966 at the law firm of Winthrop, Stimson, Putnam and Roberts, one of the partners discovered that I was Will Maguire's grandson. The firm had done some corporate work for Panhandle. The partner commented in good humor that my grandfather was "quite a guy" but that he "didn't care much about rights of minority shareholders." This somewhat gratuitous comment, no doubt true, actually captured the tough-minded Midwestern entrepreneur that I knew. Some of his own remarks remain clear in memory—especially those regarding the ways of Washington. In earlier days, conflicts of interest troubled Congress even less than they do today. My grandfather once noted in my presence that one did not even think about laying natural gas pipelines in the state of Illinois without retaining the law firm of then-minority leader of the Senate, Everett Dirksen. One sensed also that Grandpa Maguire had little patience for the extensive regulatory process that affected his business through the Federal Power Commission and other Washington agencies. (While, of course, as already described, it was some of these same agencies that helped him secure his position as Chairman and principal shareholder of Panhandle Eastern Pipeline Company, taking it out of the grasp of Columbia.) He did not live to see the broad deregulation of the energy business that has occurred in the past three decades. He, no doubt, would have been pleased.

I have in my personal files a single piece of correspondence from Grandpa Maguire. Typed on business stationery, he addresses me as an eight-year old, "Dear John" followed by a business-like colon. It relates that my mother had sent him a report card from Landon School for the Fall of my fourth grade year. My grandfather expresses his pride that I have obtained good marks— especially in arithmetic and social studies, both of which he deemed subjects that would be useful to me when I grew up. It is signed, "Granddaddy," a name I don't recall using with "Grandpa Maguire." Grandpa Maguire also demonstrated his close respect for money by giving each grandchild a birthday gift in dollars equal to the birthday achieved. (It is interesting to note that to equal today the $10 that Grandpa Maguire gave me in 1953, a grandparent would have to give more than $80 to a grandchild of 10.)

Family lore has it that Will Maguire's parents who, like most 19th century Irish immigrants were Roman Catholic, upon their deaths left whatever meager savings they had to the Church. This bequest, the story goes, caused Will Maguire to abandon whatever faith he may have had. His agnosticism notwithstanding, his widow Marian gave him a proper funeral service in St. Bartholomew's Episcopal Church in Manhattan. Nor did Will Maguire's lack of faith prevent my parents from making a substantial contribution to the Canterbury School, a Catholic boarding school attended by three generations of Smiths so far, to construct an auditorium in memory of William George Maguire. The plaque at the entrance to the Maguire Auditorium, in addition to his name, date of birth, and date of death (1965), contains the simple legend, "Strength, Persistence, Courage." Undoubtedly, these were major attributes of the man, which underpinned his extraordinary achievements as a natural gas pipeline pioneer.

Three-quarters of a century after Will Maguire's first perception of the value of natural gas and natural gas delivery pipelines as crucial economic resources, his vision finds ample validation—on a scale he could not possibly have imagined. There is now a million-mile pipeline grid delivering natural gas to towns and cities and directly to over 60,000,000 American homes. Natural gas may someday power a significant percentage of American automobiles, which could be fueled directly from home natural gas supplies. In contrast to coal and oil, combustion of natural gas emits relatively low levels of the greenhouse gas, carbon dioxide. (Already in 2007, 5,000,000 vehicles around the world ran on natural gas.)[22] In 2009, Exxon spent $31 billion to acquire XTO, a Texas natural gas company, possibly as a hedge against increasing pressures on use of oil and its products for electrical generation and automotive purposes.

In contrast to oil, for which the United States heavily depends upon imports, knowledgeable experts estimate that the United States has at least a 100-year supply of natural gas—assuming consumption at today's rates. New drilling techniques are unlocking a vast new source of "unconventional" natural gas from shale beds. Experts project that "shale gas" resources around the world may equal or even exceed current, proven natural gas resources.[23] In addition, realization is growing that the extant natural gas pipeline infrastructure may be given additional, socially beneficial uses, such as carrying captured carbon dioxide for disposal deep beneath the surface or delivering additional "green" fuels, such as hydrogen to consumers.

As a result of my kinship to Will Maguire—and my brief summer job on a pipeline surveying crew—throughout my professional career as a lawyer, I took an interest in energy matters. In 1978, Covington & Burling, where I had just become a partner, asked me to take a watching role in the development of President Carter's Comprehensive Energy Policy initiative. This initiative resulted in a series of laws, notable among them, the Power Plant and Industrial Fuel Use Act (PIFUA). In an era of Arab oil embargoes, the focus of this Act was to diminish U.S. dependence on foreign oil supplies for generation of electricity by enhancing exploitation of plentiful coal reserves in the United States. The Act essentially required all new power plants and industrial facilities to burn coal in lieu of oil or natural gas, even if constructed in areas like Oklahoma or Texas with plentiful natural gas supplies. I was tasked with leading an effort on behalf of firm clients to analyze and criticize implementing regulations under this Fuel Use Act.

Grandpa Maguire, as a fierce partisan for natural gas, would have liked other aspects of Carter's energy legislation, which began the process of deregulating the price of natural gas. He would have thought the Fuel Use Act, compelling the burning of coal in lieu of natural gas, to be asinine, which it was. Dramatically increased consciousness of the long-term risks of carbon dioxide emissions has shown the illogic of the Fuel Use Act. I have had occasion to tease my friend Tim Wirth, a former Congressman and Senator, for his 1978 support of the Fuel Use Act when, a decade later, he emerged as an early and vigorous proponent of measures to reduce emissions of greenhouse gases so as to slow the pace of global climate change.

2

John Thomas Smith

John Thomas Smith died shortly before my fourth birthday, and I have no conscious memory of him. Nonetheless, a clear portrait of him can be constructed from several sources, including the candid, handwritten journal that my father composed during the last months of my mother's life in the winter of 1987. I also rely strongly on a history of the *The General Motors Legal Staff* written by Robert A. Nitschke. Nitschke, who joined the legal office of General Motors in 1948, one year after my grandfather's retirement and death, draws extensively on interviews with executives and lawyers who worked directly with him and upon the recollections of my father, his sister Maureen, his brother Gregory, and Maureen's husband, Bernard Shanley. While the book contains some rather dry and complex legal descriptions, its central focus is upon the extraordinary lawyer and human being who was present at the creation of General Motors and served as a director and principal legal officer for three decades.[24]

Youthful Promise

J.T. was born in New Haven, Connecticut, on January 17, 1879, the son of Bernard P. and Margaret Conlon Smith. After studying in public schools in New Haven, he attended Creighton College in Omaha, Nebraska. In Omaha he lived with an uncle, who was a Catholic priest, also named John Thomas Smith. (This fact suggests that John Thomas should have been John Thomas II, which would make me J.T. III and my son John, J.T. IV. This type of numerical suffix was probably unimportant to first and second generation Irish immigrants such as John Thomas's parents, and it remains unimportant today to my son John who is content to use the simple moniker, "John Smith.")

The first record extant of John Thomas's powerful mind at work is a bound volume of his college essays entitled, *The Star of Castellar*. (The title reflects the fact that, while in Omaha, young J.T. lived on Castellar Street.) The *Star of Castellar* contains 40 essays and two poems. All have been typed meticulously. It is probable that J.T. saved handwritten college submissions and later had them transcribed into this volume. One can only speculate how many students today take sufficient pride in their work to save, compile, and print their college efforts. The topical and intellectual range of J.T.'s college output is wide. The collection contains biographical, philosophical, literary, political, and scientific essays. All are quite sophisticated. For instance, the philosophical essays include an exploration of "Buddhism and Brahmanism" and a critique of "The Effects of Cartesianism."

One of his essays entitled "Speech to a Labor Union" reflects youthful idealism in favor of the "dignity of the laboring man," while calling for harmony rather than conflict between labor and management. Later, as General Counsel of General Motors, J.T. was deeply involved in resolution of the history-making sit-down strikes of the middle 1930s as well as controversies regarding Congressional actions that led to the modern labor laws. In these events, his youthful idealism would be severely tested.

An essay of 1899 regarding the Spanish American War also reflects youthful idealism, critiquing the nation's then-current temptation to empire as corrosive to American ideals. An essay of May 1898, at the time of the emergence of "yellow journalism," is a sophisticated reflection on "the influence of the press on the Nation's life." It disapproves of the press's glorification of crime, but extols its potential to "elevate and instruct the masses." A note at the end of the essay states that it was "awarded first prize, $75." Since $75 in 1898 would be equivalent to more than $2,000 today (and $60,000 measured by relative share of gross domestic product),[25] J.T. was doubtless proud of this essay.

An intense and brilliant young man, shortly after his 20th birthday, in 1899, J.T. graduated from Creighton with honors in English, Philosophy, and Debating. He was offered a job as a reporter for a San Francisco newspaper and was on the verge of accepting it when his family directed him to return to New Haven and attend Yale Law School. There, he served as an editor of the Yale Law Journal and graduated in two years, at the age of 22, summa cum laude. To complete his legal studies in two, rather than three years, a practice that the faculty was trying to discourage by imposing severe hurdles, young J.T. took and excelled in 27 separate examinations in a three-day period. Recognizing an early drive to prosper, his classmates voted him "Most Likely to Succeed."

After passing the New York Bar in 1902, J.T. joined the venerable Wall Street firm of Alexander and Green. Subsequently, he opened his own law office in Manhattan's financial district. During his first decade after graduating from law school, J.T. entered on two engagements of lasting significance for the Smith family. The first was retention to do important legal work on behalf of bondholders who had provided capital for the construction of a railway from Guayaquil to Quito, Ecuador. The second was representation of one of the most colorful entrepreneurs/speculators of the first third of the 20th century, William C. Durant. It was through J.T.'s unlikely friendship with Durant that he became a principal officer and general counsel of the world's largest automobile company.

Ecuadorian Adventure

While still at Alexander and Green, J.T. did some work for a group of European and American bondholders who had invested in the construction and operation of a railroad in Ecuador extending from Guayaquil at sea level up to Quito at more than 9,000 feet in the Andes. This railroad, an extraordinary engineering feat at the time, attracted both the pride and interest of the government of Ecuador. In 1910, the government moved to nationalize the railroad. The result was a large claim for compensation on behalf of the investors. While J.T. was no longer at Alexander and Green, he was retained as a sole practitioner to travel to Ecuador and attend to the interests of the investors.

The trip, before completion of the Panama Canal, was a relatively arduous one—by ship to Panama, by railroad across the Isthmus, and then again by ship to Ecuador. During this journey, J.T., a gifted linguist, polished his spoken Spanish—having studied Spanish in school. Impressed by his intelligence and command of Spanish, the clients directed J.T. to take over the matter entirely and to argue a case for compensation in Spanish in Ecuadorian courts. He and his clients prevailed. In the resulting settlement, the bondholders, in lieu of cash compensation, were awarded controlling interest in other Ecuadorian ventures, including the electric utility for the city of Quito, a brewery, and a cement plant. These assets were placed in a new corporation, the Ecuadorian Corporation, Ltd. The grateful bondholders reputedly remunerated J.T. with a million dollars worth of shares in the new corporation and made him a director, a post in which he served for the balance of his life.

J.T.'s shares in the Ecuadorian Corporation passed through his estate to his heirs, including my father. When my father went to work at the State Department in 1954, he was required to divest all foreign shares. The shares transferred to his friend, William McGuirk. In 1963, following my junior year at Yale, Mr. McGuirk, by then Chairman of the Board of the Ecuadorian Corporation, offered me a job working for the corporation in Ecuador. (At the time, the President of the Ecuadorian Corporation for whom I worked was H. Norton Stevens. "Nort" was the grandson of a famous early 20th century finance wizard, E. Hope Norton. Documents regarding the Guayaquil & Quito Railroad indicate that the bondholders' investment banker was E.H. Norton & Company.) There, I was tasked with writing a history of the Corporation for the Annual Report. In doing so, I reviewed the records of the historical events recounted earlier. I also stayed for a week in Quito at the large, but decaying residence of an elderly American, with the engaging name of Forrest LaRose Yoder. Mr. Yoder, then in his 80s, had worked for the Ecuadorian Corporation and had known my grandfather, J.T., during his extended stay in Ecuador, a half century earlier. Apparently the stay did not involve "all work and no play," since Yoder fondly recalled tennis games with my grandfather.

In Ecuador I gleaned impressions of what my grandfather may have experienced as a young lawyer. Guayaquil is a seaport sprawled on the banks of a turbid river. Warehouses with bananas, coffee, and other commodities line the river, awaiting shipment. The air is humid and much of the year there is a high overcast resulting from the interplay of warm, sea level equatorial air with colder currents from both the Andes and the Pacific shoreline. Quito, in contrast, is at 9,000 feet. In 1963 it still was a city of elaborately decorated baroque churches and grand houses. Immediately on its outskirts one could view and visit towering Andean volcanoes. The air was cool and dry and the sun bright. I would be awakened in the morning by roosters, not something one encounters in the capital cities of North America. Encountering Ecuador more than a half a century earlier, J.T. Smith of New Haven and Omaha must have been stimulated to think about the rich and diverse opportunities that his excellence at the law and in languages could bring.

Durant and General Motors' Founding

At approximately the same point of his career, J.T. began legal work for William Crapo Durant, founder of General Motors. The available historical record does not make clear how the two men first met. Quite possibly they met when J.T. was working at Alexander and Green in 1903, and Durant was on an initial foray into financial speculation in New York. In 1904, Durant apparently returned to his hometown of Flint, Michigan, and became the head of a nascent automobile company, Buick. Then, in 1908, he entered discussions with other automobile manufacturers about the creation of a holding company that would effectively merge Buick and two other companies, one of which was Olds, later Oldsmobile.

My father used to recount a colorful, but probably apocryphal story of how J.T. developed a close relationship with Durant. He stated that young J.T. was sitting in his sole-practitioner's law office on Nassau Street in New York's financial district, and Durant walked in and asked him if he knew how to incorporate a New Jersey company. When asked what his fee would be, J.T. said that he wanted to be paid in stock. In any event, the record shows that the original General Motors Company was incorporated as a New Jersey entity on September 16, 1908, and that the incorporating papers were drafted by a lawyer named Hatheway and not by J.T. The record is also clear, however, that one year from the formation of this New Jersey corporation, Durant had placed the 30-year-old John Thomas Smith on its Board of Directors.[26]

Durant was not a cautious man. He quickly brought other companies into the GM fold, including Pontiac and Cadillac. Within two years of incorporation, GM had acquired a total of 25 companies, 11 of which were automobile companies and the balance were manufacturers of auto parts and accessories. Durant, in what became a pattern, soon became overextended financially and, in November 1910, General Motors was taken over by its bankers—Lee Higginson & Company. With the exception of Durant, all directors, including J.T., were forced out.

Durant persevered and by 1911 he had met and befriended Louis Chevrolet and had formed Chevrolet Motor Company, a Michigan and later New York Corporation. In 1914, Pierre duPont, President of DuPont, and John Raskob, Treasurer of DuPont, personally invested in General Motors, which was still controlled by its bankers. In the summer of 1915, Durant met with duPont and Raskob in duPont's offices in Wilmington to seek their collaboration in regaining control of GM from the bankers. J.T.

accompanied Durant at this meeting. In September of 1915, Durant incorporated the Chevrolet Motor Company of Delaware, taking over the assets of the former Chevrolet Motor companies of Michigan and New York. J.T. served as a director and secretary of this new Chevrolet Corporation, and the organizational meeting of its directors took place in J.T.'s law office. Through this new Chevrolet Company of Delaware, Durant sought to regain control of GM, and by May 1916, Durant had been able to increase Chevrolet's holdings of GM stock to more than half the shares outstanding. The bankers capitulated, leaving Durant in control. Durant was elected President of General Motors, and Pierre duPont became Chairman of the Board. A few months later, Durant formed a Delaware corporation, which became the modern GM, eventually acquiring all the assets of the original New Jersey company, as well as those of the Chevrolet Motor Company.

My grandfather served as Durant's personal advisor and legal counsel throughout these events, and the Minutes of the General Motors Corporation acknowledging his retirement in 1947 cite the fact that J.T. had been GM's counsel from inception. Also in 1916, J.T. first made the acquaintance of Alfred P. Sloan. Under the rubric of United Motors Company, Durant acquired Hyatt Motor Company of Harrison, New Jersey, which was Sloan's company. Sloan thereupon became President of United Motors in 1917. In this same time period, the initial, personal investments by Pierre duPont and Raskob expanded into investments by the DuPont Company in General Motors. For an investment of $25 million, the DuPont Company obtained a 23 percent interest in General Motors.

From the outset, J.T. was well remunerated by Durant and by General Motors. Apparently, his compensation consisted of both cash and stock. Also, working with Raskob, J.T. drafted the first General Motors "bonus plan," modeled after that of the DuPont Company. As GM thrived in the 1920s, this bonus plan, which originally gave maximum awards of 40 percent of salary, ballooned to 250 percent of salary.[27] This bonus plan and two successor plans would become the objects of a shareholders suit in the 1930s charging General Motors executives with "waste" of corporate assets by providing unreasonable compensation to officers. J.T. was a defendant in this suit and was deeply involved in the strategy for its defense.

In the period 1918–1920, Alfred P. Sloan became Vice President, a Member of the Executive Committee, and a Director of General Motors, assuming an ever-increasing role in management of the new company. He also became a substantial individual stockholder in General Motors. At the same time, Durant, who disliked management, stayed busy in his primary vocation, which was playing the stock market, as well as organizing or acquiring new companies. In 1919 he organized General Motors Acceptance Corporation, acquired a controlling interest in the Fisher Body Company, and purchased Frigidaire.

In the fall of 1920 GM's shares plummeted from $40 to a low $13. Durant, who had been actively promoting GM shares and purchasing them on 10 percent margin, could not meet margin calls from his brokers. At this point Durant was "underwater" by an amount of $27 million—a vast amount in today's currency. (Equivalent to $290 million dollars in 2008 or, taking account of percentage of GDP, approximately $4.5 billion 2008 dollars.)

As a result, Durant was forced out of General Motors, with the DuPont Company picking up Durant's GM stock, and DuPont's GM holdings grew to 38 percent of the total shares outstanding. By this time, at the urging of Alfred P. Sloan, J.T. had been formally appointed as General Motors' General Counsel. He remained with General Motors for the next 27 years, no longer attached to Durant's fallen star.[28]

Durant, undeterred by his downfall at General Motors, promptly incorporated a new company, Durant Motors. Through this entity and stock market speculation, Durant ran up another multimillion dollar fortune before the 1929 crash. J.T. apparently remained a loyal friend to Durant, and in the last years of Durant's life, together with other GM executives including Sloan, paid substantial sums to defray Durant's living expenses. Durant died in March 1947—six months before J.T.

Like Will Maguire's initial friendship with Frank Parish, that of J.T. and "Billy" Durant was an odd pairing. Durant was virtually uneducated, was a wild but creative risk taker, was irreligious, and was divorced and remarried. J.T. was a highly educated, intellectual, and prudent man who was a lifelong Catholic. Yet theirs was more than a friendship of mutual convenience. The best, although somewhat speculative, exploration of the relationship between Durant and my grandfather appears in the definitive biography of Durant by Bernard Weisberger. According to Weisberger, J.T.'s erudition was unique to an individual such as Durant who had spent his life wrapped up in business concerns and manipulation of stocks. J.T., in turn, was struck by Durant's extraordinary entrepreneurial energies.[29] In contrast to the Parish-Maguire pairing, which ended in physical violence, litigation, and enmity, the Durant-Smith friendship and mutual admiration endured.

By the time each had reached his early 40s, Will Maguire and J.T. Smith had both achieved large financial and corporate success. Each had initially benefited from an alliance with a reckless speculator. Each had also benefited from investment capital from members of the duPont family. And each was aware of the tremendous opportunities for industrial growth in post–World War I America.

While Will Maguire in 1930 faced nearly 15 years of corporate, regulatory and financial battles, J.T. Smith was embarking upon a 27-year career as Chief Legal Officer, and Member of the Executive Committee of what was to become the world's largest corporation. In this role he enjoyed a relatively stable personal life, residence in Manhattan,[30] presiding over a loyal, highly qualified legal staff, and enjoying a close personal relationship with Sloan and the other senior executives of General Motors. At the same time, he was to become involved in significant legal battles pertaining to several issues that continue to confront our society, including the consequences of unionization of automobile production and heated debates about the scale of executive compensation.

General Counsel of GM

As the first General Counsel of General Motors, J.T. enjoyed great independence of action, a close working relationship with other principal executives and an immensely rewarding legal career. In December 2007, I met a lawyer, George Comb, who had joined the GM Legal Office shortly after my grandfather's retirement in 1947 and had risen to the position of Deputy General Counsel. He ratified Robert Nitschke's perception that J.T. remained a legend at General Motors long after his retirement and death.

The office he ran bore small resemblance to the modern corporate counsel's office of the type with which I became familiar during my practice of law. First, J.T. ran the office as an independent law office. He and his subordinates were free to take on non-General Motors matters, if and as time permitted. Second, J.T. and his colleagues took direct and personal roles in litigation involving General Motors. (In the modern day, a general counsel of a large corporation and his or her staff typically manage the work of outside counsel and do not themselves appear in court.) Sagely, J.T. wanted his lawyers to have as much court experience as possible, both on GM and unrelated matters, reasoning that to give good counsel to clients, a lawyer must understand what actually happens in courtrooms and how judges and juries behave. He hired lawyers of great competence and intelligence, some of whom subsequently became leading partners in major New York law firms. Although he readily delegated substantial responsibility to his staff lawyers, he maintained the tradition that all correspondence leaving his office bear his signature line. (This practice mirrors the procedures in the U.S. Department of State where all communications leaving Washington to embassies abroad routinely carry the signature line of the Secretary of State.)

Third, and perhaps most importantly, J.T. reported on a direct line to the Chief Executive Officer of GM. According to Nitschke, J.T. wrote and preserved corporate bylaws to ratify this reporting arrangement. Indeed he commanded sufficient respect among his business colleagues that he was placed on the GM Executive Committee in 1929. Even before that time, according to Nitschke, Sloan, Donaldson Brown, and others, whose offices were one floor below that of J.T.'s, would travel up an internal staircase to visit the General Counsel's office. He enjoyed a reputation for insisting on honesty in corporate affairs and he counseled against any ethically questionable behavior, even if it was legally proper. In his autobiography, Alfred P. Sloan characterized J.T.'s advice and influence as being of "a very high order in moral and public policy matters as well as in the law."[31]

From my admittedly parochial perspective, the most successful and best managed modern corporations are ones where the general counsel function is strongly staffed and where the general counsel is welcome in the executive suite. Certainly that was the case at General Motors in the first half of the 20th century.

Although an exacting taskmaster, J.T. apparently enjoyed the respect and affection of his staff. They appreciated the breadth and rigor of his mind, and they welcomed the opportunities he furnished them for independent, meaningful legal work. Saturday office hours were frequent, and J.T. would thank those members of his staff who turned up by treating them to lunch at an excellent restaurant, Voisin, at 53rd and Park Avenue. On weekdays, J.T. would arrive by 7:00 or 7:30 in the morning and he routinely stayed until 7:00 in the evening. As a rule, he would not take papers home. The evening was for family dinner, sometimes preceded by a martini, and after dinner reading of history or philosophy.

The full range of important legal matters addressed by J.T and his staff during 1929–1947 is amply described in the Nitschke book. It will suffice for this short memoir to highlight three matters that underscore J.T.'s great capacities and character.

Opel Acquisition

In 1928, General Motors began to consider the possibility of manufacturing automobiles in Germany. On a trip with J.T. in October of 1928, Alfred P. Sloan obtained an option, good until April 1, 1929, to buy Opel. In his dealings in Germany, Sloan relied heavily on J.T.'s virtuosity in the German language. As follow-up, Sloan sent a delegation headed by J.T. back to Germany to explore the purchase of Opel. J.T. and his delegation recommended proceeding with the purchase. J.T. not only conducted the final negotiations, but also visited German banks to negotiate financing—all carried out in German. In the final negotiation, J.T. quoted Martin Luther's famous statement, "Here I stand; I cannot do otherwise." It was immediately upon the heels of this successful Opel business acquisition that Sloan placed J.T. on the Executive Committee, making him thenceforth a direct participant in the business affairs, and not simply the legal affairs, of General Motors.

During the "great recession" of 2008–2009, General Motors went into bankruptcy, an almost inconceivable development viewed from earlier years when it was a global colossus. Initially, the bankrupt company proposed to sell Opel as part of a recovery plan. Independent directors representing the interests of U.S. taxpayers, who by October of 2009 owned 60 percent of GM, determined to reverse course and retain Opel. Among other reasons, the decision was based upon recognition of Opel as a source of technology and car design ideas.[32]

Sit-Down Strike

In the mid-1930s, J.T. was thrust into a central role in resolving what has been called "the most momentous confrontation between American labor and management in [the 20th century]."[33] This dispute began when the fledgling United Auto Workers initiated a sit-down strike in Flint, Michigan, at two Fischer Body plants crucial to production of a significant percentage of General Motors automobiles. At the time, General Motors and the rest of the automotive industry had strenuously resisted unionization. It had also been able to ignore aspirational legislation, such as the National Industrial Recovery Act of 1933, which had been struck down by the Supreme Court in 1935. Similarly, the auto companies had ignored a follow-on statute, the National Labor Relations Act (the Wagner Act), expecting it to be similarly invalidated by the Supreme Court.

The sit-down strikes triggered large events, including intervention by the Roosevelt Administration, led by Secretary of Labor Frances Perkins and on one occasion by FDR himself, as well as deployment of National Guard troops by Michigan Governor (later Supreme Court Justice) Frank Murphy after a confrontation between strikers and police who opened fire with buckshot. According to the family recollections, these events included an unusual after-hours call from Alfred P. Sloan to J.T. at home during dinner. Apparently Sloan had just received a phone call from the feisty female Secretary of Labor who had berated him. He told J.T. that no one had ever spoken to him in this fashion before. J.T. advised the shaken CEO to get a good night's sleep and they would talk in the morning. Sloan responded that this was good advice.[34]

Subsequently, J.T. and other GM executives were summoned to the White House to discuss the strike impasse with the President, whose sympathies lay with the striking workers. Called upon to comment to the press at meeting's end, J.T. simply characterized FDR as having been in "good voice."[35]

As an initial move, General Motors attempted to obtain a court order to enjoin the Union members from occupation of the GM plants. The strike having begun on December 30, 1936, the legal staff worked through New Year's weekend and filed a petition for an injunction on January 2, 1937. The judge, Edward Black, issued an injunction the same day. To J.T.'s embarrassment, three days later, the United Auto Workers called a press conference to point out that Judge Black was not an objective jurist, since he owned over 3,600 shares of GM stock valued at approximately $220,000. This development rendered the injunction "dead letter." After the call-up of the National Guard and other ferment, GM agreed to begin negotiations with John L. Lewis, then the head of the Congress of Industrial Organizations (CIO). Sloan tapped Donaldson Brown, William Knutson, and J.T. to represent GM in the ensuing negotiations. According to Nitschke, J.T. took the lead.

When J.T. became convinced that a negotiating stalemate could only be overcome by legal action, the company sought a new injunction, from a new judge. The judge issued an injunction February 3, but the strikers defied the injunction. Governor Murphy tried to persuade J.T. to defer any action to implement the injunction. J.T. disagreed with the Governor, apparently believing that only the stick of strong legal action could resolve the matter. He obtained a writ commanding the Sheriff to "attach the bodies" of all the strikers and their comforters for failure to comply with the court's injunction. The Sheriff necessarily asked the Governor for assistance. The Governor in turn served John L. Lewis with a letter commanding that he take steps to restore possession of GM's plants to the company. In this context, negotiations resumed and proceeded to a settlement. Although they came from very different worlds, apparently J.T. and John L. Lewis gained respect for each other. Subsequently they continued a cordial relationship, and J.T. would stop in to see Lewis when he was in Washington.

J.T. also retained a good relationship with Governor Murphy. After J.T. argued before the Supreme Court in 1941, he received a personal note from then Justice Murphy expressing the Justice's pleasure seeing and hearing J.T. before the Court "so obviously hale and hearty." The Justice went on to say "I remember gratefully and pleasantly your efforts during the troublous days of '37."[36]

These events mark the beginning of unionization of the labor force in automotive construction in the United States. Doubtless the bargaining leverage of unions brought real benefits in wages, pensions, and health care to legions of American workers. In the early 21st century, however, it became apparent that the generosity of benefits owed to current and retired workers was a potentially crippling burden to General Motors in a world of global competition. General Motors has now been through bankruptcy and, with extensive assistance from the federal government, has emerged in 2011 as once again the world's largest automobile manufacturer.

Compensation Litigation

The financial crisis of 2007–2009 has focused broad public attention on compensation practices of large financial institutions, corporations, private equity, and hedge funds. It is notable that my grandfather was deeply involved as a defendant in a seminal compensation dispute, *Winkelman v. General Motors Corp.*, 44 F. Supp. 960. (S.D.N.Y. 1942). This famous "bonus suit" was an action brought by a small number of dissident shareholders claiming that the executives of General Motors had committed a "waste" of corporate assets through establishment and administration of certain bonus plans. As previously noted, the first of these plans had been modeled after one extant at the DuPont Corporation in 1918.[37]

It was the highly lucrative consequences of these plans that plaintiff characterized as a waste of corporate assets. J.T., together with Raskob, had been one of the principals most deeply involved in the preparation and adoption of the bonus plans. Moreover he was a significant beneficiary. Accordingly, as a practical matter, J.T. could not represent the Corporation and its executives. Indeed, he was the first witness called by attorneys for the plaintiffs and was on the stand for the first five days of the three-month-long trial.

Nevertheless, J.T. kept representation of the Corporation and the GM executives, including himself, in house by selecting one of his staff attorneys, 33-year-old David Sher, for this momentous representation. Other counsel involved in the case included so-called giants of the bar. For instance certain banker defendants from J.P. Morgan and Bankers Trust were represented by John W. Davis of Davis Polk, and the DuPont Company was represented by Judge Covington of Covington & Burling. J.T. resisted suggestions from some of these luminaries that he should replace Sher with an outside counsel of greater stature. The opposition was formidable. (One of the counsel for plaintiffs was Jerome Frank—later a Chairman of the Securities and Exchange Commission and a well regarded Court of Appeals Judge. Trial counsel for plaintiffs was Milton Pollack, later a long-term federal judge.)

Although J.T. was unable to defend the case directly for General Motors, he was present throughout much of the trial and exercised his judgment and counsel. The matter did not go to trial until nearly five years after the initial complaint. (A staff of bright young financial experts under Frederick Donner, GM's Vice President for Finance, assisted in day-to-day trial preparation. Among them was a promising 25-year old, Thomas Aquinas Murphy. He later became Chairman of the Board of GM in the 1970s. In 1976, when I served as General Counsel of the U.S. Department of Commerce, I received a flattering, personal visit from Mr. Murphy, whose staff had made him aware that I was J.T.'s grandson.)

The court eventually ruled that any claims regarding bonus awards before 1930 were untimely, while offering gratuitous dictum that the pre-1930 awards were excessive. The judge found that post-1930 awards were congruent with the value of the services rendered by the individuals receiving them, stating that "the General Motors executives had built up a great industry; managed it successfully; given employment to hundreds of thousands of skilled workers; earned tremendous profits for the stockholders and contributed largely to the prosperity of the nation." Echoing an argument heard today, the judge found the bonus arrangements were necessary to prevent the loss of talented executives who might otherwise have left the Company. The judge nonetheless found that certain accounting methods and computations were incorrect, and the net result was a judgment of $6 million including interest.

Both sides appealed and, pending appeal, the matter was settled for $4.5 million, with plaintiffs' counsel obtaining approximately $900,000 of the total in fees. (In today's values, these are non-trivial sums. Plaintiffs' counsel received approximately $22 million in 2009 dollars. GM settled for approximately $60 million in today's terms. The amount was paid by 34 GM executives and not the Corporation.) At the time of the settlement/appeal period, J.T. recommended that each individual defendant obtain separate representation. Alfred P. Sloan was represented by Fred Wood of Cravath, and Raskob by Arthur Dean of Sullivan & Cromwell. J.T. was in favor of full prosecution of appeal and against settlement. However, his own counsel, David Sher, as well as several of the other prestigious counsel were in favor of settlement. The matter was put to the Board of General Motors for decision. J.T. insisted that Sher accompany him to the Board meeting so that Sher could express his views about the merits of settlement, even though they diverged from the views of his "client," J.T.[38]

In an unguarded moment, my father once stated that his father was a paragon in almost every respect except that he might have had too great a drive to make money. From the vantage of future generations who have benefited from his energies in this respect, this appears a curious perception. In any event, the *Winkelman* case highlights that J.T. and the other senior executives of General Motors were not averse to robust compensation for their labors.

J.T. reached GM's mandatory retirement age (then 68) on June 30, 1947. He remained a director and a member of the Corporation's Financial Policy Committee after his retirement. A corporate resolution upon his retirement noted that Alfred P. Sloan reminded the Board that "Mr. Smith was one of the Corporation's real pioneers and was the oldest remaining official in terms of service." The resolution stated that J.T. had participated in the "original organization" of the Corporation and that of equal importance to his service as general counsel had been "his sound judgment in dealing with the business affairs of the Corporation."

3

More about J.T.

The foregoing outline of J.T.'s legal career can only hint at his brilliance as a lawyer. It does not cover his several arguments before the Supreme Court. Among them was a case still studied in law schools, *Klaxon Co. v. Stentor Elec. Mfg. Co.*, 313 U.S. 487 (1941).[39] Apparently, oral argument extended over two days, a Thursday and a Friday. The following Monday, J.T. began his five days on the witness stand in the previously discussed *Winkelman* executive compensation matter. At the time, J.T. was 62 years old. He made his final Supreme Court argument at the age of 65. Justice Stanley F. Reed once told Bernard Shanley, J.T.'s son-in-law, that J.T. was "one of the most impressive lawyers to appear before the Court" and that "it wasn't necessary to ask him any questions, and nobody ever went to sleep."[40]

Doubtless, J.T. derived great personal satisfaction from his professional endeavor and his virtuosity as advocate and counselor. Having practiced law for three decades in one of the nation's premier law firms (and one of the few outside law firms employed by J.T.), I have some sense of the extraordinary caliber of J.T. as a lawyer and human being. He was what we in the legal profession call a "lawyer's lawyer." Encompassed by this term are characteristics such as rigor of intellect, capacity for hard work, deep respect for the institutions and instrumentalities of the law, creativity grounded firmly in ethics and morality, fearlessness before adversaries and tribunals, capacity to speak and write clearly and persuasively and with deep respect for language, and unfailing civility to colleagues and opponents.

Life outside the Law

Although, as remarked by Justice Joseph Story, the law is a "jealous mistress" requiring "a long and constant courtship," J.T. lived a rich and productive life beyond the boundaries of his law office. As previously noted, in June 1910 at the relatively ripe age of 30, J.T. married Mary Agnes Smith, a second cousin whom he had known since childhood in New Haven. A single piece of correspondence between J.T. and Mary survives. It is a postcard, free of any endearments, sent by J.T. from Germany in 1908 to Mary Agnes Smith of New Haven. It remarks on the presence in Germany of numerous American school teachers, presumably a light-hearted reference to Mary's then occupation. They produced three children during the first four years of their marriage—Maureen, Gregory, and my father, Gerard Coad Smith.[41]

Initially, they lived on the Upper West Side of Manhattan. Subsequently they moved to 92nd Street and Fifth Avenue and, in 1936, to 19 East 72nd Street. The young couple's social life focused on attendance at the opera and companionship with William Durant and his second wife, Caroline. Hands-on care of the three young children was relegated to a governess, Miss Michel. Beyond the Durant tie, consistent with the times in which Irish Catholics were the object of social discrimination, the J.T. Smiths' social circle comprised other well-to-do Catholics. Mary Smith and the children spent summers on the Atlantic shore of New Jersey in Asbury Park, near where Durant maintained a palatial summer house in Deal. J.T. would commute on weekends.

Notwithstanding his love of reading and the life of the mind, J.T. apparently was an active tennis player and golfer. My father's diary records that J.T. played tennis until he was 50, and, upon his retirement from the game, he had never been defeated by his son Gerard, who was, I can attest, a darn good tennis player. A silver flask retained by the family shows J.T. as the winner of a golf tournament at Deal in the summer of 1920—although the trophy may reflect victory at one of the unofficial and informal "tournaments" organized by William Durant, a keen but not terribly expert golfer.

There is not much record of Mary Smith's life. According to my father's diary, she was quite devout, took an interest in liturgical art and suffered long periods of ill health, including the consequences of a botched gallbladder operation. Surviving home movies and photographs show a "handsome" woman with clear, intelligent eyes and dignified manner. She had musical talent and played the piano—a skill that has not been manifest in younger generations. She died, still in her early 60s in 1943, due to complications from the earlier gallbladder operation.

J.T., while a lifelong Catholic, took a more minimalist approach to his faith, fulfilling the Catholic requirement of "Easter duty" receiving the sacraments of Penance and the Eucharist at least once a year during the Easter season. Mary Smith speculated to her children that J.T. had received an overdose of religion when residing with his priest uncle in Omaha while attending Creighton College.

Whatever J.T.'s degree of piety, he contributed generously to Catholic education. He donated funds to enable construction of the current chapel at Canterbury School. Likewise, he contributed the funds to build the Thomas More Chapel at Yale University. Further, he helped fund a fellowship to allow a prominent French Catholic philosopher, Jacques Maritain, to reside at Princeton during World War II. Another of J.T.'s generous impulses was paying the law school tuition for the son of a family friend from New York Catholic circles, R. Sargent ("Sarge") Shriver, whose family had suffered financial reverses in the crash of '29 and ensuing Depression. Shriver became a Kennedy in-law, founding Director of the Peace Corps, and in 1972 candidate for Vice President of the United States.[42]

According to my father's diary, J.T. was essentially a shy man. For all his worldly success, he didn't feel comfortable with New York "club men" who had enjoyed wealth for several generations. Nor, one senses, did he aspire to a grander social circle than that he enjoyed with other Irish Catholics in Manhattan and at the Jersey Shore. Nevertheless, as his fortune grew, and with a probable goad from Mary and the three children now in their late teens, J.T. purchased a magnificent 14-acre estate in Southampton, Long Island, in 1932. He renamed the estate "Certosa," an Italian word meaning a Cistercian monastery—and so ended the family's summers on the Jersey Shore. This Italianate villa, previously named "Red Maples," had been originally constructed in 1908 at a cost of $500,000 (approximately $12 million in today's world, using simple inflation, and more than $200 million, using a fraction of GDP), although depression circumstances enabled J.T. to buy the estate at a lesser sum, $320,000. The villa was 250 feet long and 65 feet wide on two floors, suggesting living space in excess of 30,000 square feet. The property included a two-acre sunken garden and a rose garden with 4,000 rose bushes, a superintendent's house and a substantial garage.[43]

Eventually, J.T., the non-"clubman," enjoyed membership in the Southampton Beach Club, the Meadow Club, the National Golf Links of America, and the Shinnecock Hills Golf Club, now among the most coveted memberships in the world. In 1936 my aunt Maureen was married in Southampton, and a grand reception was held at Certosa. Attendees included Alfred E. Smith, former Governor of New York and the defeated Irish Catholic, Democratic Presidential candidate in 1928. Invitations to this event were important—at least to some. (As previously noted, my father's middle name "Coad" recognizes a longtime friend of J.T.'s, William Coad. The two had a falling-out and never reconciled, when Coad did not respond to his invitation to Maureen's wedding. He later stated that the invitation was not received. In any event, in later life, my father preferred using just the initial "C" rather than the full Coad in his middle name.) Sarge Shriver's biographer records that Shriver first met Jack Kennedy's older brother, Joseph Kennedy Jr., at parties in the late 1930s at Certosa.[44]

My father's diary recounts that his father was the single largest influence in his life. And, as my father's son, I have been able to discern, and try to practice, the benefits of this influence. J.T. was not a prescriptive man and did not seek to command the behavior of his children. Rather, he tried to lead by example. An extreme form of this practice was that he set no curfew for children old enough to drive and go out to parties and nightspots. But, he did have a "rule" that all in residence with him would be prompt to breakfast at 7:30 a.m.

J.T. read widely and took a broad interest in international affairs. As already noted, he was a gifted linguist, with working command of German, French, Spanish, and Italian. His scholarship had included years of study of both Latin and Greek. My father remembers his father spending a quiet Sunday afternoon, exercising his gray matter by translating Greek poetry directly into German, a pursuit somewhat more demanding than watching NFL football. J.T. was generous to his children, giving them large allowances to encourage independence of action and judgment. He "joint ventured" with my father on the purchase of a 72-foot sailing yacht, the *Innisfail*, when my father was still in his 20s. J.T. liked yachts and enjoyed being on as well as beside the ocean. He indulged my father in a series of fishing boat charters, in Long Island, Florida, and the Bahamas, while my father pursued a fascination with bill fishing in the 1930s.

As with succeeding generations, J.T. enjoyed good food and wine and comfortable lodgings and, as with later generations, he knew the value of starting the day with exercise, usually a substantial walk from home to work, as a way of both sharpening the mind and counterbalancing fine dining. Apparently, he drank little or no alcohol until the advent of prohibition in 1919. He deemed prohibition an intolerable and unjustified governmental interference with human freedom, and he promptly became a scofflaw—

along with a vast number of other Americans. Thereafter, he would enjoy a cocktail at the end of the day—as have succeeding generations.

For all his intellect and probity, J.T. had a keen sense of humor—exercised with a degree of learning. The poor puns that my generation can't resist may be a genetic residue of this feature of J.T. My father would cite as evidence of his father's humor a story of confused identity. In 1938, the Vatican honored a man named John Thomas Smith by making him a "Knight of Saint Gregory," a type of honorary chamberlain to the Pope. The redoubtable parish priest in Southampton, Father Killeen, wrote J.T. to congratulate him. In the event, the honoree turned out to be a different John Thomas Smith, a manufacturer from Brooklyn, who had the misfortune to die several days after receiving the Pope's honor. J.T. wrote Father Killeen to apprise him of the mistaken identity and to note the other John Thomas's sudden demise. A copy of my grandfather's letter saved by Killeen and furnished by him to my father 30 years later begins in Ciceronian Latin—"Odi Persico et honoris," apparently a saying originally in Greek (Thucydides) meaning "Hate Persians and honors." J.T. goes on to say, "It was bad enough to be mistaken for the real Chamberlain, tragically sad for him notified on Monday and mortified on Saturday." (J.T. was used to confusion caused by his plain name. Once when he was seated in the Carleton Hotel in Washington, there was a repeated "page" for "Mr. Smith." His colleague became anxious when J.T. ignored the page. J.T. explained that he never responded to a page, the odds being very strong that the call was for a different Mr. Smith.)[45]

While a lifelong resident of the East Coast (with the exception of four years in Omaha), J.T. had an abiding affection for California. Part of the attraction was, doubtless, the fact that in 1917, he became the majority stockholder in a California gold mine, The Argonaut Mine. Family lore has it that one of his clients could not pay a bill for services and, in lieu of payment, gave J.T. shares in the mine. J.T. placed his brother Joseph in charge of the mine, but remained as the principal shareholder and an officer of Argonaut for the 30-year balance of his life. The company avoided the "injustice" of double taxation on earnings and dividends by purchasing GM stock in lieu of distributing profits as dividends and also paid J.T. a not insignificant monthly salary. It was probably Argonaut business that first took J.T. to California in 1910, a path that he pursued regularly, delighting in the atmosphere and climate. Some of my father's fondest memories of youth are accompanying his father on trips to California.

Involvement in the fortunes of the Argonaut Mine also brought a measure of tragedy and a debt of conscience. On August 25, 1922, the mine experienced an explosion and fire in which 47 miners died in the worst gold mining tragedy in California history. My father's diary makes a cryptic reference to the event, and, included in his personal papers at his death, was a set of grim photographs of the ensuing funeral proceedings. At the time, mining activities were lightly regulated, and such safety regulations as did exist were not enforced out of deference to the economic strength of the mining industry in the area of the Sierra "Mother Load." Nevertheless, an investigation by a Special Committee appointed by the Governor of California attributed the disaster to scanting on safety practices by mine management. J.T. was closely involved in these events. A recent book contains a gripping narrative of the tragic event and the protracted suspense of the unsuccessful efforts over two weeks' time to find and rescue the trapped miners.[46] With the outcome of the explosion and fire still in doubt and the prospect that the 47 men might still be rescued, J.T. sent a telegram to the mine's general manager directing that he "[s]pare no expense or money to save [the] men and mitigate the disaster their families face, the welfare of the mine being the last and least consideration."[47] This advice to spare no expense and to place the men's welfare in paramount position is, of course, the instinctive work of a fine lawyer. But it must also represent the heartfelt product of J.T.'s conscience.

A stained glass window in the Chapel at Canterbury School built with funds from J.T. testifies to his California connection. It carries a representation of a Franciscan monk, Fra Junipero Serra, an important figure in establishing missions in 18th-century California. The glass panel contains a map of California, the names of early missions, and J.T.'s motto, *Carpe Diem*.[48]

In 1936 J.T. purchased real estate in Manhattan at the corner of 72nd Street and Madison Avenue. Taking advantage of deflated depression economic circumstances, J.T. was able both to buy the land and construct a luxury apartment house by paying $2.25 million out of his own pocket ($35,000,000 in 2009 terms or nearly $500 million in terms of relative share of GDP). The architects were the prominent Rosario Candela and Mott Schmidt. The resulting 15-story apartment building remains distinctive today for its discrete art moderne line and by its relatively compact and luxurious style—containing 34 units—20 of which are duplexes. Students of the subject generally consider 19 East 72nd Street as the last of the top luxury buildings constructed in New York—at least until the recent boom in super luxurious apartments in the midtown area.[49] J.T. and Mary occupied the penthouse duplex that had a terrace. J.T. would enjoy sitting on this terrace and viewing the city skyline. He was heard to comment that, "this town has been good to us," certainly not an understatement.

Three months after his mandatory retirement from General Motors in 1947, J.T. was again visiting California. After attending a Stanford football game on September 22, he died in his sleep of an apparent heart attack at the St. Francis Hotel in San Francisco.

J.T.'s counsel and business judgment helped launch General Motors into the top echelon of 20th-century global corporations. GM flourished by stimulating and rewarding consumer demand for ever more powerful and stylish automobiles, which consumed increasing quantities of gasoline. At the time, all these developments, including the resulting obsolescence of public transport, such as trolley cars, appeared right and just. Modern concerns about the public health and welfare consequences of emissions from tailpipes of proliferating numbers of cars and trucks were nonexistent before the 1960s. And, as large domestic oil resources were discovered and developed in Texas, the nation did not worry about dependence on insecure sources of foreign crude oil.

As this and future generations wrestle with the dilemmas of climate change, as well as control of imported supplies of crude oil by foreign dictators and "Islamic Republics," the creation and flourishing of American automotive culture deserve a fresh look. As newly prosperous nations such as China and India, with immense populations seek to emulate the automotive culture pioneered by the United States, the prospect is for hundreds of millions of additional automobiles, further compounding the issues of fuel scarcity and climate change. (In 2009 the Chinese purchased more motor vehicles than did Americans.) But it is beyond dispute that General Motors in the 20th century contributed mightily to the growth and welfare of the U.S. and global economies. When Charlie Wilson, then President of GM, was nominated by President Eisenhower to serve as Secretary of Defense, his 1953 confirmation hearing resulted in a famous "misquote." The press stated that Wilson had told the Senate Armed Services Committee, "What's good for General Motors is good for the country." What he actually said, when asked whether his corporate service presented a potential conflict for a public servant, was "For years I thought that what was good for our country was good for General Motors, and vice versa."[50]

4

My Father, Gerard C. Smith

Aristotle equated the "good life" with the notion of a "happy life." As necessities for a lasting happiness, Aristotle identified "good birth, good health, good looks, good luck, good reputation, good friends, good money and goodness."[51] My father was blessed with all these Aristotelian attributes, and he put them to constructive use. In addition he set an extraordinary example for his children and grandchildren.

In sharp contrast to my two grandfathers, my father spent his youth in very comfortable circumstances. His challenge in life was not to make a fortune—his father had taken care of that—but rather to avoid squandering the opportunities furnished him by a fortunate birth. (J.T. left an estate of approximately $25 million. It is reasonable to assume that each of his three children, after taxes, inherited approximately $4 million. In today's terms this amount is equivalent to approximately $40 million measured by the CPI and $240 million in terms of relative share of the GDP.)

In the first part of his life, until age 36, Dad reaped the rewards of his privileged circumstances: attending private schools, Yale University, and Yale Law School; sailing, skiing, playing polo, tennis, and golf; chartering deep-sea fishing boats; and touring Europe. In 1950, however, Dad began a career of exceptional and productive public service, much of which focused on the promise and peril of nuclear technology and nuclear weapons. To this task he brought the benefits of a first-class, liberal education; the sense of personal security and balance afforded by independent financial means; and the example of his father's questing intellect. He also had the benefit of my mother's unstinting affection, companionship, and determination. He allowed the advantages of birth to be an asset for public service rather than to become a detriment and distraction. That said, he enjoyed a life of many opportunities and comforts, while striving until his death at the age of 80 to limit the risks to this nation and to the planet posed by nuclear weapons.

Many of the details of my father's public career appear in a short memoir entitled *Disarming Diplomat*[52] that he completed in 1994, in the last months of his life. Further detail on his most significant public service as head of the U.S. Delegation to the first Strategic Arms Limitation Talks (SALT) with the Soviet Union, in 1969–1973, appear in his book *Doubletalk*.[53] Still further reflections on his public career can be found in the "Festschrift" prepared by friends and colleagues on the occasion of his 75th birthday, entitled *Gerard C. Smith: A Career in Progress*.[54] As a matter of reticence and personal propriety, Dad omitted extensive personal detail from his memoir. Instead, he offered a daunting menu of discussion of such topics as Atoms for Peace, Multilateral Force (MLF), SALT, and the nuclear Non-Proliferation Treaty (NPT), leavened with only a modest amount of personal detail. Accordingly, I will not encumber this short book with extensive historical exposition. Rather, I attempt to paint a more personal picture of my father than do these previous volumes, while nonetheless sketching the broad outlines of his public contributions.

Childhood

Dad was born on May 4, 1914. At the time, his parents, as well as his older siblings, lived on the Upper West Side of Manhattan. When he wrote his stream-of-conscious diary entries in the early winter of 1986–1987 by my mother's bedside, my father recorded his earliest memories as being "about 1917." These memories date to the entry of the United States into World War I in the spring of 1917, when he turned three. He also recalls being sent to promote the sale of war bonds on the steps of the New York Public Library dressed in a soldier suit. His mother called him "Baby," an endearment that transmuted into "Waddy," a nickname used by his brother Gregory and family friend José Ferrer, well into my father's 60s. His early memories include the gift of a gold watch from his uncle Terry; his mother playing the piano; his father traveling to Ecuador and returning using large Spanish words; his father's weekend drafting legal papers on a yellow legal pad; his parents' departure for numerous operas and a stack of librettos saved.

Dad further remembers his mother's brother Vincent, a doctor, giving him a shot during the Spanish flu epidemic 1918–1919; his governess Miss

Michel; and his first opportunity to wear long pants in 1924. He also remembers holiday visits from W.C. Durant; receiving a catcher's mitt for his birthday in 1919; and soldiers being thrown into the pool at Allenhurst, New Jersey, preparing them for crossing the Atlantic for World War I service in the summers of 1917–1918; and seeing the French Naval Fleet in the Hudson River with large searchlights in 1921.

Dad initially attended a Catholic School named Loyola in upper Manhattan. Then, from 1923 to 1927, he attended St. Bernard's School, a rigorous and, in 2009, still thriving Episcopal day school on East 98th Street in Manhattan. Apparently his parents' respect for excellence in education trumped their belief in Catholic education. Dad noted in his journal that the day would begin with the Lord's Prayer and that he would stop, consistent with his Catholic faith, with the line "deliver us from evil," since at that time Catholics did not say "for thine is the kingdom, the power and the glory forever and ever." Other St. Bernard's memories include a dressing-down from the stern headmaster, J.G. Jenkins, for leaving early one day; an unsuccessful role in a Shakespeare play; shooting baskets in the gym; and skating on a frozen school yard. Dad lists Mr. Jenkins as a significant formative influence, inculcating values of integrity, "British fair play," sportsmanship, and the importance of not being a quitter and not "letting the side down."

Canterbury School

A move from the Upper West Side to 1115 Fifth Avenue (at 93rd Street) in 1926 made St. Bernard's at East 98th Street more readily accessible. As St. Bernard's only went through the eighth grade, Dad and his classmates had to transfer elsewhere for later education. At the time, most young New Yorkers at St. Bernard's would proceed to boarding schools such as Groton and St. Paul's. In 1926, for an Irish Catholic like Dad, this was not a comfortable option. Instead, he enrolled at Canterbury School in New Milford, Connecticut, a lay Catholic school already attended by his older brother Gregory (and subsequently by two further generations of Smiths). At the time, Canterbury was a relatively small school, founded in 1916 to provide a first-class preparatory education to Catholics who were either not welcome or not comfortable at more established preparatory schools. Canterbury was run or "ruled" by an extraordinary figure, Nelson Hume, a dominating personality who led daily chapel and who was reputed to monitor, individually, the behavior and habits of every young man at the school.

There, my father was strongly influenced by two teachers, Philip Brodie, a former Rhodes Scholar from Alabama, and Ed Mack, a history teacher. Both were still alive when I attended Canterbury in 1956–1960, and the elderly Mr. Brodie confused me with my father at the time of my graduation in 1960. Mr. Mack encouraged Dad to think of history as a tool to understand the present and the future. He helped my father write a paper regarding the first five-year economic plan prepared by the Soviet Union, in which Dad opined that the plan would fail, since Russians were dreamers, not doers. Neither my father nor Mr. Mack could then have realized that a significant portion of my father's later public career would be taken up by negotiation with non-dreamy representatives of a nuclear-armed Soviet Union. My father remarks that he admired Mr. Mack because he was a man, like J.T., having "no pretense."

In addition to studying history and Latin, my father played baseball, starting as catcher on the varsity team in his junior or fifth form year. In his senior year, Mr. Jenkins's injunction against quitting notwithstanding, he resigned from the baseball team in protest of a firing of the coach. His place as catcher was filled by a younger student and family friend, "Sarge" Shriver. (In 1982 Canterbury convened a graduate "colloquium" to help enhance the school's image after a lackluster 1970s and the stewardship of an unsuccessful headmaster. The new headmaster in 1982, my history teacher and friend, Rod Clarke, selected Dad and Sarge Shriver to chair the event.)

While at Canterbury he participated in Catholic "retreats," a period of a day or more dedicated to silence, reflection, and inspirational sermons by intelligent priests. He remembered especially a retreat led by a Father Donovan, a Dominican priest and the brother of "Wild Bill" Donovan, who became the head of the Office of Strategic Services (predecessor to the CIA) in the Second World War. At one point, my father even wondered whether he had a "vocation"—that is, a calling to be a Catholic priest. Luckily for all of us, he decided that he did not have such a celibate calling. During my father's final year at Canterbury a young Irish Catholic, John F. Kennedy, attended Canterbury as a first-year student. He became ill and was withdrawn before the year was out. The regimen at Canterbury was not Spartan. Until the beginning of the Second World War, meals at Canterbury were excellent, and were served by a staff of Filipino waiters. (When I attended 30 years later, the food was indifferent, and students took turns waiting on tables.)

As I am able to imagine my Smith grandfather's life in Ecuador in 1910—having lived there myself in the summer of 1963, so too can I envisage my father's environment (meals aside) at Canterbury School, after attending it myself, 1956–1960. The school, in Western Connecticut, sits atop a hill above the town of New Milford. It enjoys a view of the Berkshire Mountain foothills and of the Housatonic River Valley. Autumn mornings are crisp with glorious foliage. Mist often sits above the river. Winters are extensive with persistent snow cover and gray skies. Spring, while not early, is treasured. The dormitories are simple, stucco buildings—the dining hall a handsome paneled affair. The environment was strictly "male," the exception being a handful of faculty wives who would attend dinner. Accountability was ensured by calling the roll of the entire school at least once a day. (In my freshman year, 1960–1961, there were five Smiths at the school, including a James Smith. Hence the roll call included Smith, A., Smith, J., Smith, J.T., Smith, R., and Smith, W. As a result, at the age of 12, I became "J.T." rather than John Smith.) The gymnasium is at the highest point of the campus, and, in winter after showering, one's hair would freeze on the walk to chapel, dinner, or the dormitory below. Academics were rigorous but not punitive—and every day reinforced Catholic faith from, among other things, compulsory attendance at chapel.

As noted in the prior chapter, J.T. donated funds to Canterbury for the construction of a handsome chapel. This chapel was under construction during my father's tenure at the school and was completed by his graduation in 1931. Though Canterbury doubtless had a strong and beneficial effect on my father's upbringing, his diaries and personal reminisces are somewhat "thin" on this period of his life. They suggest that at this stage in his upbringing, he was more interested in vacation than the rigors of school—a not unhealthy or atypical attitude. His diary describes long and enjoyable summers on the Jersey Shore playing tennis, golf, and polo, and fishing and swimming in the Atlantic. It also includes reference to such simple boyhood pleasures as placing coins on railroad tracks to see them flattened by passing trains, the joys of summer ice cream and hayrides. The family had a German Shepherd named "Toby"—but only on the Jersey Shore during the summer. My father's diary reflects puzzlement as to what happened to this admirable creature during the balance of the year. Suffice it to say Toby did not live with the Smith family in a New York apartment.

During the time my father attended Canterbury, in 1928–1929, he spent an extended period in Europe, where he learned to ski at St. Moritz, while his father was engaged in the negotiations for acquisition of Opel by General Motors. My father's memories of this stay in St. Moritz appear more affectionate than his memories of being "nestled in the foothills of the Berkshires" at Canterbury.

Other extra-scholastic interests included California, where his father would go with some regularity on business for the Argonaut Mine. According to his diary, Dad first felt the "spell" of California while accompanying his father on a drive down from the Sierras to the Coast in 1924, when he would have been 10 years old. He goes on to remember later visits to California—the glamour of Hollywood, playing tennis on cement courts at Pasadena, visiting Catalina Island, and riding the Southern Pacific from San Francisco to Los Angeles. Also in 1924, my father made his first ocean crossing, when the entire Smith family sailed from New York to Europe on a vessel called the *Leviathan*. My father was impressed by the ship's swimming pool and the sight of the great hull cutting through the water—as well as an ice carving of a swan in the dining salon.

Yale College

Upon graduation from Canterbury in 1931, my father journeyed to New Haven to attend Yale. He records no thoughts regarding the fact that, in returning to New Haven, he was returning to family roots. The polo, golf, and tennis playing, 17-year old Gerard Smith approached New Haven with a great deal more worldliness and wealth than had characterized the status of his father when he left, a poor but prodigiously talented graduate of Yale Law School three decades earlier.

My father's diary is quite reticent regarding his four years as an undergraduate at Yale. He majored in history and began a lifelong interest in naval matters, writing a long paper on the Battle of Jutland. (This battle involved the only fleet-to-fleet naval combat—between the British and the Germans—during the First World War.) Seeking to emulate J.T.'s erudition, Dad continued to study Latin all four years of college, bringing his total Latin studies to 12 years. He took an interest in Roman history but claimed never to have "mastered it"—even after studying, in Latin, Suetonius, Horace, Catullus, Plautus, Tacitus, and Cicero. It is likely that he obtained a better grasp of both Latin and Roman history than any but a very few modern-day college scholars. In my father's junior year he was accepted into Pierson College, one of the most prestigious of the new "residential colleges" established at Yale during his tenure.

If my father's diary is to be credited, his favorite memory of these undergraduate years was playing polo during his first two years at Yale. He was part of a practice squad that would scrimmage the Yale Varsity, comprising legendary players such as Mike Phipps and Stu Igelhart. He recounts that, at the end of these scrimmages, he would be so tired as to be virtually unable to crawl into bed. He comments that he could not have imagined at that time that he would later (in 1972) be awarded an honorary degree by Yale for his subsequent public service. Perhaps tongue in cheek, my father's diary comments that these polo scrimmages were "more fun than all that came later." My father's diary also adverts to football weekends and drinking homemade gin with orange juice before the end of prohibition. My father's polo career ended when his otherwise permissive father determined that young Gerard was devoting too much energy to polo and not enough to his studies. At the time, students wishing to play polo had to bear the cost of maintaining a string of polo ponies, and J.T. decided it was no longer appropriate to subsidize my father's string.

Young Sports Fisherman

Polo to one side, one senses that my father's Yale undergraduate years were neither particularly productive nor happy. His journal suggests that he was socially awkward. For instance, he confesses that he did not know how to dance—a requisite skill for social success in the 1930s. (He ultimately remedied this defect by taking dancing lessons at the age of 26 at an Arthur Murray Studio.) His polo playing curtailed, Dad took up a new interest that could be pursued during college vacations—fishing for marlin and sailfish from chartered boats, first in Miami and in Long Island, and subsequently in the Bahamas at Bimini. There, while on vacation from Yale Law School, my father caught a 14-foot long, 600-pound blue marlin. Living large, as he did as a young man, he had this leviathan mounted and placed on the wall of the staircase in J.T.'s Southampton villa, Certosa. After Certosa was torn down (deemed too large and costly to operate after the Second World War), my father's great fish ended up hanging behind a bar in Montauk Point, Long Island. More than sixty years later, the location of this great trophy is unknown.

A remarkable record of my father's "romance" with deep-sea fishing survives in the form of a letter to his mother and father, written in Miami Beach, Florida, in December 1934 during his senior year at Yale, when he was 20. Even then, missives from 20-year-olds to parents were rare. It begins "believe it or not, I'm writing you a letter for the first time in many years." The letter proudly describes the catch of Dad's first sailfish. It is worth quoting at some length for it amply conveys Dad's fascination:

[B]y Castor and Pollux, it was the greatest of all thrills to see a fin slicing through the wake—a strike: then you gave him lots of line and bang you snap on the drag and forcibly set the hook in his leathery jaws and in a split second he's taken 200 yards (count 'em) of line and you can't do a thing about it.

The fish once landed after a half hour struggle is described as follows:

[A] glorious cyllinder [sic] of astonishing blue and gray pigmentation— a long ferocious bill, a streamlined body and a large eye which looks up at you from the fish box and seems to say reproachfully—why don't you "collitch guys" leave us alone.

Then, to assuage any concerns that John Thomas may have had regarding Dad's frivolous pursuits, the student/fisherman reports that he is halfway through Churchill's *World Crisis*. He analyzes Churchill's treatment of the World War I Dardanelles/Gallipoli disaster, noting that Churchill's apologies suggest more culpability on Churchill's part than the historical record could otherwise attribute to him.

The letter then is testament not only to Dad's love of fishing and the sea, but also to his emerging interest in history and world events. He finishes with reassurances to his mother that the fishing boat is safely equipped and that fishing took place in view of high-rises in Miami. This reassurance was ironic in light of an adventure Dad would undergo four and a half years later in the Bahamas.

My father's fascination with "billfishing" led him to spend an entire summer, seeking to catch a broadbill swordfish on rod and reel. (In those days, most swordfish were taken by use of harpoons.) In this quest, my father drove each morning from Southampton to Montauk, Long Island (a distance of 25 miles), to spend the day on a charter boat. In more than seventy days of fishing, my father did not land a single swordfish. J.T.'s underwriting of a summer-long fishing charter on behalf of my father is testament to his generosity toward his children. My father's Ahab-like quest for a swordfish possibly testifies to an admirable discipline and determination that would later sustain him in more difficult undertakings, such as strategic arms limitation negotiations and persistent efforts to limit proliferation of nuclear weapons.

A year after his graduation from Yale Law School, my father had a life-altering fishing adventure. In July 1939, he set off from New York with his sister, Maureen, and her husband, Bernard (my uncle "Barney") Shanley, by steamer to Nassau in the Bahamas. There, my 25-year old father and the Shanleys boarded a charter boat, the *Northern Star*. The plan was to run *Northern Star* from Nassau to Bimini, a journey of approximately 130 miles through then little traveled waters above the Bahama Bank. Ten hours into this journey, the two engines of the *Northern Star* sputtered and quit, while the young charter party was still 40 miles from Bimini. Apparently, a thief had siphoned a significant portion of the 150 gallons of fuel previously loaded aboard *Northern Star*, while it was at rest in Nassau. *Northern Star* drifted for several days. Flares and rifle shots failed to obtain the attention of a regularly scheduled Pan Am Clipper flight that passed each day near the horizon. As food and water ran low, those aboard had time to reflect on mortality. Eventually, after a favorable wind shift, the charter party adopted the expedient of sewing together sheets from the boat's bunks and lashing them to the bamboo poles or "outriggers" used for fishing. They then "sailed" to safety in Bimini.

My father recorded the details of this adventure in a small, privately published book, *All at Sea*. At the book's end, my father, while expressing skepticism about "moralizing epilogues," offers the thought that he came out of this experience a different person. Surviving the adversity of a summer week adrift at sea and uncertain of rescue had built up in him a store of confidence of the sort that "experience alone can engender."[55]

In Bimini, my father would stay at an inn called The Compleat Angler, also a haunt of Ernest Hemingway. Dad was doubtless glad for a stiff drink, a good meal, and a night's rest at this inn upon completion of the adventure described in *All at Sea*. Eager to share the happier features of his fishing adventures, my father took his children to Bimini as one stop on a spring vacation cruise aboard a chartered yacht in the early 1960s. There we met the proprietress, Helen Duncombe, who greeted my father fondly after a nearly quarter century absence.

Sons try to emulate admirable fathers. Though neither I nor my two brothers have had the time or the resources to do as much fishing as my father did in his 20s, all three of us have retained a fascination for deep-sea fishing. My brother Hugh has pursued the sport off Costa Rica in recent years. My brother Gerry served as captain of the "Yale Fishing Team." And, in my youth, I had some wonderful fishing adventures off the Pacific Coast of Panama, off Ecuador, and in the Sea of Cortez off Baja, California. In my case, these experiences have been more than adequate to enable me to understand the delight and fascination my father must have felt in this sport.

Yale Law School

My father followed his father's footsteps and attended Yale Law School. Again, his journal is quite reticent about academic life during these years (1935–1938). At least two of his professors, Fritz Kessler and Myres McDougal, were still active at Yale Law School when I attended 30 years later. The former was a renowned contracts law professor who spoke with a thick German accent, had a twinkle in his eye, and was not averse to consuming a martini at lunch. I fondly recall him using the expression "If my memory serves . . .," and then after a short pause following up with the statement "and it does." McDougal, who had been a property law professor in my father's day, became a leading scholar on international law. Ten years after graduating from law school, I had occasion to work with him when I was part of the U.S. delegation to the U.N. Law of the Sea Conference.

Whatever the reason for my father's reticence about his law school days, the family's ties to this extraordinary educational institution are long and deep. (The attendance of the law school by my nephew and Godson, Gerard F. Griffin in the class of 1995, marked the fourth generation of the family to be educated at this exceptional institution.) While I was still a student there, my father and others endowed a professorship in honor of my grandfather's memory. The first holder of the John Thomas Smith Professorship of Law was Guido Calibresi, later Dean of the Law School and now a distinguished judge on the U.S. Court of Appeals for the Second Circuit. (I studied under Guido and, with three colleagues, rented his farm in Woodbridge, Connecticut, during our second year in law school when Guido was on sabbatical.) I also served with Guido on the Board of the St. Thomas More Catholic Center at Yale, the chapel at which had been built with funds from John Thomas Smith.

Guido, in turn, while Dean of the Yale Law School, suggested that a Chair be endowed in honor of my father. Guido made this suggestion in 1990, while my father was still alive. Dad initially opposed the notion of an endowed Chair in the name of a living person. He succumbed to Guido's logic that many friends who would want to contribute might no longer be alive if the project waited until my father's death. Also, to expand the appeal of the idea to my father, Guido suggested the Chair be named after my mother (who died in 1987) as well as my father. The initial occupant of the Gerard C. and Bernice L. Smith Chair of Law was Harold Koh, who himself served with distinction as Dean of Yale Law School and, at this writing, is the Legal Advisor to the State Department.

Early Profession and Marriage

After graduating from Yale School in 1938, my father took the New York Bar exam and went to work for his father on the legal staff of General Motors. At this time, my father also took over as President of the Argonaut Mining Company, which gave him occasion for new trips to California, which he enjoyed. One senses that Dad did not flourish in the role of a junior lawyer on his own father's legal staff. (Modern principles against nepotism inhibit such awkward situations.) In any event, Dad worked principally for a GM lawyer named George Brooks. He was a stern mentor, who impressed on Dad the paramount importance of thorough preparation of legal cases and the use of clear, no-nonsense language. Dad's journal lists George Brooks as one of the people who had the greatest influence on him when he was a young man. Others that he lists include: J.T. (the largest single influence); Ed Mack, the Canterbury history teacher; Mr. Jenkins of St. Bernard's; and Father James Keller, who taught my father the expression that it is "better to light one candle than to curse the darkness." According to Robert Nitschke, Brooks was a man of many parts. He had put himself through Fordham Law School by teaching high school Greek and Latin and lecturing at Seton Hall College. Subsequently he had obtained a Master of Law degree from NYU and privately practiced law for four years before joining the GM legal staff in 1934.[56]

Whatever the rigors of working on his father's legal staff, Dad's prewar life left time for fishing in the Bahamas, cruises with J.T. aboard Alfred P. Sloan's yacht, the *René*, tennis and golf in Southampton and, eventually, in 1940, much needed dancing lessons. In 1940, a mutual friend introduced him to my mother, Bernice Latrobe Maguire, an attractive, auburn-haired, strong-minded, strong-willed, and intelligent woman. A contemporaneous diary entry by my father records the meeting and the unenthusiastic comment, "ugh." Nevertheless, he quickly overcame his initial reaction and, by the winter of 1941, my mother and father were journeying (with proper chaperonage) by overnight train to Canada for skiing at Mt. Tremblant. A graduate of Smith College and former Midwesterner (having grown up in St. Louis and Chicago), Will Maguire's third daughter, "Tubby," in 1940 was working in New York as a director of publicity for the department store, Lord & Taylor.

After the snows melted, romance proceeded aboard the *Innisfail*. As previously mentioned, my grandfather, who shared his son's love of the ocean, purchased *Innisfail* for my father in 1940. "Innisfail," which is an ancient name for Ireland, was also the name of a privately controlled corporation, the Innisfail Corporation, to which J.T. had sold GM shares at a loss in the early 1930s in search of a personal tax benefit. Litigation between J.T. and the Commissioner of Internal Revenue regarding the legitimacy of these losses went all the way to the Supreme Court, where J.T. lost.[57]

On Memorial Day weekend in May 1941, my father proposed to my mother, while anchored off Solomon's Island where the Patuxent River enters the Chesapeake Bay. Also aboard the *Innisfail* were my father's Southampton friends, John and Audrey Baker. Martinis marked the celebration when mother accepted. They were married in a small ceremony August 9, 1941, at St. Ignatius Loyola Church on Park Avenue and 83d Street in New York. My mother undertook instruction as a Catholic, and the day before the wedding she was baptized a Catholic. This was likely a significant step for the daughter of a Christian Scientist mother and agnostic father. Mother remained a Catholic, but one sensed that the root of her faith was her devotion to my father rather than any profound appreciation for the doctrines of the Church.

From the wedding reception, bride and groom proceeded by car to Montauk, Long Island, to board the *Innisfail*—after stopping briefly at Certosa to call upon Mary Smith, whose infirmity had prevented her attendance at the wedding. Their honeymoon cruise took them to Block Island, Nantucket, and then on to the coast of Maine—Boothbay Harbor, Rockland, Northeast Harbor, and Bar Harbor. Anchored in Nantucket Harbor with my father on a chartered sailboat in the summer of 1987 after mother's death, we spotted the now fashionable Inn called the White Elephant. Dad recalled that, at my mother's urging after two days of honeymoon aboard the *Innisfail*, they inquired at the White Elephant about the availability of a room. They thought the quoted price of $7 per night to be scandalous. (A room today in August at the White Elephant costs 100 times this amount.)

Navy Service and Young Family

Earlier in 1940, my father, anticipating that the United States would be drawn into the Second World War, had sought and obtained a commission as an ensign in the Navy, and wedding pictures show him resplendent in the white summer uniform of a Naval Ensign. After honeymooning, he and my mother returned to his posting in Washington, D.C. There, in the short period before Pearl Harbor, my father kept the *Innisfail* on the Potomac River and would take his commanding officer out for luncheon cruises. It was a different era, and it is a safe bet that not many 27-year-old junior officers in today's Navy have 72-foot yachts at their personal disposition. After Pearl Harbor, my grandfather and father donated *Innisfail* to the United States for such service as she might render.

By his own assessment, my father did not have a "heroic war." Though he volunteered for sea combat duty, the Navy kept him in Washington, applying his legal training to problems of contractual procurement of important defense systems, including radar. My father speculates that the Navy disqualified him for combat service due to a heart condition from arrhythmia (diagnosed when he was about 19 years of age). During his four and a half years of service in Washington my father, as a naval reserve officer, received promotion on a routine basis from Ensign to Lieutenant JG, and finally to Lieutenant. A journal from this period, in which Dad made episodic entries, records rather uninteresting meetings about contractual issues. It also demonstrates that Dad enjoyed enough free time, even during war, to attempt to teach himself celestial navigation—his mind doubtless running to the sea—either for active duty or possibly for a return to the life of yachting.

My father and mother took up residence in D.C.'s Kalorama district, which became their neighborhood for most of their married life: first at 2540 Massachusetts Avenue; then 2409 California Street; then in 1950 at 2425 Kalorama Road; and finally, from 1965 until after my mother's death in 1987, at 2425 Tracy Place. My parents valued this fine neighborhood for its quiet streets, tall trees, substantial houses, embassy residences, and congenial, sophisticated neighbors. Once we children appeared, there was ready access to the Bancroft Street playground and to Montrose Park. A mile's walk would place Dad at his Navy, and later his State Department offices. A half-mile walk would place him at early Mass at St. Matthew's Cathedral adjacent to Connecticut Avenue.

My sister Sheila was born seven months after Pearl Harbor, on July 13, 1942, and I was born on October 22, 1943. As the mild pejorative goes, by our 15-month separation, we are "Irish twins." Our passports reflect that neither of us was born in Washington. Our parents, sophisticated Manhattanites, were distrustful of the quality of medicine in Washington, D.C., and my mother was sent to reside uneasily with her parents-in-law in New York to await our respective arrivals.

My father recalls wartime Washington with little enthusiasm—although my parents made some lifelong friends, including Harry Covington, the son of Judge Covington, founder of Covington & Burling and counsel to DuPont; Alfred Moran, a well-known citizen of New Orleans with a major tugboat company in his background; Paul and Kitty Swett, a Smith College friend of mother's; John Avirett, a somewhat older naval colleague of Dad's; and Turner and Jane McBaine. In addition, through the McBaines, my parents would see another of my mother's Smith College acquaintances, Julia Child. Food and gasoline were under ration, and my father records, shock of all shocks, that good wine and whiskey were scarce.

Of these World War II acquaintances, John Avirett proved the most consequential, if not the most famous. He was an up and coming Baltimore lawyer before the War and later became the managing partner of Baltimore's most established law firm, Piper, Marbury. More importantly, as the war was ending, he suggested that my father consider purchasing a Maryland farm. In the spring of 1945, "Uncle" John and my father (without my mother) visited Ratcliffe Manor, outside Easton, Maryland, comprising a 1750 Georgian manor house, extensive boxwood gardens, barns and tenant houses, and approximately 500 acres of farmland, bordered by miles of waterfront on the Tred Avon River. When the real estate agent told my father that there was active interest in the place and that he was to show it again that same day, Dad confronted the choice of moving promptly to purchase without consulting my mother. Uncle John advised him to proceed, and he did. Ratcliffe Manor remained the family's center of gravity for a half a century thereafter.

In the short contribution that Uncle John made to the *Festschrift* that I helped organize for Dad's 75th birthday, he recollects not only the hurried and successful purchase of Ratcliffe Manor, but also meeting John Thomas Smith. The occasion was a side trip when Dad and Uncle John visited New York on Navy business. At the time, J.T. was in Southampton. He was sitting in his study reading Karl Marx's *Das Kapital* in German. J.T. opined that young men like Uncle John and my father should pay close heed to this book by the philosophical founder of Communism because they would "certainly have to deal with the Russians."[58]

Ratcliffe Manor, Manhattan,
the Welkin, and the Ark

Upon my father's discharge from the Navy, at War's end, the family moved to Ratcliffe Manor, where we lived from September 1945 until the autumn of 1946. Among my earliest memories is my mother's return from the hospital, a month before my third birthday, with my younger brother, Gerry, born September 10, 1946. (Gerry's full name is Gerard Lawrence Smith, with Lawrence substituting for the out-of-favor "Coad." Lawrence was my mother's grandfather's name, and a congratulatory telegram from Will Maguire on this occasion praised selection of Gerry's middle name.) Sheila cried because she had wanted a sister. Gerry cried as only a new baby in unfamiliar circumstances can. I remember interruption of my dinner, cherry-flavored Jell-o, and a temporarily, very noisy household.

During his year in Maryland, my father began active management of the farm, took long walks and augmented his exercise by chopping and sawing wood. In the latter endeavor, he was guided by a wonderful grandson of slaves, Wilson Ayers, who, with his wife and eight children, lived in a tenant house on Ratcliffe Manor. Wilson's wife, Sarah, cooked and, through the years, Wilson and Sarah's children became playmates to the Smith children. Wilson and Sarah's daughter, Barbara, upon their deaths, took over management of the household and provided unstinting, loving care to both my mother and father in their final infirmities. Wilson's son Robert, and his grandson, Keith, still help maintain Ratcliffe Manor (under new ownership since 1995), making the tenure of the Ayerses significantly more sustained than that of the Smiths.

My father readily determined that life as a full-time "gentleman farmer" would not be a fulfilling one. In the fall of 1946, the family moved to New York City and took up residence in J.T.'s building at 19 East 72nd Street. My father, without excessive enthusiasm, resumed the practice of law, first in partnership with a college and law school friend, Kevin McInnerny, then briefly with his own father from the date of his GM retirement until his death a few months later, and lastly, on his own. Upon his father's death in 1948, Dad's legal practice focused on the details of my grandfather's very substantial estate. This inheritance must have eroded any residual zeal my father might have had for general legal practice.

Dad compensated for any professional disappointment by enjoying a very high quality of life for one in his early to mid-30s. In addition to Ratcliffe Manor and 19 East 72nd Street, he acquired a 60-foot ocean sailing yacht, which he christened the *Welkin* (meaning in Middle English, "the vault of heaven"). She had been named the *Orient* by her prior owner, John Nicholas Brown of Rhode Island, and had competed in the Trans-Pacific race. With a favorable breeze and a calm sea, she could sail at 14 knots (or 16 miles per hour). *Welkin* was manned by a captain and a steward. She spent the fall, winter, and spring on the Chesapeake and in the summer was moored in Sag Harbor, Long Island. My sense is that Dad used her mostly for "day" sails with friends and not for long ocean passages or racing. She was a very fine day sailor, indeed. A small photograph of *Welkin* under sail found in my father's desk bears the handwritten caption, "Remember these days."

Unfortunately, my memories of sailing aboard *Welkin* are scant, as she was sold before my sixth birthday. Cruises with small children aboard were an exception—for good and sufficient reason. Indeed, my only clear memory of a sail aboard the *Welkin* is a day on which I made myself a pest to the adults. At about the age of four, I was given a pirate costume. Dressed in this pirate regalia, and brandishing a toy gun with the manic indiscretion of a four-year-old, I sufficiently disrupted the peace of the martini-drinking and sandwich-eating adults that I was told the Coast Guard had been called to remove the pirate menace. I recall retreating in fear of removal by the Coast Guard. In fact, I am unsure whether I ever wore my pirate costume again.

Having sailed on the protected waters of Long Island Sound and Gardiners Bay, as well the Chesapeake Bay, I have an appreciation of the delight that my parents must have felt, married with the wind and sea on an ocean-racing yacht in sparkling days, imagining an unbounded future with war ended, youthful energies, and bright prospects at every horizon.

Those delights notwithstanding, my father sold the *Welkin*, and, in 1949, purchased a large, yellow, shingle-style house on the dunes of Southampton, ideally located across the street from the 20 grass tennis courts of the Meadow Club and an easy walk to the Beach Club. Due to the ability of this house to withstand hurricane tides, my parents named it "The Ark." The Ark was a luminous example of "shingle-style" architecture that burgeoned in the early 20th century. With approximately 12,000 square feet of living space, the house had eight bedrooms, seven of which faced the Atlantic Ocean, two living rooms, north and south sun parlors, a large "playroom" adorned with heads of African animals bagged by the prior owner, a dining room, and extensive kitchen and pantries and maids' quarters. The Ark served as the family's summer home from 1949 to 1979. During the first twenty years of this period, my mother would normally take up residence shortly before the Fourth of July and remain in Southampton until after

Labor Day, with my father commuting from Washington for weekends as well as vacation weeks.

The house was close to the ocean, and the Atlantic was a constant presence. With a strong southerly wind, one could almost feel ocean spray when sitting on the oceanside terrace. At other times, the waves would spike sharply, and waking in a second-floor bedroom, one could feel the house shaking. The north side windows looked over the lawn tennis courts of the Meadow Club. The more constant sound of the ocean would be punctuated by the sounds of rackets striking balls or, depending upon the time of day, the noise of lawnmowers manicuring the lawn tennis courts. The Ark provided Sheila, John, Gerry, and Hugh (born in 1954) Arcadian summer circumstance.

I have clear memories of life at 19 East 72nd Street. Some are of nightmares typical of a three- or four-year-old. Others are of trips to Central Park to the sailboat pond and to the zoo. On one traumatic occasion, a baboon spat a mouthful of dirty water on me. More pleasantly, my sister Sheila and I would be taken by our English nanny, Miss Beatrice Trinder, to matinees of Broadway plays, armed with phone-book "yellow pages" as a kind of booster seat. In particular, I remember *Annie Get Your Gun*. From my window, I could watch snow fall and the excitement of wedding parties entering and leaving St. James Episcopal Church across Madison Avenue. Two favorite books read to Sheila and me repeatedly were E.B. White's *Stuart Little*, and Dr. Seuss's *Horton the Elephant*. (The former featured an exciting sailboat race that took place in the familiar Central Park pond that I visited each day in fair weather.)

I have but the haziest memories of the beginning of nursery school and kindergarten—with my sister Sheila. In the fall of 1949, at the age of five, I entered first grade at St. Bernard's where my father had studied. Apparently my parents had tried to enter me a year earlier, when I would have been four turning five. The redoubtable Mr. Jenkins advised them of the obvious—that I belonged in kindergarten or even nursery school. My memories of St. Bernard's include boldly singing "Onward Christian Soldiers," a well-run classroom led by a kind, but firm Miss Ferguson, and friendship with Jonathan Mayhew Wainwright, who had cachet due to the fact that his Uncle was a famous World War II general, "Skinny" Wainwright, who had been the U.S. Commander on Bataan and survived the famous "death march." At a spring "field day," I won a running race and the prize was a copy of *The Wind in the Willows*, in which the rambunctious Mr. Toad made a lasting impression.

During this four-year New York stage, my sister Sheila and I were close. Gerry, but an infant and toddler, was much less of a presence. (Gerry really caught my attention somewhat later in life. After our move to Washington, in the early 1950s, he managed to throw a heavy wooden block in my direction hitting me squarely in the "groin." Gerry later proved to be an excellent tennis player and golfer, and his strength and untoward accuracy at block throwing probably presaged these later, more constructive athletic accomplishments.)

On fall and spring (and some winter) weekends the family would journey to Ratcliffe Manor—by train to Wilmington, Delaware, and then by car to Easton. I have memories of cozy fires in the library, cold winter weather, and the advent of spring signaled by forsythia blossoms. In spring and fall, we would play inside the 10-foot-tall, 200-year-old boxwoods that adorned the back lawn and provided a magical world of filtered sunbeams. At some point in this period, my parents dubbed me "Gink" due to a propensity to cry out at night demanding a "gink of water." Shortly thereafter my father bought a small powerboat and, in my "honor" christened her the *Gink*.

International Beginnings

As reflected in a journal that he kept in 1950, my father's mind turned increasingly to consequential, international matters. Possibly fulfilling J.T.'s advice to him and to John Avirett, he began to prepare to "deal with the Russians," by spending most of his free time studying the Russian language. His diary on January 6, 1950, records the question of "what effect should atom (and now hydrogen bomb) have on our handling of our lives?" An entry on January 20, 1950, indicates that Dad favored proceeding with development of a hydrogen bomb, but that mother was less certain of the correctness of this course. (President Truman had announced in late September 1949 that the United States had determined that the Soviet Union had tested a nuclear device, and a formerly secret policy debate on development of the hydrogen bomb became public in the fall of 1949.)

Dad's journal indicates, however, there was time for dinners and bridge games with friends, journeys to Ratcliffe Manor, attendance at the opera and summer golf, tennis and ocean bathing in Southampton. In addition, in early 1950, Dad and his sister Maureen began to plan a trip to Europe. The first idea was to ski in the Alps at Davos. However, my parents in their mid-30s decided that skiing would be too strenuous (after a 10-year hiatus caused by the War and the arrival of a young family). As a result, Dad, mother, and the Shanleys decided to tour, rather than ski. As recounted in my father's journal, he and my mother entrusted the three of us to a governess, and on March 3 boarded the Queen Mary to cross the Atlantic for a six-week visit to Europe.

My parents began their visit in Paris, where they spent two weeks. During this time, they ate at the apartment of their wartime Washington friend, Julia Child, who cooked. As reflected in his diary, my father found Julia's husband to be somewhat to the "left" in his political views, and the two of them argued. My father recorded no evaluation of the cuisine prepared by this now most famous of chefs. Dad was attuned to the political situation, and social unrest, spurred on by Communists, was in the air. Later they ventured to Rome, where my father's diary mentions that, while he was calmly buying shirts, soldiers were controlling a mob outside. From Rome they proceeded to Florence, then to the Cote d'Azure in the South of France. Europe still wore a depressed, postwar mantle, and fortunate Americans, such as my parents, could travel in great style, at relatively modest expense given the value of the dollar. They returned, again by ocean liner, the *Ile de'France*, doubtless glad to be home again and reunited with their children.

In the spring and summer of 1950, Dad resumed his charmed, but unfulfilling life in Manhattan, Easton, and Southampton. On June 25, 1950 the Korean War began, and Dad's diary started to reflect his concerns with its implications for the U.S.-Soviet relationship. On July 9, 1950, Dad noted that "Russian leaders are as worried (probably) over Korea as American." Then, three days later, Dad speculated that the United States would have to pull out of Korea and rely on air and naval strikes until marshalling the ground troops to land in Korea in 1951. Then, in somewhat ignorant fashion, his diary asked: "Why not scorch the earth of Korea with some A-bombs after due warning to N Koreans—not to kill but to prevent them coming further."

The Atomic Energy Commission

In the late summer of 1950, a family friend, Thomas E. Murray, whom Truman had appointed as a Commissioner on the Atomic Energy Commission (AEC) in March 1950, invited Dad to Washington, D.C., to serve as his Executive Assistant. Unfulfilled by his legal practice and looking for a way to make a larger contribution to the nation's welfare, the 36-year-old Gerard Smith jumped at the chance to return to Washington and work in what was at the time one of the most important agencies of government. Dad thereupon began a 40-year career in wrestling with the problems of nuclear weapons, nuclear proliferation, and nuclear power. Dad's government service at the AEC began October 1, 1950.

Murray was an engineer by training, and a businessman who had been a Director of Chrysler Corporation and the Bank of New York. He knew J.T. and Dad from both business and social circumstance. The Murrays, active and devout Catholics, were a leading force in Southampton, Long Island. This large and dynamic family with many children, as well as the related McDonnell family, moved to Southampton in 1929, greatly increasing the Catholic "footprint" in the resort, a more tolerant domain than the more glitzy Newport, Rhode Island. [59]

Created by the Atomic Energy Act of 1946, the AEC had assumed responsibility for all of the facilities and programs of the Manhattan Engineering District, which had developed the atom bomb during the Second World War. These responsibilities included stewardship of the nation's then small arsenal of nuclear weapons. The five-member Commission also had responsibility for developing peaceful uses for nuclear power. From its inception in 1947 until September of 1949, when the United States determined that Russia had developed a capacity to build an atom bomb, the Commission, its Military Liaison Committee and its General Advisory Committee, comprising eminent scientists and engineers, and chaired by Robert Oppenheimer who had led the successful World War II effort to build an atomic bomb, had been wrestling with the questions of whether to build an arsenal of such weapons, and if so how large. They did so with oversight from an extraordinarily powerful Congressional Joint Committee on Atomic Energy chaired by Senator Brien McMahon, the principal sponsor of the Atomic Energy Act.

The first Chairman of the AEC was David Lilienthal, former Director of the Tennessee Valley Authority, a liberal New Dealer and highly accomplished public servant. Lilienthal's Chairmanship had been undercut by another commissioner, Admiral Lewis L. Strauss, a conservative Republican and former partner of the investment banking firm, Kuhn Loeb. The latter was a very smart, self-made man, highly adept at bureaucratic and political manipulation. He was also deeply skeptical about the Soviet Union and the likelihood of any meaningful control of nuclear weapons. He would play a large role in development of U.S. nuclear policy in the Eisenhower Administration.[60]

Efforts in the immediate postwar period to develop international control of nuclear weapons had foundered. In the month immediately following the U.S. use of atom bombs on Hiroshima and Nagasaki, the Truman Administration debated possible sharing of some level of nuclear information with the Soviet Union (our World War II ally) in an effort to forestall a nuclear arms race. Robert Oppenheimer favored this approach, as did former Secretary of War, Henry Stimson. In the absence of political support, this initiative failed. In 1946, Dean Acheson and David Lilienthal co-chaired a study regarding controls and safeguards respecting atomic energy. Oppenheimer's was the dominant voice on the study committee. The resulting report proposed turning the U.S. monopoly of nuclear weapons technology, as well as the then quite small U.S. nuclear arsenal, over to a new international sovereign authority, the Atomic Development Authority. This Authority in coordination with the newly created United Nations would control development of atomic energy for peaceful purposes and would prevent proliferation of harmful nuclear weapons arsenals.

To advance this proposal, President Truman called upon Bernard Baruch. Before presenting it to the United Nations, Baruch made a number of elaborations and modifications that provoked Soviet opposition, and the plan proved essentially stillborn. (It is doubtful, in any event, that the Acheson-Lilienthal Plan would have been viable, even if not adulterated by Baruch.)[61]

Debate had emerged whether to proceed with a "Super" or thermonuclear weapon 1,000 times as powerful as an atomic bomb. Oppenheimer consistently opposed building the "Super," which was promoted by physicist Edward Teller, supported by Lewis Strauss. Oppenheimer believed that if the United States proceeded with such a weapon, the Soviet Union would mirror our action to America's net detriment. This debate, as a practical matter, ended once the United States discovered that the Russians had successfully exploded a nuclear device in August 1949. Pursuit of a thermonuclear weapon by the United States could assuage political and public concerns about the Soviet acquisition of the atomic bomb.[62]

In the late 1940s before my father's entry into government service, two men gained prominence in governmental debates about nuclear weapons policy and the U.S. posture toward the Soviet Union. Both preceded my father as Director of the State Department's Policy Planning Staff: George Kennan, from April 1947 until January 1950, and Paul Nitze, from 1950 until the end of the Truman Administration in January 1953. As detailed by the latter's grandson, Nicholas Thompson, in a fascinating joint biography,[63] the two men diverged sharply in policy beliefs during these debates. Kennan joined Oppenheimer opposing the utility and morality of thermonuclear weapons. Nitze favored aggressive development and deployment of nuclear weapons. My father's career would intersect those of both Nitze and Kennan. In 1957, he succeeded both men as Director of Policy of Policy Planning at the State Department. Nitze and my father worked together during the first Strategic Arms Limitation Talks in 1970–1972. My father later joined Kennan in the publication of an article in *Foreign Affairs* in 1982 urging a radical shift in U.S. nuclear weapons policy.

My father's role as Commissioner Murray's Executive Assistant was to make sure that he read the papers that he needed to read and was ready for all agenda items of the meetings of the Commission. In addition, my father helped draft Commissioner Murray's speeches—22 in number during the four years of my father's apprenticeship at the AEC. He also undertook special projects, such as seeking means to ensure foreign sources of supply of uranium from places such as Spain and South Africa.

My father's diary acknowledges that he was "lucky" to receive an appointment to work at the AEC in 1950. Even though he had no background in physics or science, he quickly discovered that very few people in government had full confidence that they knew "what was up." Dad soon felt that he had about as much knowledge as the next nonscientist dealing with the issues of atomic energy. His Navy experience during the Second World War had given him some confidence in the "business end" of government, as well as an appreciation of the importance of relations with military officers. He doubtless also benefited from his fortunate, family background. For instance, when asked by Commissioner Murray to identify candidates for the post of General Manager of the Commission, Dad felt comfortable calling Alfred P. Sloan, then Chairman of GM, to ask his advice. He also noted that his good fortune included the fact that his father was acquainted with Lewis Strauss, who served as Chairman of the AEC once appointed by President Eisenhower in 1953. Apparently, Strauss and J.T. had invested together in an unsuccessful gold mining venture in Virginia.

Dad records that he had little doubt at this time that the United States should be the first to obtain "more/better/bigger weapons" and only subsequently to put them under some sensible control. He thus carried through on his early 1950 instinct that the United States should move ahead with the hydrogen bomb. At the same time he began lifelong ruminations about the morality of nuclear deterrence, that is, whether there was any conceivable scenario under which the United States would be justified in using nuclear weapons again and, if not, whether it was proper to maintain for purposes of deterrence the threat of using such a weapon.

His concerns in this regard were reinforced when his professional responsibilities took him to witness two atmospheric nuclear tests on the atoll of Eniwetok in the Pacific, the first in 1951 and the second in 1952. Senator Henry ("Scoop") Jackson of Washington was part of the Congressional contingent witnessing the 1952 test. Shaken by witnessing the scale of the atmospheric explosion, Jackson turned to my father and asked "Gerry, where is the nearest bar?" My father long maintained that those charged with policy regarding the development and potential use of nuclear weapons should be made to witness such tests. He later urged Secretary of State Dulles and President Eisenhower to witness a test, but he was not successful. Of course, witnessing such a test, did not automatically lead to prudence. Scoop Jackson remained a lifelong "hawk" regarding nuclear weapons— strongly influenced by defense intellectuals such as Albert Wohlstetter and staff aides such as Richard Perle. To the best of my knowledge, neither of these men, or the majority of "defense intellectuals" who gained expanding policy influence during the Cold War, ever witnessed an atmospheric nuclear explosion. (The United States and Russia ceased such atmospheric tests pursuant to the Limited Test Ban Treaty of 1963.)

Dad spent three and a half years working for Commissioner Murray at the AEC. In addition to witnessing nuclear tests, my father underwent other formative experiences during this period. He became a close friend and admirer of another Murray assistant, William McGuirk, a former Naval Academy graduate and investment banker. McGuirk left the Commission in 1952 and spent most of his life in Baltimore, becoming that city's leading citizen, serving as President of the Mercantile Bank and Trust Company, and Chief Executive of the *Baltimore Sun*. He and his wife raised a family of 15 children (two of whom were adopted). (As a troubled teenager, my wife's sister, Emlen Tydings, spent a year living with the McGuirk family, further expanding an extraordinary household.)

As already noted, Bill McGuirk furnished me summer employment in Ecuador in 1963, allowing me the opportunity to trace my grandfather's Ecuadorian footsteps. McGuirk contributed a cogent chapter to the 1989 *Festschrift* in honor of my father's 75th birthday. There, he illuminates some of the roles my father played at the AEC. One included intervening on behalf of a Navy captain, Hyman Rickover, who had been passed over for promotion to Rear Admiral in 1951 and 1952 and therefore faced mandatory retirement from the Navy. My father, who strongly respected Rickover's immense intelligence and unrelenting energies, persuaded Commissioner Murray to intervene with President Truman to rectify the situation. As is well known, Rickover remained in naval uniform for decades more and was the genius behind the development of the country's "nuclear navy." (Rickover ended his career as a Four-Star Admiral, with the longest service as an officer in the history of the Navy.)

During my father's tenure at the AEC, the Pentagon and the powerful Congressional Joint Committee on Atomic Energy pressed hard for continued expansion of the nation's nuclear weapons arsenal. Included in this growth were so-called tactical nuclear weapons, favored by the U.S. Army, to allow it a role in nuclear weapons deployment and by European leaders as a counterbalance to presumed Soviet conventional forces advantages. Robert Oppenheimer participated in studies of these growth demands, and in 1951–1952 favored tactical nuclear weapons and the acquisition of more and better fission bombs, in part to discourage expansive development of thermonuclear weapons. In the end, the country pursued all these avenues. Commissioner Murray, a fervent anti-Communist, endorsed rapid expansion of the nuclear arsenal to eliminate any chance that the country would lag behind the Soviets. At the time, my father was also imbued with strong suspicions of the Soviet Union and had no problem supporting Murray's aggressive policies. As already noted, my father's enthusiasm for nuclear weapons was, however, tempered by the experience of witnessing actual nuclear explosions.

In May 1953, Dad visited the headquarters of the Strategic Air Command in Omaha, Nebraska. His host was Lieutenant General James Walsh, SAC's Head of Intelligence and Dad's personal friend. During this visit, Dad met and talked with General Curtis LeMay, architect of the savage bombing of Japan during the Second World War and now Commander of SAC. He also took time to visit the church on Castellar Street in Omaha where J.T. had lived during his years at Creighton College more than half a century earlier. As an outgrowth of this visit, General Walsh, a devout Catholic, learned that neither my mother nor my sister Sheila had yet received the Catholic sacrament of Confirmation. General Walsh arranged a confirmation ceremony at SAC by a visiting Catholic Bishop, and General LeMay gave a reception to honor the event. Later, when my father became a senior arms control negotiator and was criticized for being too much of a "dove," he would be tempted to answer his critics, "How many of your family have been confirmed at SAC headquarters?"

I had occasion to visit SAC headquarters 20 years later, when serving as Executive Assistant to Secretary of Defense, Elliot Richardson. As part of the Secretary's staff, I received very gracious treatment and a detailed briefing on the extraordinary and redundant capabilities that the United States had developed for use of nuclear weapons. In one of these briefings, an officer suggested that we had the capacity in a nuclear exchange to "make the rubble bounce." It was thus apparent by 1973 that the uniformed military found the country's nuclear arsenal more than sufficient, leaving it to politicians and civilian defense intellectuals to argue for development of even more numerous, sophisticated, and expensive weapons.

While at the AEC, Dad witnessed the initiation of a security investigation of Robert Oppenheimer. Although Oppenheimer had been instrumental in the development of the first atomic bomb as civilian head of the Manhattan Project during World War II, he had been known at the time to have flirted with communism in the 1930s. Hence, the new investigation was not based upon any "new" news. (Indeed, Oppenheimer had undergone thorough investigation and renewal of his top-tier security clearance in 1947, with signoff by J. Edgar Hoover personally.) Rather, it was based upon resurgence of anti-Communist hysteria after Russia demonstrated an ability to develop its own nuclear weapon, and after disclosure in 1949 of Soviet penetration of the Manhattan Project by Klaus Fuchs and others. This anti-Communist paranoia was fueled by the demagogue, Senator Joseph McCarthy. Moreover, Oppenheimer had argued courageously against development of thermonuclear weapons, on the basis that there was no morally conceivable utility to weapons of such power.

The upshot was that the Commission moved ahead with an investigation of whether Oppenheimer should be denied a security clearance, which would effectively remove him from the councils of government regarding nuclear weapons, a subject on which he had unsurpassed expertise. In 1954 (shortly after Dad left the AEC for a job at the State Department), based upon an extraordinarily unfair proceeding, the Commission decided to withdraw Oppenheimer's clearance. The Commission by a 4-1 vote affirmed a determination by a special security panel, which found Oppenheimer to present an unacceptable security risk. The panel determined, however, that he was not "disloyal" to the United States. Commissioner Murray filed a dissent arguing that the Commission had not gone far enough and that it should have concluded that Oppenheimer was disloyal to the United States. Dad did not share Murray's pro-McCarthy sentiment and pleaded with him to omit the disloyalty language. Dad's relations with his former mentor soured from that point forward.

Recent scholarship indicates that the "persecution" of Oppenheimer was aided and masterminded by Lewis Strauss. In confederation with J. Edgar

Hoover, he saw that Oppenheimer's consultations with his counsel were bugged and that the prosecutor, later Federal Judge Roger Robb, received daily reports on Oppenheimer's discussions with his lawyer before and during the proceedings. The three-member panel had frequent and prolonged ex parte meetings with Robb, who furnished materials to the panel that were not shared with Oppenheimer's counsel. This mode of proceeding grossly offends any and all standards of due process and shocks the conscience.[64]

The only Commissioner who opposed the decision to strip Oppenheimer's clearance was Henry Smyth, a former physics professor at Princeton. His dissent had been supported and written by a young staffer, Phil Farley. Farley's actions were highly courageous in the paranoid times in which these events took place. Although his actions could have been prejudicial to his career, Farley emerged as a long-time, highly skilled public servant at the State Department. Later he ably served as my father's deputy special assistant for nuclear affairs at the State Department and subsequently as his Deputy Director of the Arms Control and Disarmament Administration in the Nixon Administration.

Upon the election of President Eisenhower in 1952, Commissioner Murray lost special access to the White House that he had enjoyed under his friend, President Truman. Eisenhower appointed Strauss as Chairman of the AEC, and he became preeminent in the government's councils on nuclear policy, even dealing with the White House without any consultation with his fellow commissioners. Strauss had extraordinary self-confidence, and a naive faith in science. He opposed any moratorium on nuclear testing.

Commissioner Murray was a strong proponent of harnessing nuclear technology for generation of power—both to propel naval vessels and for civilian electrical purposes. At the same time Murray and other commissioners were aware that peaceful use of the new technology would need to be accompanied by safeguards to prevent use of power generation facilities and materials to enable proliferation of nuclear weapons programs. Upon Strauss's appointment as Chairman of the AEC, Murray and he clashed on a range of issues—even though the two men had congruent views on the Soviet threat and the desirability of using nuclear power to generate electricity. Strauss did not respect the need to coordinate with fellow commissioners. At Strauss's initiative, in December 1953, President Eisenhower announced an "Atoms for Peace" program endorsing use of nuclear power reactors worldwide and the creation of an International Atomic Energy Agency to coordinate the spread of peaceful use of atomic energy. The proposal failed to pay proper heed to the design of safeguards against proliferation. Strauss had given no notice to the balance of the Commission about the President's initiative. Murray was outraged not to have been consulted, and Commissioner Henry Smyth characterized the proposal as "thoroughly dishonest,"[65] for failing to address proliferation risks.

My father managed to maintain equilibrium in this vexed political environment, holding the respect of both his immediate superior, Murray, as well as the powerful new Chairman, Strauss. He was still sufficiently "junior" that he had no inkling of Strauss's Mephistophelean persecution of Oppenheimer. Indeed, in 1953, when a vacancy occurred on the Commission, both Murray and Strauss separately sounded out my father about his willingness to become an AEC commissioner—a high compliment to a 39-year old with three years' tenure on the AEC staff. Then, in February 1954, Strauss asked whether my father would be interested in becoming Special Assistant for Atomic Energy to Secretary of State John Foster Dulles. This post appealed to my father as it would provide him a new vantage point from which to pursue his growing concerns about nuclear weapons and nuclear weapons proliferation. It also allowed my father, a Republican, to implement the advice of his brother-in-law, Bernard Shanley, a White House aide to Eisenhower, to "get on the Administration team." (Dad also noted that Strauss's support for him in this new position was not entirely altruistic. Strauss and Murray were at loggerheads, and Strauss knew that Dad was part of the problem, insofar as he drafted Murray's speeches, some of which took policy positions contrary to those of Strauss.)

S

Life in Washington in the Early 50s

Upon relocation to Washington in September 1950, our family settled into a fine fieldstone house at 2425 Kalorama Road. As a possible harbinger of my father's future career, it had previously been the residence of soon-to-be Secretary of State John Foster Dulles, rented to him by the Richard Griffins, who in 1967 would become sister Sheila's in-laws upon her marriage to Richard B. Griffin Jr. We found that our New York education gave us a head start in D.C. schools. I had completed first grade at St. Bernard's in New York and was soon deemed too advanced for second grade in D.C. Accordingly, I found myself at the age of six, about to turn seven, entering third grade. I remember my mother working patiently with me as I struggled to bring my rudimentary reading skills to third-grade level.

Sheila and I (and Gerry as he became older) enjoyed the newfound freedom of having the run of the neighborhood, in contrast to the more tightly controlled circumstance of living in a New York apartment building. We had no need for a key. In these simpler times our house remained unlocked in daytime. In 1953, my father's sister, Maureen, Uncle Barney, and their five children moved in on the same block of Kalorama Road, and Dad's brother, Gregory, and his wife, Peggy, moved in a block away on Kalorama Circle with their three children. Moving to Washington made Ratcliffe Manor more accessible, although, until completion of the Chesapeake Bay Bridge in July 1952, we needed to take a ferry to cross the bay.

While Dad worked on vital public issues, Sheila and I began education in earnest. In the fall of 1951, we both entered fourth grade, I at Landon School in Bethesda, Maryland, and Sheila at Stone Ridge, a Catholic girl's school, also in Bethesda. Brother Gerry would follow me to Landon in due course. My parents chose Landon in preference to D.C.'s then most prestigious boys' day school, St. Albans, even though the latter was within walking distance from Kalorama Road. Purportedly, my father was concerned that St. Albans was an Episcopal school and hence an inappropriate environment for Catholics like his sons. (Curiously, this same concern had not extended to St. Bernard's in New York.)

Landon, in the early 1950s, provided a rigorous academic and social environment. The all-male classes were sternly administered. Teachers would dole out corporal punishment to slackers—usually a ruler across the palm of the hand, but on occasion sterner measures were used. The fall sport was tackle football, and, at the age of seven, I began a nine-year participation in this rough, but enjoyable sport. In the winter, we played soccer, outdoors in snow, mud, and ice. Spring brought the relative respite of baseball, although undiagnosed nearsightedness on my part brought terror to waiting in right field for fly balls, the depth of which I could not judge. The academic pace was stern. I recall laboring over weekend assignments of "500-word compositions" in fourth and fifth grades. By seventh and eighth grades, I was studying Latin and algebra.

Just as nuclear weapons haunted my father's professional endeavors, they loomed large in the consciousness of schoolboys. I recall feeling a measure of terror when sirens would sound in the city for we lived in fear of a potential Russian nuclear attack. This fear was not in any way assuaged by participation in actual air raid drills at school. Nor was I comforted by a school assembly to witness television coverage of an actual atmospheric nuclear test. On a more positive note, I recall the excitement we felt at school on receiving news of the death of Joseph Stalin in March 1953.

Transportation to and from school entailed a half hour ride each way in a school bus. These rides were quite enjoyable and provided an opportunity for social interactions with a cross section of the student body. The bus ride allowed a glimpse each day of various neighborhoods as the bus made its way from Kalorama near the center of the city, out through Cleveland Park, Reno Road, Chevy Chase, and on to Bethesda. In the 1970s, there was broad national debate about the consequences of "school busing" as a way of mitigating segregation in public education. Parents argued that "busing" children long distances was dangerous, time-consuming, unjust, and potentially detrimental to their health and welfare. As a survivor of five years of busing to an elite suburban school, I remained skeptical about the merits of these "anti-busing" arguments.

This same timeframe marks my first growth of political consciousness. I had a friend and neighbor, Ralph Worthington Keith, who also attended Landon and rode the bus with me. He and his family took me as their guest to the Army-Navy game in Philadelphia in November 1951. We traveled by train directly to Veteran's Stadium. After leaving the train, as we walked toward the stadium, we passed the railway car of President Harry Truman. He appeared at the back of the car. A small crowd assembled and simply stared at the quite unpopular President. I remember reflecting that it seemed strange that the President of the United States should be treated so coolly. I have no memory of the actual football game, but the image of the unapplauded Truman remains with me. The 1952 election, which marked the end of the Democrats' 20-year hold on the presidency, brought great excitement in my childish milieu. We collected campaign buttons reflecting support variously for Robert Taft and "Ike" Eisenhower, and occasionally for Stevenson and Kefauver. Donkeys and elephants proliferated. Living in Washington, D.C., thus engendered a lifelong interest in the quirks and color of our political process. This excitement helped countervail, somewhat, the emotional dread of nuclear annihilation.

Also during this timeframe, I began several constructive hobbies, including collection of stamps and toy soldiers. Both hobbies stimulated an interest in history and geography. When I left for boarding school in the fall of 1956, these collections languished and were handed on to younger siblings. Like most members of my generation, I also developed an interest in emerging "rock and roll" music. I can recall listening by radio to a black disc jockey with the improbable name, Lord Fauntleroy Bandy. (I read recently that the son of the Turkish Ambassador, who lived three blocks away somewhat earlier, also listened to Bandy. Ahmed Ertegun, founder of Atlantic Records, put his education by Lord Fauntleroy to good use and grew up to be a prodigiously successful music entrepreneur.)

My brother, Hugh Maguire Smith, was born in May 1954, giving Sheila another opportunity to lament the lack of a sister and otherwise providing new excitement to the Smith household. My mother was 42, somewhat senior for childbirth in those days.

At a relatively young age I developed a strong interest in recreational reading—a passion that endures to this day. I began at the age of nine or ten to devour the books of Howard Pease, who wrote stories about a young man who would ship out to sea on tramp freighters and experience nautical adventures. From Pease, I graduated about the age of eleven to the Horatio Hornblower narratives of C.S. Forester, and during this same period, at the relatively young age of ten turning eleven, I developed an "interest" in the opposite sex. My nautical and romantic interests were perfectly complemented in February of my eighth-grade year. My parents took my sister Sheila and me out of school for a two-week period to accompany them on a cruise from New York to Venezuela and Columbia and back on a ship belonging to the Grace Line. The ship was relatively small and I can still remember the February Atlantic in a full gale. The seas were high enough that the ship's propeller would come out of the water and turn in the air causing the entire vessel to shake. I was intrigued by a fellow passenger, a now nameless brunette of around 12 or 13, who wore a becoming "peasant blouse."

Sheila and I were soon to take another voyage. In the summer of 1957, chaperoned loosely by our aunt Elizabeth ("Libby") Maguire, we were treated to a six-week voyage aboard a Norwegian-American Line ship, the *Bergensfjord*, which made its way across the Atlantic, cruised the fjords of Norway up to the North Cape to view the midnight sun, and then proceeded to Stockholm, Helsinki, Hamburg, Antwerp, and then home to New York. The ship contained a robust population of other young people and I lost my heart to an attractive, intelligent 15-year-old blond from Greensboro, North Carolina, named Laurinda King. Consistent with the plot of the popular movie, *An Affair to Remember*, starring Cary Grant and Deborah Kerr, we agreed to meet some years hence at the top of the Empire State Building. The young woman ended up as president of her class at Sweetbriar College and married a doctor. In 1968, after her marriage, she wrote me in jest to remind me that I had missed our Empire State rendezvous.

Both these ocean voyages engendered in Sheila and me a lifelong joy in seafaring. With air travel supplanting ocean passages and cruise vessels resembling massive luxury hotels, future generations will be unlikely to experience the thrill of a rough sea or the highly civilized amenities of an old fashioned ocean voyage.

* * * * *

Reflection—Religion and "Last Things"

The early 1950s marked my first full consciousness of religion. Indeed, the Catholic Church considers the age of seven as the beginning of the "age of reason." In the spring of 1951, I received my "first communion" at Sts. Peter and Paul Catholic Church in Easton, Maryland. My godfather, Uncle

Gregory, was present and marked the event by a gift of monogrammed golden cufflinks—an odd present for one so young. These cufflinks have long since been lost, but, maybe as Uncle Gregory intended, they are not forgotten. Gold was not a bad symbol of my family's relationship to the Church. J.T. and my father were generous to the Catholic Church, the former endowing chapels at Canterbury School and at Yale and the latter donating significant sums to Catholic causes through the years. But neither was inclined personally to social service efforts or to close community with other parishioners. My father even resigned from the elite "Knights of Malta," and he commented that his brother Gregory was wiser never to have joined. Presumably, he disliked its somewhat pompous approach to good works and its ostentatious "white tie and medals" approach to camaraderie.

My mother was discomforted by one of the 1960s reforms of The Second Vatican Council. It called for members of the congregation to greet co-congregants with a handshake or other "sign of peace." I used to tease my mother that her reluctance to have contact with strangers at Mass was at odds with the manifestly communal spirit of Christianity. My mother's somewhat elitist approach to her faith manifested itself elsewhere. During a family debate at a summer dinner in the late 1960s, Mother expressed her horror at "hippies" with unkempt beards, sandals, and robes. Never one to resist debate, I noted that most artistic representations of Christ portrayed him with a beard, sandals, and robes. Mother exploded with anger and threatened to expel me from the household. Fortunately for me, her evening anger typically disappeared the next morning.

In any event, the Roman Catholic Church remained an important feature in the lives of my Smith grandfather and my father, and remains a strong influence in the life of my sister Sheila and, to a lesser extent, that of my brothers Gerry and Hugh. The Church was an important influence on my life, when young, and remains for me a stimulus to thought and intellectual exploration. However, denied access to the sacraments of the Church due to divorce and remarriage, I no longer attend church on any regular basis. As I write this book in my sixties, my thoughts increasingly turn to the subject of death, and I compare the teachings of the Church with the reflections of ancient and modern philosophers on the ultimate questions of the existence of Deity and the prospects for an afterlife.

My religious education had several sources. First and foremost was my father. Not only did he set an example by regular attendance at church and the sacraments, he would also take his children aside on Sunday mornings for gentle instruction in what he called "philosophy class." I was sent to

Sunday School to prepare for first communion, where I was drilled in the catechism of the Catholic Church. Later, at the ages of 12 to 16 when I attended Canterbury School, several courses in religion were mandatory. The most useful and persuasive was a senior year course in ethics. The curriculum embraced four years of study of history—with ancient history involving exposure to the Old Testament, and medieval history consisting of large amounts of Church history, including readings regarding Saints Augustine, Thomas Aquinas, and Francis of Assisi. This curriculum, in turn, was reinforced by daily chapel and annual "retreats."

My religious education transpired before the wide-ranging reforms of Pope John XX III in 1963. The mass was recited in Latin, with the priest's back turned to the congregation. Before receiving Communion a good Catholic needed to attend to the sacrament of "confession." After mumbling one's usually jejune sins to a priest inside a confessional, a young man experienced a great weight lifted upon receipt of absolution.[66] Fridays were meatless, an injunction that extended even to a family favorite, onion soup, on grounds that it had meat stock. Only Catholics would be eligible for salvation. Certain books and movies were proscribed.

During my childhood in the 1950s, we lived in three different places each year and attended several different Catholic churches. Each had its own "flavor." When in Washington, D.C., the family would attend mass either at St. Matthew's Cathedral or at St. Thomas Apostle. The former is a massive, Romanesque structure, administered by highly sophisticated priests, and mass there often included glorious music. St. Thomas was more of a conventional parish church. When in Easton, Maryland, on Sundays, we attended Sts. Peter and Paul Church. There, a rather worldly Monsignor, Joseph Irwin, presided. He delivered lengthy sermons, consisting largely of appeals for contributions to enable the parish to build a parochial school. Irwin succeeded in this mission, and the school remains an important part of the community a half century later. He succeeded rather less well in inspiring genuine religious fervor in me. In summers, in Southampton, we attended the Church of the Sacred Heart. The parish priest was Monsignor Joseph Killeen—a large, red-faced, gray-haired, archetypical Irish prelate with an old country accent. He would deliver fire and brimstone sermons that were too lengthy for beautiful July days.

I experienced my deepest religious feelings while at Canterbury School, where distractions were minimized and religion was a relatively constant presence. I can remember fervent prayer in advance of important athletic contests—if not academic exams. I also remember being genuinely and deeply moved by a midnight mass on Easter weekend, as the lights were turned off and each of us lit a beeswax candle while reciting the Latin "lumen Christi." Once, on a chilly spring afternoon, I prayed intently to the Virgin Mary before pole vaulting at a track meet. Before unleashing my personal best vault, I thought I felt a mysterious presence beside me.

Then, as now, the Catholic Church reflected a preoccupation with human sexuality and its consequences. Rome had declared the use of artificial contraception—even by married couples—a serious sin. Until overturned by the Supreme Court in 1965, the law of the State of Connecticut, where I spent 11 years at school, college and law school, made sale of contraceptives unlawful. Reputedly, in the early 1960s my father's sister, Aunt Maureen, commented to her older children that they shouldn't engage in premarital sexual relations, but if they did, they certainly should not use contraception! Although Rome has not relented in its proscription of contraception, its edict is widely ignored by American Catholics. The concern of the American Catholic Church focuses now on the more substantial issue of abortion and the somewhat curious issue of the use of otherwise to-be discarded embryonic tissue for purposes of embryonic stem cell research. In parallel, the Catholic Church has been shaken, first in the United States and more recently in Europe, by revelations of scandalous sexual abuse of juveniles by Catholic priests. This sad phenomenon may suggest that the Church's preoccupation with sexuality may need reevaluation.

The emphasis of the Catholic Church, and one presupposes other faiths, on channeling sexual energy toward marriage and in attempting to preserve some of the mystery of sexuality for discovery in adulthood is entirely appropriate. But, given the immense access to sexually explicit material afforded by the Internet, new and different means to restore the mystery of human sexuality need to be found.

Other, more laudable attributes of the Church's teaching are not easy to reconcile with the modern ethos of greed that afflicts the United States. The church reflects a steady awareness of the need to lift up the earth's poor, sick, and dispossessed. Indeed, any sober reading of the New Testament reflects that Jesus Christ was a radical "redistributionist." My father would take note of the biblical injunction that it is "easier for a camel to pass through the eye of a needle than for a rich man to enter the Kingdom of Heaven." I was bemused by a response given by then presidential candidate George W. Bush in 2000 to a question as to who was his favorite "political philosopher." This emphatically non-bookish president, who liked to wear his religion on his sleeve, facilely responded that his favorite political philosopher was

"Jesus Christ." Bush's economic and military policies during his eight-year presidency did not reflect consistent application of the political philosophy of the Lord. (In one respect, Bush deserves credit for following the Lord's philosophy, and that was in vastly increasing aid to Africa, especially with respect to the scourge of AIDS.)

In the United States, the press and pundits often overlook the radical nature of the Church's teaching on economic and social matters. I can recall being invited to witness a speech by Pope John Paul II, in 1979 on the south lawn of the White House. While he reiterated the Church's stern opposition to abortion, a major part of his speech was given to a plea for more equitable international economic policies that would redistribute the wealth of the first world in the direction of the oppressed of the third. The reporting the next day on the Pope's address spoke only to his position on abortion and omitted mention of his radical economic message.

The most powerful, single factor that caused me to retain my Catholic faith, at least until my 40s, was the example set by my father. His faith was good and true—reinforced by practically daily attendance at mass, extensive reading of Catholic texts, history, and philosophy. He did not flaunt his faith, but was nonetheless unafraid to demonstrate his commitment to the Church. He made close friendships with some of the leading intellectuals in the American Catholic Church. In his early career the church's detestation of "Godless" communism buttressed my father's morale as a career "cold warrior." In later years, as my father puzzled over the ultimate morality of nuclear weapons, he wrote a letter to the Pope suggesting that the Catholic mass be modified to include a closing prayer seeking the abolition of nuclear weapons. He received a polite but noncommittal response from a Vatican bureaucrat.

While unashamed and confident in his Catholic faith, Dad bristled a bit at the label, "Irish Catholic." His father's great economic success had enabled the family to rise above the social prejudices that afflicted immigrant Catholics in the first half of the 20th century, and being typecast as an "Irish Catholic" irritated Dad. Paul Nitze, in his memoir, referred to Dad as an "Irish Catholic." Dad took offense, noting that in his book about SALT, he had not seen fit to describe his colleague Nitze as a "German Lutheran."

For all my father's erudition, sophistication, and professional accomplishment, he was content to adhere to basic tenets of the Catholic faith as recorded in the New Testament and as promulgated by Rome. Thus, for instance, he believed that at the end of time deceased souls would be reunited with their earthly bodies, and, hence, he and my mother would be reunited as themselves in some future eternity. The month after my mother died in the winter of 1987, Dad chartered a sailing yacht in the Caribbean. I recall standing on deck with him one evening admiring the stars. The night sky having stimulated thoughts of eternity, and with my mother's death fresh in mind, Dad asked me whether I believed in resurrection of the dead. I told him I found it an exceedingly difficult concept. He commented, not contentiously, that this doctrine of faith had to be correct or "all was lost."

In the intervening years, I have had occasion to reflect further on this starlit discussion. At the time, I took it as evidence of admirable but simple faith on my father's part. Later reading persuades me that my father was grappling with a much more sophisticated point of Christian doctrine. The late Richard John Neuhaus points out that philosophers through the ages have addressed the issue of whether the "I" of the mind and "soul" is truly separable from the human body. He comes down on the side of St. Paul that resurrection of the dead is an essential element of Christian belief.[67]

A memorable exception to my father's adherence to the dictates of his faith was his skepticism regarding the Church's preoccupation with the issue of abortion. His scholarship had shown him that until relatively recently (circa 1850) the Church had not proscribed first-term abortions. He found that the Church's prohibition of abortion even in cases of rape and incest to be misguided. He did not live long enough to ponder the debate about embryonic stem cell research. But I can speculate that he would have been puzzled by it. He wanted his Church to be a strong force against the development and proliferation of nuclear weapons, which had the potential to end the human race. The Church's focus on contraception and abortion he found to be a diversion of the Church's energies and moral authority away from more fundamental issues. He was heartened when the American Catholic Bishops wrestled in the early 1980s with the whole question of the morality of the nuclear arms race. Nevertheless, he was disappointed when the Bishops ended up affirming the morality of limited use of nuclear weapons for purely military purposes. By my father's life's end, he had decided there could be no conceivable, morally acceptable use of nuclear weapons.[68]

A few days before my father's death on the Fourth of July 1994, Father Robert Coine visited his hospital room to administer the sacraments, which include a final confession. My sister and I left the room. Upon Father Coine's departure, we rejoined my father. To my surprise, in some of his last conscious words to me he remarked, "That was quite some mumbo jumbo that was just staged for me." I responded that Sheila and I assumed he would want to receive the sacraments. Dad replied: "Oh John, you have always exaggerated my religiosity." I can only attribute this curious remark to the state of Dad's medications. Certainly he was against ostentatious flaunting of his faith as implied by the term "religiosity." Nevertheless, he was a dedicated and admirable practitioner of the faith of his fathers. I am not.

Ironically, Dad's last words to me, a day later, were "God bless you." I had sneezed while seated in his hospital room. Not fully awake, my father responded with reflexive and characteristic courtesy—a benediction nonetheless.

I deeply respect sophisticated individuals like my father who exercise the discipline and imagination to be devoutly religious. Their beliefs bring structure, coherence, and purpose to their lives and provide relatively clear moral boundaries on behavior. I have difficulty, however, with the religious beliefs of less sophisticated individuals who, contrary to overwhelming evidence, insist on such things as the literal veracity of the Biblical creation narrative and oppose sound scientific endeavor that contradicts what they see as Biblical truth. I also respect a significant number of my friends who appear ready to face death bravely without the comfort of the religious promise of an afterlife and redemption. And, I worry about the fact that I have not been a good steward of my children's religious or moral education. All three of my sons have had the moral benefit of attendance at Episcopal schools, but their interest in religion is at best modest. My example has been a far less steady one than my father's was for me.

Although my father set a tremendous example, he was sufficiently humble to doubt the power of his example. Thus I find in my records a handwritten note from him dated March 31, 1989, expressing a concern that he had been "remiss as a parent and grandparent in not trying harder to stress the paramountcy of . . . post-world destiny," and expressing the hope that I would make up for his "deficiencies in this respect." The same letter expresses a concern that his descendants would "lapse into 21st century paganism." At the same time he acknowledges that he has "some idea of the problems that people of [my] generation and the next face in trying to keep the faith—and pass it on."

These ruminations regarding the importance and effect of religion in my family's lives lead necessarily to some thoughts on the state of religion in the modern world that my children and grandchildren confront.

Although polls report that a large percentage of the American people embrace religion—a large fraction still believing in the literal truth of the Book of Genesis—increasingly those of fortunate birth or privileged education receive little or no religious education. A 2010 *Newsweek* article reports upon an ongoing debate at Harvard University whether undergraduate students should be required to take at least one course in a category loosely labeled "Reason and Faith." Such courses would explore big issues in religion and the intersection of religious and scientific/secular forces in American society. The Harvard faculty has not achieved agreement on such a requirement.[69]

While the impasse in Harvard faculty debates about the acceptability of exposure of undergraduates to religious thinking reflects a kind of neutrality, recent years have seen the publication of powerful, best-selling criticisms of religion. Notable among them is *The End of Faith* by Sam Harris.[70] The author, a PhD neuroscientist, elucidates what he perceives as the profound dangers of all three Abrahamic, Monotheistic religions, Christianity, Judaism, and Islam. He highlights the intolerance of certain of these religions' scriptural prescriptions and argues passionately that a world with weapons of mass destruction can ill afford to structure its conduct based upon 2,000-year-old texts. In his view "our religious traditions are intellectually defunct and politically ruinous." A lively and broad-reaching book by the late polymath, Christopher Hitchens, entitled *God Is Not Great* plows similar ground. Hitchens concludes that "Human decency is not derived from religion. It precedes it."[71]

Another book of note is *The Evolution of God* by Robert Wright.[72] The author traces the development of human religions starting with shamanism, through the Old and New Testaments and the Koran and discerns an increasingly robust morality in religious doctrine and practice as history moves forward. He posits that, while the doctrine of any one religion is unlikely to be divinely correct, the pattern of evolving religion toward greater morality may itself be proof of a deity outside of time.

Another, nonscriptural source of "belief" can be found in the work of Baruch Spinoza who pursued scientific and philosophical investigations in 17th-century Holland. Spinoza did not accept a conventional Judaic or Christian God, but perceived a kind of divinity in the complex workings of the universe, an approach that essentially denies the existence of a conventional "religious" god.[73] A leading biographer has cited Einstein for embracing the God of Spinoza. When asked by a Jewish rabbi whether he believed in God, Einstein responded: "I believe in Spinoza's God, who reveals himself in the lawful harmony of all that exists, but not in a God who concerns himself with the fate and doings of mankind."[74]

I can no longer accept doctrinal religion. I am persuaded nonetheless that it is wrong to try to expunge all religious considerations from one's life. My reading and experience persuade me that there remains much that is mysterious and not explicable by reason or its handmaiden scientific inquiry. To my thinking, religion should be a recognition and celebration of mystery.

Sam Harris's book is strong in its elucidation of the dangers of literal, dogmatic religion. It is less robust in its prescription of alternatives. Nonetheless, Harris points preferentially to Eastern religions, such as Buddhism predicated on search for self-knowledge through meditation. Harris embraces mysticism, describing it as "rational enterprise," that is, exploring the "roiling mystery of the world" without preconceptions. Religion, in contrast, comprises "bad concepts held in place of good ones for all time."[75]

A recent book by a former Catholic priest, Paul Knitter, goes part way down the path urged by Harris. It bears the provocative title, *Without Buddha I Could Not Be a Christian*. He confronts the vexing "problem of evil," that is, if God is good and loving, why does God allow humans free will to commit "morally evil" acts on one another such as genocides, torture, sexual abuse? Why does he allow "natural evils" such as earthquakes, tsunamis, epidemics, and the like? Knitter refuses to believe that the latter are properly characterized as "acts of God." Part of the problem, Knitter believes, is our insistence on anthropomorphizing "God" to be like an omniscient, omnipotent "person." He suggests instead that one should conceive of God as a "pervading spirit." Thus catastrophic natural events are not caused or allowed by God. They just happen as part of the natural order of things.[76] As to moral evil, Knitter finds an answer in Buddhist belief that harmful human actions are founded not in "evil" but stem in "ignorance." Buddhist "enlightenment" is an antidote to such ignorance and the harmful actions it causes.[77]

Knitter also raises questions about the nature of "eternal life." In contrast to my father and Richard John Neuhaus, he rejects the notion of continuation of personhood (and by implication reunion of earthly body and soul). He states "life after death will no longer be life lived as individuals."[78] He rejects the vision of heaven in which he would "live as an individual along with billions of other individuals," as "selfish" or "egocentric." He supposes that the mystery of life after death will be "so unexpectedly and wonderfully different" as to be indescribable in personal terms.[79] Celebrating mystery he states that he wants the opening hymn at his funeral to be Paul Simon's "The Sound of Silence."[80]

Paul Knitter's ability to rethink fundamental Christian concepts through a comparative examination of Buddhist practices has illuminated for me both the encrusted illusions of traditional Catholicism and the opportunities for religious faith directed toward eradication of ignorance and openness to mystery.

James Carse's profound book, *The Religious Case against Belief*, makes a distinction between "belief systems" and "religion." The former are what we would conventionally call "religions." They are characterized by orthodoxy, certainty, and hostility toward different or competing beliefs. True religion, in contrast, recognizes ignorance about great mysteries such as what happens at death or why there is evil in the world. Carse states: "By virtue of the ignorance inherent in its long conversation with itself, each religion can behold another only with wonder."[81] Carse's pluralistic conception of true religion as open-minded, humble, questing in the direction of the mysterious and the unknowable strikes me as valid and desirable. While Carse posits a religious approach quite different from the catechisms of my youth, it is not without representation within the vast history and literature of Catholicism. For instance, a now largely forgotten Cardinal, mathematician, and theologian in 15th-century Germany, Nicolaus of Cusa, entitled his masterpiece, "On Learned Ignorance." Later he produced a plea for "Peace among the Faiths," expressing moral outrage against human slaughter of Muslims or Jews in the name of God. Nicolaus believed that the most profound thing humans can "know" about God is God's unknowability.[82]

In recent years, there has been lively discussion as to whether reconciliation is possible between the findings and doctrines of modern science, on the one hand, and traditional religion on the other. Beyond dispute, the vast increase in our scientific understanding of the planet and of the universe in the past 250 years contradicts fundamentalist perceptions of religion. Nonetheless, one consequence of science is to discover new mysteries. To the extent religion acknowledges and celebrates mystery, religion and science are compatible. As pointed out by physicist and philosopher, Freeman Dyson, "[e]ven physics, the most exacting, the most firmly established branch of science, is still full of mysteries. . . . Science is the sum total of a great multitude of mysteries."[83]

In *The Case for God*, Karen Armstrong,[84] makes a much more detailed presentation of essentially the same point. According to Armstrong, modern orthodoxy of the sort described by Sam Harris, Christopher Hitchens and others invoking a prescribing, active, anthropomorphic God is inconsistent with the true roots of the great religions. From the beginning they emphasized the unknowability of God. She warns against those who are "stridently virtuous, aggressively orthodox, and contemptuous of the ungodly."[85] She cites the example of the Buddha, who showed that the path to peace and harmony with one's fellow creatures consists of "systematically cutting off egotism at the root."[86] She warns against "born again" conversions and calls instead for "slow, incremental and imperceptible transformation" through "habitual practice of compassion and the Golden Rule."[87]

Much of the same lesson is conveyed in a commencement speech by the late "postmodern" author, David Foster Wallace, delivered at Kenyon College in 2005. Wallace stated:

> In the day-to-day trenches of adult life, there is actually no such thing as atheism. There is no such thing as not worshiping. Everybody worships. The only choice we get is *what* to worship. And an outstanding reason for choosing some sort of God or spiritual-type thing to worship . . . is that pretty much anything else you worship will eat you alive. If you worship money and things . . . then you will never have enough. Worship your own body and beauty and sexual allure and you will always feel ugly, and when time and age start showing, you will die a million deaths before they finally plant you. . . . Worship your intellect, being seen as smart—you will end up feeling stupid, a fraud, always on the verge of being found out.[88]

My children and grandchildren will find that as the years pass and they shed the invincibility of youth, thoughts turn to death, which presents the unavoidable question, "Is this all that there is?" Plato reports that Socrates, confronting a death sentence, expressed equanimity. Either he would be entering on a perfect, uninterrupted and perpetual night's sleep or he would find his way to an afterlife in which he would have the privilege of conversing with greats such as Homer who went before him.[89] Dad was also struck by Socrates' final reflections. A diary entry of January 14, 1961, contains a reminder: "Send children Socrates' dying words in Plato's *Apology*." Dad was 47 at the time, and this entry evidences his scholarly and reflective mind. I was 17, and I have no memory of receiving a copy. I finally read—and was deeply affected by *Apology*—as a participant in a St. John's College "Senior Seminar" in 2008 at the age of 65.

My father, in a letter in February 1979, reminded me of the so-called wager of the French philosopher and mathematician (and inventor of mathematical "probability" theory), Blaise Pascal. Pascal reasoned that belief in God was a wise wager. If it turned out there was no God, not much would be lost—in the terms of the wager. If, however, there is a God and an eternal life, the wagerer would hit the jackpot. Pascal doubtless was counseling belief in God and adherence to the prescriptions of the Catholic Church. His wager remains a "good plan" if it simply includes maintenance of an open and questing mind regarding the existence of a God and conforming one's behavior to simple consensus moral norms such as doing unto others as you would have them do unto you, and being generous within your means to those less fortunate than yourselves.

By these words, I pass on to my children and grandchildren an admonition to keep an open mind and be alert to mystery and the need to live moral and compassionate lives, to abjure selfishness and, if you want to embark on Pascal's wager, by all means, do so.

6

State Department — Round One

Dad began service as Special Assistant for Atomic Energy Affairs to Secretary of State John Foster Dulles in April 1954. Three and a half years later he became Assistant Secretary of State for Policy Planning, where he served until the end of the Eisenhower Administration in January 1961. In these posts, he enjoyed increasing responsibility and involvement with respect to the enduring issues of the nuclear age.[90] As he gained the confidence of Dulles, Dad had direct personal contact not only with Dulles, but also with President Eisenhower, Vice President Nixon, Nelson Rockefeller, and Curtis LeMay. More importantly, Dad befriended and worked with a group of extraordinarily talented State Department officers. Two of them, his predecessor as Director of Policy Planning, Bob Bowie, and Henry Owen (a successor head of Policy Planning), became close lifelong friends, as well as professional collaborators. Indeed, Dad, in his journal, with typical self-effacement, attributes a significant measure of his professional success to Henry Owen, who died at the age of 91 in November 2011.

Initially, Dad's State Department responsibilities centered on implementation of Eisenhower's "Atoms for Peace" program, including planning for the establishment of the International Atomic Energy Agency (IAEA). (Twenty-five years later Dad would find himself as the U.S. representative on this agency's board of governors.) The Soviet Union, then the only nation other than the United States with a nuclear weapons capacity, was appalled by the "Atoms for Peace" initiative. Dulles received a strongly worded message from Soviet Foreign Minister Molotov asking what possible motive the United States could have for spreading "nuclear materials" around the world. Ironically, the Soviets were more prescient than the United States on this score. Nearly half a century later we are still pondering the best means to obtain the potential benefits of nuclear power while limiting the risk that materials used in generation of electricity will be diverted into weapons programs.

Another persistent issue was atmospheric testing of nuclear weapons. During the 1950s both the United States and the Soviet Union tested increasingly powerful nuclear devices. One U.S. test of a 15-megaton hydrogen bomb in 1954 in the Marshall Islands led to radiation poisoning of 27 Japanese fishermen aboard the *Lucky Dragon,* which unluckily strayed near an exclusion zone, 95 miles downwind of the test. There was no need to belabor the irony that Japanese citizens once again had suffered from an American nuclear weapon. Release in 1955 of a report on the potentially adverse effects of atmospheric nuclear testing led to periodic exploration of the feasibility of a ban on nuclear testing, both as a bilateral matter with the Soviets and as a possible UN initiative. Lewis Strauss at the AEC fiercely opposed any such initiative. Progress was further impeded by a perennial concern that the Soviet Union could not be trusted and that, in the absence of robust verification measures, it would be able to cheat on any testing limits. The issue was further muddied during the 1956 presidential campaign when the Democratic candidate, Adlai Stevenson, advocated testing limits. In the mid-1950s, the United Kingdom began testing its own nuclear weapons—adding to the problem of dispersion of radioactive material in the atmosphere.

After efforts at a formal agreement on limiting atmospheric nuclear testing failed, the United States and the Soviet Union agreed informally in 1958 on a testing moratorium, with both sides reserving the right to resume testing. This moratorium ended when tensions escalated several years later, and the Soviets exploded a large-yield device. Eventually, an atmospheric test ban treaty was agreed in 1962 in the Kennedy Administration.

Throughout the 1950s, the United States wrestled with the practical implications of its nuclear weapons capacity. Dulles is famous for endorsing a doctrine of so-called massive retaliation. In the event of a feared Soviet invasion of Western Europe using conventional forces, in theory the United States would unleash the full weight of its nuclear arsenal against the Soviet Union. From the outset, there were legitimate doubts in Europe regarding the willingness of the United States to execute such potentially catastrophic measures when its own national security was not more directly threatened. For this reason, European countries, such as the United Kingdom and subsequently France, pursued development of their own nuclear weapons. The United Kingdom did so with the active support of the United States. France did so notwithstanding American discouragement. Skepticism about the viability of "massive retaliation" also led to development of so-called tactical nuclear weapons that could be deployed in Europe, and even on the battlefield. As Special Assistant for Atomic Energy and subsequently as Director of Policy Planning, Dad was centrally involved in these deliberations.

During this period my father grew in his understanding of the potentially catastrophic consequences of use of nuclear weapons. He believed in the corollary proposition that the United States needed to maintain robust conventional forces in lieu of undue reliance on nuclear weapons. Relatively early in his tenure as Special Assistant for Atomic Energy he had occasion to disabuse Dulles of any illusions regarding the employment of nuclear strikes. In a memorandum to file dated March 16, 1955, Dad reports that he had admonished the Secretary after Dulles stated at a press conference that "tactical" nuclear weapons could be employed with modest consequence. Dad pointed out that even such tactical weapons could present significant untoward consequences due to fallout. In this same discussion, Dad reminded the Secretary that Air Force plans for bomber strikes on Russia would result in casualties "in the tens of millions." Dad was at pains to remind the Secretary that no level of "nuclear warfare" could be conducted without "tremendous destruction to civilians.["][91]

Although it is not widely recognized, Dulles, in his final years as Secretary dropped his support for "massive retaliation." Beginning in the spring of 1958, in meetings with the Pentagon, Dulles argued for expanding conventional forces to defend Europe, as well as vigorous exploration of means to provide Europeans with "tactical nuclear weapons" to employ in their own defense. He also suggested exploring "wider internationalization of nuclear capacities within NATO.["][92]

In this same period, on several occasions, the United States actually considered using nuclear weapons—not in Europe, but in Asia. On two occasions, when the People's Republic of China threatened Taiwan and began shelling Quemoy and Matsu, Taiwanese islands close to the mainland coast, the United States gave active consideration to nuclear strikes at China. On the first occasion, in 1954, Dad's predecessor as the Director of Policy Planning, Bob Bowie, briefed Dulles on the potentially horrendous casualties that would result, and this tactic was not pursued. The same problem flared again during my father's tenure as Director of Policy Planning. He had occasion to remind Dulles's Under Secretary, Christian Herter, of the potential consequences of this tactic. In a memorandum dated August 13, 1958, Dad, in sober bureaucratic language, stated as follows:

> [C]urrent JCS war plans call for the defense of Quemoy and Matsu by nuclear strikes deep into Communist China, including military targets in the Shanghai-Hangchow-Nanking and Canton complexes where population density is extremely high. . . . While nuclear strikes would be with "low yield" weapons, this would include weapons having a yield comparable to the 20 KT weapons dropped on Hiroshima and Nagasaki. It is my judgment that before such hostilities were over there would be millions of non-combatant casualties. . . . In light of the above considerations, it seems to me that the U.S. does not have a politically feasible capability to defend Quemoy and Matsu. I question whether, in the event of an attack on Quemoy and Matsu, we should or will run the very grave risk of general nuclear war attendant on our present military planning.[93]

During the late 1950s, tensions with the Soviet Union escalated. Khrushchev demanded a resolution of the status of the City of Berlin. (At the end of World War II the City of Berlin had been divided into zones by the victors. The United States' presence in and access to Berlin, located in the Soviet dominion of East Germany, continued as a source of great tension between the Cold War "Superpowers.") Further, the United States worried that the Russians had gained a large technological advantage with the successful launch of Sputnik on October 4, 1957. The following month the Gaither Committee produced a classified report, principally authored by Paul Nitze, which contended (erroneously) that the United States was falling behind the Soviets in strategic weapons capacity and urged that the United States increase strategic offensive weapons, anti-missile defenses, fallout shelters and conventional forces. Eisenhower disagreed and counseled against unwarranted panic.

The myth that the Soviets enjoyed an advantage in nuclear-capable missiles—the "missile gap"—gained currency as the 1960 election approached. (Dad's good friend, General James Walsh, the Chief of the Air Force Intelligence, was a proponent of this missile gap theory.) In fact, President Eisenhower may have known this gap to be a myth, due to the extraordinary intelligence that the United States was gathering through U-2 spy planes. Eisenhower did not reveal this highly classified reconnaissance capacity as a way of rebutting the false claims of a missile gap. The Soviets finally managed to shoot down a U-2 in the spring of 1960, shortly before a potentially important summit meeting involving the Soviet Union, the United States, France, and England to discuss the Berlin issue. Khrushchev used this event as a pretext for scuttling the Conference and with it the hopes for a near-term peaceful resolution on tensions centering on Berlin. Dad was part of the U.S. delegation to this Conference and remembers firsthand the distress expressed by Eisenhower at his treatment by Khrushchev. Referring to the brutal Soviet suppression of a democratic uprising in Hungary in 1956, Eisenhower said of his tongue lashing by Khrushchev: "You might have thought we had done a Hungary."[94]

Although my father's duties in the 1950s at the State Department involved the existential dilemmas of a nuclear armed world, his life was not without personal comfort and glamour. In the 1950s, professional life was not as consuming as it is today. Dad left home around 8:15 a.m. to walk to the State Department. Usually, his first commitment was a Secretarial staff meeting at the rather civilized hour of 9:15. Dad was usually home before 7:00 p.m. Weekends were spent at Ratcliffe Manor. Summer "vacation" allowed a week or two in which Dad joined the family in Southampton—in addition to most weekends. In this period, Dad had invested in Maryland Airlines, a charter service run in Easton by Bill Newnam, who would ease Dad's weekend commutes from Washington to Easton or Southampton.

Dad's professional duties were not without glamour, as well. He traveled the world with Secretary Dulles. In addition to numerous trips to European capitals, he traveled in the Far East. While still a relatively young and junior officer of the State Department, Dad met and spoke with notable historical figures including Chiang Kai-shek and his U.S.-educated wife, British Prime Minister Harold Macmillan, and French President Charles de Gaulle.

The President nominated Dad to be Assistant Secretary of State and Director of the Policy Planning Staff in August 1957, and he took up duties in this post October 1957. (Actual Senate confirmation did not occur until January 1958.) Dad undertook this post with humility, in recognition of the extraordinary caliber of his predecessors, George Kennan, Paul Nitze, and Bob Bowie. Ironically, a decade earlier, when the post of Director of Policy Planning was first created, Dad had suggested to his father that he bring his great mental acumen to the post. J.T. dismissed the idea due to his advancing years and, in any event, Truman appointed Kennan to the post. Dad notes that in 1947 he could not have imagined that he, and not his formidable father, would be Director of Policy Planning only a decade later.

In this post Dad cemented a lifelong friendship and collaboration with Henry Owen, a member of the Policy Planning Staff and later its Director. Dad's journal has a separate entry entitled "the Owen influence" in which he selflessly credits Owen with a major role in many of Dad's subsequent accomplishments. Among these, during Dad's tenure as Director of Policy Planning, was promotion of the idea of a "hot line" between Washington and Moscow to allow direct communication in the event of an escalation of world tensions, as well as the idea of vastly expanded economic aid to Latin America. Both the "hot line" and enhanced aid to Latin America in the form of the "Alliance for Progress" were adopted by the subsequent Kennedy Administration. Dad received a letter from President Kennedy acknowledging his contribution to the creation of the hot line. Dad subsequently requested that Henry Owen be the sole eulogist at his funeral—a role that Henry discharged with his usual intellectual force and grace. Owen became a Catholic, supposedly due to Dad's influence. While querying whether Henry's claim regarding his influence was valid, Dad notes that if true "it was only a fair exchange for all of his help."

My Teenaged Perspective on the State Department

In September 1956, before my father's promotion to Director of Policy Planning, I began four years at Canterbury School. Thus, with the exception of school vacation, I was quite detached from the rhythms of my parents' day-to-day lives. My father's example nonetheless remained a constant influence. As best I could from my remote Connecticut location, I followed events in the world. In my senior year I wrote pretentiously sophisticated editorials for the school newspaper about foreign policy. In junior year, I participated in a "model UN" activity—perhaps because it enabled the rare treat of a day at a girls' school in Farmington, Connecticut. I spent much of the day catching up with an attractive friend from Washington, D.C., Wendy Green, whose father also worked in the State Department. At dinner the following evening, one of my favorite faculty members, James Breen, who had accompanied us to Farmington, asked me good-humoredly what "that blond had to do with foreign policy." I took juvenile satisfaction in replying that her father was a senior officer of the State Department. I also managed to win a graduation prize for the best senior history essay—a paper on diplomatic recognition of the Soviet Union by the United States in 1933, for which I had been provided useful documents by the State Department's historian.

In other respects, my four years at Canterbury were deeply formative and rewarding. Due to the quality of education at Landon School in Washington, I arrived at Canterbury with an academic head start. Although still 12 years old upon my arrival, I found that much of the English and math curriculum was familiar territory. I was able, therefore, to achieve a fast start academically and to flourish throughout my four years. The education imparted by Canterbury was excellent, including four years of rigorous history, English and math, as well as courses in chemistry, physics and foreign language. Upon graduation, in addition to the history essay award, I earned the "John Thomas Smith Award for Excellence in the Study of English"—a stark example of the ties that may abound between and among generations.

My most sustained intersection with my father's career as an Assistant Secretary of State occurred in the summer of 1959. During this summer, my sister Sheila and I embarked on a tour of Europe again chaperoned by my mother's sister, Aunt Libby. We crossed the ocean on a Cunard Liner from Montreal to Southampton, England. We proceeded to Claridge's Hotel in London. There, in the lobby lounge, as a 15-year-old, I tried to order a beer but was informed, "I'm sorry, sir, we don't serve beer here. How about a nice gin and tonic." I was also deeply impressed by women in short skirts on London's streets, as well as by the bawdiness of the West End performance of "Irma la Deuce," a light-hearted musical about a prostitute. From London we went by boat and train to Paris, then on by train to Cologne, Germany. We took a steamer up the Rhine to Munich. From there we traveled by train to Italy, where we luxuriated at the Lido in Venice, then from Venice on to Florence and Rome.

After this "grand tour" of European luxury hotels, restaurants, art galleries, and cathedrals, we proceeded to Geneva, where we joined our parents. There, Dad spent much of the summer of 1959 as part of a high level delegation negotiating with the Russians, including Foreign Minister Gromyko, in search of a resolution to the festering subject of Berlin. Sheila and I enjoyed dining on roast chicken and French fries at lakeside restaurants, taking steamer excursions to Lausanne, and lunching and waterskiing at the lakeside villa of the famous jeweler, Cartier. Cartier's daughter Marianne Claudel, an American divorced from French intellectual Paul Claudel, had befriended the U.S. delegation. She entertained warmly and generously. Her glamorous, bikini-clad daughters were present. The oldest, Dominique, had appeared on the cover of *Paris Match* as the love interest of Victor Emmanuel, the heir to the Italian throne. The prince was present at our Sunday lunches at Cartier's villa. The younger, Marie, waterskied recklessly, and I injured myself in an effort to emulate her skill. We became close friends when Marie reappeared in Easton, Maryland, in the summer of 1982. I showed Marie the scar from my Lake Geneva misadventure 23 years earlier, and we, with our respective children, began waterskiing together again.

Before beginning Yale, I returned to Geneva to work in the summer of 1960 at a clerical post at the International Labor Office (ILO), a UN agency headed by a family friend, David Morse. The work was menial (operation of a mimeograph machine) and unlike the golden days of the previous summer, the weather was largely gray and rainy. My then romantic interest, Joanne Field, the daughter of Chicago publisher Marshall Field, was spending the summer in Lausanne, and I wasted much time in transit between Geneva and Lausanne before a hurtful "breakup" at midsummer. My residence with a fine Belgian family, the Pacquets, compensated somehow for an otherwise dreary experience.

In these youthfully idyllic days, Sheila and I little realized that Dad was haunted by a feeling that failure to resolve the Berlin crisis could actually result in a war between the Soviet Union and the United States. Eisenhower's eventual invitation to Khrushchev to visit the United States temporarily defused the crisis.[95] Dad's journal notes that the protracted Geneva proceedings didn't accomplish much but sufficed nonetheless as an example of Churchill's admonition that "jaw/jaw" is better than "war/war."

While in Geneva, my parents became attracted to the idea that I should take a year off after Canterbury and before college, to attend an elite Swiss boarding school, le Rosey. There, I could have learned to ski and to speak French and, not incidentally, meet sons of other influential and prosperous parents from all over the world. At 16 years of age, I thought I knew better and argued strenuously that I wanted to start college with personal friends who would be entering at the same time in the fall of 1960. My parents consulted the headmaster of Canterbury as to whether I was mature enough to attend college. Since, at the time, I was a class leader, captain of the swimming team, and chairman of the school newspaper, the headmaster could hardly give my parents the judgment they wished. Accordingly, I proceeded to Yale upon my graduation from Canterbury instead of spending a year hobnobbing with elites in Switzerland. I have had occasion to regret this immature and short-sighted decision—not the least in 1989 when my law firm asked me to open a Brussels, Belgium, office. A knowledge of French and network of acquaintances from education in Europe might then have been quite valuable.

7

The 60s

My generation recalls the 1960s with special acuity. It was a decade of large events and large changes of national mood and direction. For purposes of this narrative, I begin the "60s" with John F. Kennedy's election as President in November 1960. I end with Richard Nixon's election as President in 1968. In this eight-year interval, the nation experienced the abortive Bay of Pigs invasion (1961); the Cuban missile crisis (1962); the assassination of President Kennedy (1963); the escalation of the war in Vietnam (beginning in 1964–1965); the Civil Rights battle in the South; and the assassination of Martin Luther King and subsequently that of Robert F. Kennedy (both 1968). Paralleling these events was the development of a "counterculture," eager to experiment with drugs, caustic regarding "establishment"[96] figures and mores, and vehemently opposed to the U.S. involvement in Vietnam. The forces of the counterculture and the establishment clashed in mass sit-ins, marches, seizures of university administration buildings and, most notably, in a riotous Democratic Convention in Chicago in 1968. By the time U.S. involvement in Vietnam ended in 1975, the establishment figures who had advocated this war were significantly discredited and some of the social changes catalyzed by the counterculture became norms.

The 1960s also marked the first decade that I witnessed with adult sensitivities. A product of my wealthy, secure, relatively carefree, Republican background, I remained firmly rooted in established political culture. The possible exception was that, like other members of my generation, I readily realized the merits of the civil rights revolution. (Growing up on the Eastern Shore of Maryland, I had witnessed first-hand the implementation of segregation; some of my closest playmates have been the children of the extraordinary, African American Ayers family that helped manage Ratcliffe Manor.) Accordingly, against the turbulent backdrop of the 60s, my life remained remarkably stable—anchored in the traditions and examples of my parents and grandparents. I spent seven years in New Haven, first at Yale College and then Yale Law School. I worked in the summer of 1962 for Grandpa Maguire's Panhandle Eastern Pipeline Corporation and the summer of 1963 for the Ecuadorian Corporation, established by John Thomas Smith.

At dinner table discussions, my parents were unwavering in the view that the U.S. involvement in Vietnam was justified and would achieve the objective of stemming Communist expansion. Although I did not challenge my parents' establishment views on the topic, my enthusiasm for the Vietnam War was sufficiently modest that I did not seek an active military role in Southeast Asia. Instead, upon graduation from Yale Law School in 1967, and in order not to be drafted, I obtained a position affording me a two-year commission as an Air Force Officer, sponsored by the Central Intelligence Agency, in which I would subsequently become a "career trainee." Thus, in yet another reflection of my father's example, I embarked on a potential career in public service.

Before returning in somewhat greater detail to my personal development in the 1960s, it is appropriate to describe my father's endeavors during the same period. Indeed, it was during the 1960s that I first had the maturity to understand and appreciate the importance of my father's engagement with nuclear issues. Again, anyone wishing a more detailed look at my father's career in this period should refer to his memoir.[97]

GCS—Multilateral Force and Interplay Magazine

My father's tenure as Assistant Secretary of State for Policy Planning ended on January 19, 1961. He left the State Department assuming that his public service career might be over. However, he was soon back in harness. In the summer of 1961, he was hired as a State Department consultant as a new Berlin crisis emerged. The Soviet Union's threat to cut off Western access to West Berlin stimulated my father's thinking on two, interrelated issues: First was the question of how the United States and its NATO allies could best respond to Soviet threats without relying upon the questionable threat of massive use of nuclear weapons. Second, and related, was the question of how the United States could reassure skeptical European allies that it was willing to incur the risk of nuclear war affecting U.S. soil in the name of defense of Europe.

On the first question, my father circulated within the new administration a paper that he had written during his six months out of government. Drawing upon work done by the Policy Planning Staff during the prior Berlin crisis in 1959, Dad advocated use of naval resources to blockade Soviet access to the oceans as a means of bringing counter pressure in the event of the Soviet Union denial of Western access to Berlin. Dad recognized that such a strategy could lead to war but urged that it was a vastly preferable approach, when compared to direct use of conventional, much less nuclear weapons. My father shared his thinking with Arthur Krock, a prominent columnist for the *New York Times*. Krock published an op-ed piece endorsing and quoting liberally from my father's views.[98]

In any event, the Berlin crisis of the early 60s abated with the construction of the Berlin Wall and with probable recognition by the Soviet Union of the United States' nuclear superiority—the vaunted "missile gap" having been revealed as a gap in favor of the United States, not the Soviet Union. Nevertheless, the awareness by the Soviet Union of the United States' superiority led Khrushchev to deploy nuclear-armed missiles in Cuba. Notwithstanding more belligerent advice from many sources, including Dean Acheson and military leaders, President Kennedy decided upon a "quarantine" or Naval blockade. This step (together with a secret agreement to withdraw then recently emplaced U.S. missiles in Turkey on the Soviet border), led to a resolution of the most dangerous nuclear confrontation of the Cold War era. My father has noted that the means adopted by President Kennedy were consistent with those recommended by him a year earlier as the best way short of war to limit Soviet expansionism.[99]

The danger of nuclear confrontation during the Cuban missile crisis was acute. Historical dialogue and investigation involving participants in these momentous events has amply illuminated the precipitous conditions we were facing. One story that emerges from post–Cold War discussions is especially hair-raising. According to scholar, Michael Krepon, the U.S. Naval quarantine detected a Soviet submarine that did not surface as required by the quarantine. A U.S. vessel dropped depth charges. The three Russian officers aboard the submarine, which was equipped with nuclear-tipped torpedoes, did not have means to communicate with Soviet command authority as to a course of action. They caucused to decide whether to use its nuclear torpedoes. By a vote of two to one, the officers decided to surface and not to fire the torpedoes. By the single vote of a junior Soviet naval officer, under great stress, the world averted the unknown consequence of the use of a nuclear weapon in the midst of the Cuban crisis.[100]

In the spring of 1962, Dad was asked to undertake diplomacy with our European allies regarding the possible creation of a so-called multilateral force (MLF). The MLF idea had been percolating for several years at the State and Defense Departments. Now relegated to historical footnotes, the MLF, in the period 1962–1965, was an important issue as the United States wrestled with the challenges of providing a plausible nuclear deterrent to protect Europe while seeking to limit nuclear weapons proliferation as European nations such as England and France developed their own nuclear weapons capacities. The MLF, to be jointly manned by NATO nations, would be a force of seaborne intermediate range, nuclear armed missiles. Decisions regarding any use would be shared by the United States and its NATO allies. But, by giving the NATO allies a direct say in potential use, MLF would reassure them that there would be a robust "nuclear umbrella" in the event of Soviet hostilities toward Western Europe. Moreover, its proponents thought the MLF would have beneficial effect in stimulating greater political integration in Europe.

President Kennedy was ambivalent about the idea but authorized its advancement. As first announced in the spring of 1961, the MLF was to comprise five Polaris submarines. The President undercut its viability, however, by agreeing with the British at Nassau in late 1962 to enable British nuclear submarines to carry U.S.-supplied Polaris missiles. Granting the Brits this special privilege undercut prospects for participation in the MLF by the Brits and less favored European allies. Dad's friend Admiral Rickover posed a further obstacle to any submarine-based MLF. He adamantly opposed sharing the Navy's nuclear missile—and sensitive command and control technology—with other nations. He succeeded in persuading President Kennedy to abandon a submarine-based approach to MLF.

As it eventually evolved, the MLF contemplated deployment of seaborne missiles on surface vessels, jointly owned, manned, and controlled by the U.S. and its NATO allies. The MLF faced powerful obstacles; Secretary of Defense McNamara was a skeptic; the still powerful Joint Congressional Committee on Atomic Energy had strong misgivings about any sharing of U.S. nuclear capacities with third parties; the Russians hated the idea, characterizing it as a step toward giving the West Germans a nuclear weapons capacity; and France under de Gaulle cherished both its individual nuclear deterrent and the prospect of basing future European order on bilateral cooperation between Germany and France, and not one orchestrated by the United States and NATO.

After Kennedy's assassination in November 1963, the new President, Lyndon Johnson, was keenly alert to potential opposition in the U.S. Congress. This factor, combined with Defense Department ambivalence and European equivocation, doomed the MLF. In December 1964, my father resigned as head of the MLF Task Force at the State Department. Among the letters my father received upon the event of his resignation was one from Harvard Professor, and sometime State Department consultant, Henry Kissinger. Kissinger noted that he had not supported MLF, but was greatly impressed by the "dignity, efficiency and sense of honor" with which my father had performed his duties.[101] My father was destined to have further, extensive dealings with Kissinger during the Nixon administration.

During this same period of my father's career, my siblings Sheila and Gerry and I were variously at college and boarding school. (Hugh, aged 6–10, was still at home.) To keep up family communication, my father adopted the expedient of dictating "circular letters" addressed to the three of us away at school. Copies of these letters survive. They comprise a mix of family news, encouragement to academic excellence, and quotations from my father's self-improvement reading. Illustrative is "Circular Letter No. 6," dated April 13, 1962, in which Dad seeks our recommendations for future spring vacation travels. He asks that our recommendations exhibit "good sense." He then quotes from René Descartes who stated, "Good sense is of all things in the world the most equally distributed, for everybody thinks himself so abundantly provided with it that even those most difficult to please in other matters do not commonly desire more of it than they already possess." Dad then goes on to recount that our Christian Scientist grandmother, Ballo, had recently addressed seven-year-old Hugh with a Christian Science aphorism—"You know you are a perfect child of God." Hugh replied, "That's what everybody says." "Circular Letter No. 3," dated January 22, 1962, quotes Napoleon as having said "Let China sleep. When she wakes up, the world will be sorry." It goes on to recommend that we children read the UN Charter. It concludes with the datum that there were 1,352 swimming pools in fourth century Rome. Occasionally, the circular letters would express Dad's discouragement that the letters apparently elicited no response. Doubtless we youngsters were preoccupied with our educational and social lives. We also were shy about framing adequate responses to our Dad's impressive mix of humor and erudition.

The year 1965 found Dad again without government employment. At the urging of Henry Owen and Bob Bowie, as well as Bob Schaetzel, another State Department colleague, Dad became the founder and publisher of a magazine called *Interplay*. The title drew snickers given its similarity to the ever fascinating word, "intercourse," but *Interplay* was a serious venture. A journal of opinion and analysis, it focused on the growing economic and cultural interrelationships among European and North American countries. It had a glittering international advisory board and a highly qualified British journalist, Anthony Hartley, as Editor. The contributors included prominent journalists, statesmen, and academicians such as David Broder, Henry Fairlie, William Pfaff, Joseph Kraft, John McCloy, Zbigniew Brzezinski, and my now longtime friend, John Newhouse. Its Deputy Editor was James Chace, who went on to edit *Foreign Affairs* and to write an award-winning biography of Dean Acheson.[102]

Dad underwrote much of the cost of this venture, with help from his brother Gregory and his sister Maureen. As with many small publishing ventures, its chief economic result was to lose money, but it furnished its investors with desirable tax losses. An internet search for information about *Interplay* today reveals almost nothing, and copies of editions of *Interplay* are quite rare. But, at the time, the magazine published important and provocative articles with a distinctly "Atlantic" cast. Not insignificantly, it foreshadowed the later effort of David Rockefeller in establishing the Trilateral Commission, in which my father was to play a role beginning in 1973.

8

J.T.S. II, Yale Years

While my father wrestled in government with the issues of nuclear proliferation and the maintenance of the credibility of the U.S. deterrent, and
dealt at a relatively high level with European statesmen and subsequently
with *Interplay* magazine, I was preoccupied with tracing family footsteps at
Yale College and subsequently at Yale Law School. A brief summary of my
seven years in New Haven may be appropriate consistent with the theme
of a "generational reflection."

Yale College

When I arrived at Yale College at the age of 16 in September of 1960,[103]
Yale was quite similar to the College that my father had attended three
decades earlier and dissimilar to the Yale of today, or even the Yale of a decade later. It was all male. Students wore coats and ties to classes and meals.
There were even Saturday morning classes for those insufficiently clever
at scheduling to avoid such indignity. Women were not allowed inside
dormitories after 10 p.m. Fraternities flourished. Alcoholic beverages were
ubiquitous; illegal drugs unknown. Yale's effort to emulate the "college"
system of Oxford and Cambridge with individual residential colleges as
centers for both social and academic endeavor—begun in the 1930s—was
still a work in progress.

I entered Yale with a secure, if not a complacent, attitude. I had received
an excellent education at Canterbury and had established "advanced place-
ment credits" in both English and European History. I had been honored
by the award of a Yale National Honorary Scholarship—consisting of a

letter and a check for $50. The letter explained that Yale had marked me as a student of special promise. I regret to say that I did not completely fulfill this promise. I entered with two close friends from Southampton summers. One, Terry Moulton, would become part of my rooming group for all four years, and the other, Billy Morton, would participate in an eight-man rooming arrangement during my sophomore to senior years. (My zeal to attend college with these two summer friends had been the basis for my foolish rejection of a year in Switzerland.) Each of these two men brought friendships from their respective boarding schools. Also, I was acquainted with the three other members from my class at Canterbury who attended Yale in my year, as well as five or six members of my grade school classes at Landon. (Admission to elite colleges was a much simpler matter in 1960 than it is today. Of my class of 44 boys at Canterbury, approximately half attended Yale, Harvard, Princeton, and Georgetown.) My sister Sheila's attendance at nearby Briarcliff Junior College provided an avenue for introduction to attractive women.

As a reflection of my father's interests and career, I signed up for an upper class course on the diplomatic history of the United States. There, I wrote a first semester paper regarding the interplay of realism and idealism in American 20th-century foreign policy, which garnered an A. I was somewhat less successful in my emulation of my father in the study of Russian, where I labored for a C+ under the tutelage of an impressive Russian lady author later recognized as one of the great Russian short story writers of the 20th century—Nina Nikolaevna Berberova. Berberova had fled the Russian Revolution in 1922 and lived in France until 1951.

A dry recounting of my courses would add little interest to this short book. But a few highlights deserve mention. In my sophomore year I took a course in Modern American Political History. The professor, John Morton Blum, was universally admired by my generation of Yale students. He was an unabashed New Deal Democrat, a charismatic lecturer and a hugely stimulating professor. I remember his speaking extemporaneously on the day that the news was received of the death of Eleanor Roosevelt. He persuaded us of the large historical consequence of this ungainly woman. In my junior and senior year I pursued an "honors" history curriculum, focusing again on diplomatic history. My professor was Gaddis Smith, who later became a head of the Yale History Department. I wrote an honors essay focusing on President Woodrow Wilson's role at the Conference of Versailles at the end of the First World War. One further high point was History of Modern Architecture taught by Vincent Scully. This course, outside my normal field of interest and study, was of the utmost worth, giving me a modest ability to appreciate architecture wherever I later lived or traveled.

My principal academic regret is that I did not pursue courses in either economics or statistics. Both disciplines became an important part of my practice of regulatory law in later years. I actually took one semester of an introductory economics course. I had an instructor from Yugoslavia, who was particularly difficult to understand. At the end of the first semester, assuming I had done poorly, I sought and obtained his permission to drop the course. Later, I learned with pleasant surprise that my first semester grade in economics had been a high one.

In my senior year, I took History of American Oratory under Professor Roland Osterweiss. This course was undemanding in that it required no exam, no extensive reading, or other travail. It did require each student, once a month, to make a short speech in class, and it was on these speeches that one's grade principally depended. Osterweiss imparted valuable lessons about the proper structure for a speech, and the course proved useful as well in providing practice in speaking on one's feet. An underclassman two years my junior and a member of my fraternity, John Kerry, took me aside one day to volunteer some pointers on improving my speeches in Osterweiss's class. Although I was ambivalent about receiving guidance from an underclassman, he almost became President of the United States, at least in part due to his polish as a speaker and debater. Joe Lieberman, United States Senator and 2000 candidate for Vice President, was a classmate and excelled as the Chairman of the *Yale Daily News* and as a fledgling politician. The Gore/Lieberman ticket actually won the popular vote but, after the intervention of the Supreme Court, lost in the electoral college. Lieberman subsequently ran unsuccessfully in the Democratic presidential primaries in 2004, with John Kerry emerging as the nominee.

Yale College in the early 1960s offered myriad opportunities that I am ashamed I did not pursue. In addition to courses not taken—and especially a Shakespeare course by the leading scholar, Maynard Mack—I did not participate adequately in extracurricular activities. My athletic endeavors were woefully small, consisting principally of an occasional game of squash. I did participate in several intramural football games in my sophomore year on behalf of my residential college. My football "career" ended after three games with a concussion and a night in the Yale infirmary. Nor did I gravitate to the Catholic Center at Yale, Thomas More House, even though the Saint Thomas More Chapel had been constructed in the late 1930s with money donated by my grandfather, John Thomas Smith. I would attend Sunday Mass, but my attendance record was at best imperfect.

In the 1960s, entering sophomore year, a student was allowed to form a "rooming group" of as many as eight men to be assigned to a single suite of rooms in one of the residential colleges. I joined my friend Terry Moulton and two other friends of his from the Hill School, and Billy Morton, together with three friends of his from St. Paul's School, and the eight of us were assigned to Jonathan Edwards College. Seven of the eight of us "rushed" and joined a fraternity known as "The Fence Club." Thereupon this social fraternity occupied a disproportionate amount of my time as an undergraduate.

In its day, "Fence" was considered the "preppiest" of the undergraduate fraternities. The preponderance of its members had attended elite boarding schools. Some of the membership were athletes, but typically in "preppy" sports, such as ice hockey, crew, squash, and tennis. The advantages of membership included the ability to run a charge account for drinks and dinners, play pool and billiards, entertain one's weekend dates at parties, often including live bands, in an atmosphere that was an odd meld of the decorous and the raucous. Each spring there was a renowned party which included a fountain device that cascaded gin and juice—the notorious "gin fountain." In my junior year, this weekend featured the live band of Rock and Roll Hall of Famer, Bo Diddley. Although the drinking age in Connecticut was 21, Fence, like other Yale fraternities, served liquor with liberality to all members and guests under the benign gaze of the professional manager or "permitee," John Huggins, a wise and distinguished gentleman from Nevis in the British West Indies. On occasion, a distinguished alumnus of Yale (1950) and the Fence Club, William F. Buckley, would pay the Club a visit.[104]

At the end of the sophomore year, each class of the Fence Club would elect a slate of officers to preside during junior year. At the age of 18, I found myself elected to be President of Fence—further testament to the liberality of administration of the drinking laws. I did not campaign for this office. It seems quite plausible that my election reflected "block voting" by six of my roommates, who also were members. Further proof of the strength of the block was that my friend and roommate, Terry Moulton, became Vice President. The duties of President of Fence were not onerous, although Terry and I had responsibility on Saturday nights to ensure that there were no crashers at club parties and that lingerers were shown the door at closing time. As president I worked closely with John Huggins, whom I greatly admired.

Each year the fraternity permitees, all of whom were black, entertained fraternity presidents at a dinner. I learned from Huggins the ages of some of the other permitees, who were surprisingly old. In an unguarded moment I told Huggins that I had difficulty telling the age of black people. Huggins laughed gently and pointed out that he had the same problems with "us white gentlemen." His rejoinder was sophisticated—genuinely ironic given the fact that he served liquor to many who were underage, but also a polite pushback to my racial gaucherie.

In the spring of my junior year, doubtless as a result of serving as President of Fence, I was "tapped" by a senior society, Wolf's Head. Membership in this institution provided the richest extracurricular experience that I had as a Yale undergraduate. Public attention to the system of senior societies at Yale has long focused on the most famous one, Skull and Bones, where both Presidents Bush, as well as John Kerry, were members, but the other six senior societies furnished an analogous experience. Each senior society selected 15 seniors who had distinguished themselves academically, athletically, or in extracurricular fashion. All recruited throughout Yale College, breaking the parochialism of individual residential colleges and fraternities. Each senior society occupied its own "tomb," a dedicated building where the 15 privileged seniors could fraternize and study, and from which all nonmembers were rigorously excluded. Societies would meet for dinner on Thursday and Sunday evenings. They placed emphasis on public speaking (to the other 14 members) through a variety of mechanisms. And, to the best of my belief, each required that all members deliver an extensive oral "personal history" open to comment and criticism by the other 14. Wolf's Head occupied an especially fine building designed by prominent architect James Gamble Rogers, located near the center of the Yale campus. Rumors that Wolf's Head had an indoor swimming pool, alas, proved false.

Reflecting its founding in the 19th century, Wolf's Head involved a modest amount of mumbo jumbo focusing on Egyptology. But its real purpose was to allow 15 men from widely varying backgrounds to come to know and appreciate each other in a manner that would not be possible outside its walls. Like other senior societies, Wolf's Head also provided an opportunity to network with distinguished or successful graduates. Some of the most distinguished would return on Sunday evenings to talk about their careers. Wolf's Head continues to thrive to this day. Each class now contains men and women, and the degree of "diversity" among "wolves" has expanded radically.

Despite its function in expanding intellectual, cultural, and social horizons, Yale College in the early 1960s also provided a cocoon, or interlocking set of cocoons. We were engaged with our classes, fraternities, girlfriends, football weekends, road trips to women's colleges, and senior societies. We did not spend a great deal of time reflecting on developments of the world outside. For instance, I am bemused to confess that I have no memory of what I was doing or thinking at the time of the Cuban Missile Crisis in the autumn of my junior year. All were conscious of the hostilities in Vietnam, but the United States did not commit serious forces to Vietnam until the winter of 1965, when I was in my first year of law school. Several of my friends, however, attended "platoon leader class" at Quantico in preparation to become marine officers. Other less adventurous friends took heart from commentators who speculated that the military draft, which had been in place since the Korean War, would be ended by 1966.

We were conscious of the civil rights ferment in the South, but none of my close acquaintances participated in freedom rides and rights protests. As did our professors, most of us found the rhetoric and example of President Kennedy inspiring. Just as a new generation will likely recall the precise circumstances when they heard about the destruction of the World Trade Center on September 11, 2001, members of my generation remember precisely where they were and what they thought upon learning the news of Kennedy's assassination on November 22, 1963. (I was in an early afternoon lecture on French history. Someone entered the classroom and handed the Professor a note. The color drained from his face and he imparted the news of Kennedy's shooting and dismissed the class.) In retrospect, this event was for me and others a call to wider consciousness previously avoided in Yale's cocoons.

In the autumn of my senior year I applied to and was admitted to Yale Law School. My junior year marks placed me in the top 10 percent of my class. My law school aptitude scores were respectable if not exceptional. The fact that I was a third generation descendant of graduates of the Law School, who had distinguished themselves and been generous to the School, probably did not hurt my chances for admission.

College vacations and summers provided other opportunities for growth. As already mentioned, in the summer of 1962, I worked for Grandpa Maguire's Panhandle Eastern Pipeline Company, assisting on a pipeline survey crew in Western Kansas and subsequently in Western Missouri. There I worked and socialized with individuals quite different from the occupants of my Yale milieu. The diversity of experience gained by working on the pipeline was highlighted when I purchased a *Time* magazine one day while living in a motel in Greensburg, Kansas, and saw a report on the debutante party at England's Blenheim Palace of Serena Russell, a contemporary from Southampton, Long Island, and niece of Winston Churchill.[105] I had been invited to this party (attended by 1,100 people), but had declined due to my summer employment. Indeed, Blenheim was a long way from Western Kansas.

As already described, in the summer of 1963 I lived and worked in Ecuador for the Ecuadorian Corporation, retracing the steps of my other grandfather. As my departure for Ecuador approached, my father told his friend and contemporary, Sarge Shriver, then Director of the newly created Peace Corps, that I would be spending the summer in Ecuador. Shriver invited me to his office. There he asked me to gather information about what the Peace Corps representatives were doing in Ecuador and how their efforts were being received. I did so and wrote a short memorandum for Shriver upon my return. I immediately received a letter of thanks and commendation from this ebullient and generous man. (I don't recall the details of my report to Shriver. If memory serves, I was constructively critical of some agricultural assistance efforts that seemed to lack focus and intensity.)

In the summer after my Yale graduation in 1964, I traveled with my sister Sheila and brother Gerry to South America. Gerry and I went first and fished for marlin for several days off the Pacific Coast of Panama. We then joined up with Sheila and traveled to Ecuador, Peru, Bolivia, Argentina, and Brazil. In Peru we visited the city of Manchu Pichu, the so-called Lost City of the Incas. We stayed at a small hotel at the actual site and were the only guests. Accordingly, the morning after our arrival we had the entire site to ourselves for several hours prior to the return of a train with numerous tourists. We also visited the Peruvian Amazon and took a steamer across Lake Titicaca from Peru to Bolivia. Our experiences in the Andes and on the Amazon live larger in memory than our more urban adventures in Buenos Aires, Rio de Janeiro, Sao Paulo, and Brasilia.

I am struck in retrospect that, before my 21st birthday, I had lived and worked in Switzerland and Ecuador and had toured Scandinavia, Western Europe, and South America, all grand opportunities, more or less taken for granted.

Yale Law School

Yale Law School provided a much more serious intellectual climate than had Yale College. I attended in the belief that a law school education would provide a good general background for addressing public policy issues. Like my father, I aspired to public service in the international realm, and I did not anticipate spending a career in a corporate law firm. Yale Law School, in contrast to its chief competitor, Harvard Law School, was known for probing the policy underpinnings of law and for affording its students a broad degree of discretion in selection of courses. Consistent with my lack of interest in private practice of law, I chose not to take certain basic courses, including Evidence, Legal Accounting, or Commercial Law. As I had as an undergraduate, I gravitated to courses that had an international aspect, spending a significant portion of my third year in law school in a seminar and writing program on regulation of international trade.

At the Law School, I soon encountered the footprints of John Thomas Smith. In an introductory course on income taxation, we studied *Higgins v. Smith*, the Second Circuit Court of Appeals decision disapproving the tax-loss scheme that my grandfather had created to sell depreciated General Motors shares to the wholly owned Innisfail Corporation.[106] And in an introductory course on Federal Civil Procedure, we read *Klaxon v. Stentor*, in which my grandfather prevailed on General Motors' behalf in the Supreme Court.[107] My father's footprints were less evident. He had not spent much of his career in the practice of law. But, as previously noted, he was fondly remembered by at least two of my professors, Fritz Kessler and Myers MacDougal.

Then, as now, Yale Law School had a faculty of extraordinary capacities and highly memorable personalities. My first semester course in Contracts was taught with suitable incomprehensibility by Leon Lipson, an expert on Russian law, who had the demeanor of a Soviet commissar. Lipson was rigorous in use of the Socratic method in which students were provided questions but not answers. Students were called upon to stand up and answer questions about the significance of particular cases. One of the most eager participants was Jeffrey Greenfield, who went on to be a highly regarded journalist and author. Jeff, with cause, considered himself something of a star performer in this contracts class. However, on the final class before exams in January 1965, Greenfield volunteered an answer that Professor Lipson did not like. Looking sternly down from his podium, Lipson offered the following, wonderful admonition: "Mr. Greenfield—your answer reminds me of the fabled 13th chime, inaccurate and misleading in and of itself—and casting doubt upon the 12 that went before." I have long relished Lipson's statement as good counsel against excessive intellectual exuberance.

I was fortunate in the first semester of my first year to be assigned to a seminar on Constitutional Law taught by the extraordinary Charles Reich. In 1970, Reich gained notoriety for his bestselling *The Greening of America*, in which he celebrated the rise of the counterculture as a beneficial revolution that would allow all that was best in the American experience to overwhelm the faults and prejudices of the establishment. Many looked askance at this paean to hippiedom by a Yale Law School professor. Those of us who had spent the fall of 1964 examining the Constitution under Reich's tutelage were less surprised. (One of my seminar mates was an earnest prior Peace Corps volunteer, Paul Tsongas—yet another contemporary who later ran for President.) For all his eccentricity, Reich was a superb teacher. We spent the first two weeks of the class examining a single case, *Marbury v. Madison*, in which Justice Marshall established the right of the Supreme Court to conduct constitutional review of legislation. The facts in this case and the context in which it arose were quite complex. Reich drilled us class after class to achieve a more perfect understanding of the facts—a critical skill in any future legal endeavor. Reich also had a capacity, after long discussion of a particular area of constitutional law, to sum up with a few pithy, lucid sentences all that had seemed protracted and complex.

Under Reich's guidance, I wrote a legal memorandum assessing the legality of warrantless electronic eavesdropping. I concluded that such activities offended the Fourth Amendment's bar to warrantless search and seizure. My analysis of Fourth Amendment case law proved useful nine years later when I became embroiled in the Watergate matter, working with Attorney General Elliot Richardson.

Another leading professor at the time was the late Alexander Bickel, who taught Administrative Law and Advanced Constitutional Law. He was a highly thoughtful and articulate proponent of "judicial restraint"— a doctrine that accords Congress wide discretion to legislate and seeks to conserve the legitimacy of judicial decision making by avoiding decisions except when absolutely necessary. Especially, the Court should avoid essentially political questions not implicating fundamental Constitutional principles. Although in present day it is conservative Republicans who rail against "activist judges," the true disciple of Bickel on today's Court is Justice Breyer, and the archetypical case that Bickel's philosophy would identify as inappropriate for Supreme Court decision making was that regarding the vote count in Florida in the election of 2000, *Bush v. Gore*.[108] In his dissent Justice Breyer quoted Bickel extensively.

In my second year I studied Antitrust Law under Robert Bork, who was to go on to prominence as Solicitor General of the United States, the man who did Nixon's bidding in dismissing Special Prosecutor Archie Cox in the "Saturday Night Massacre," a failed nominee for the Supreme Court, and, subsequently, as a searing critic of what he perceives as the degradation of the moral fabric of the United States. I was to have an opportunity to work with Bork only a few years later when I served in the Justice Department under Elliot Richardson. As will be shown, Alex Bickel also played a small role in the events of the Saturday Night Massacre.

Another star of the Law School faculty was Guido Calabresi, who taught a wide range of subjects. I took from him a memorable course on a relatively dry subject—gift and estate tax. He was a master of the Socratic teaching technique and a man of the widest imagination and capacities. As already noted, Calabresi later became the first John Thomas Smith Professor of Law and subsequently Dean of the Law School. It is noteworthy that Guido was quick to discern the great capacities of both Bill Clinton and Hillary Rodham when they were students at Yale Law School a few years after me. It was the Clintons who promoted Calabresi's candidacy for a federal judgeship.

Although I made numerous friends as a Yale undergraduate, friendships formed at Law School have proved more sustained. Principal among them is Alan R. McFarland. Alan and I had been in the same class at Yale College but had not been well acquainted. However, early in on our first year of Law School we discovered a mutuality of interest and outlook. We had some of the same professors, most notably Reich for Constitutional Law. We became fast friends and remain so to this day. Our continuing ties are substantial. I introduced Alan to his first wife and through her, I met John and Will's mother. Alan and I are godparents to each of our oldest sons. Alan's second wife, whom he met through me and Ben's mother, is godmother to Ben. Through Alan, I met Alfred Rankin Jr. Al had been in the same fraternity with Alan at Yale College, but was a year ahead of both of us at Yale Law School. In my second year at Law School, as mentioned previously, Alan McFarland, Alfred Rankin, Luke Sadler, and I lived very comfortably in the farmhouse of Professor Calabresi. I am a godfather to Alfred's glorious daughter, Clara. Alfred is married to Viki Griffin, sister to my sister Sheila's late husband, Dick.

Three other law school friends deserve mention. All three were academic stars in Al Rankin's class. The first is Ed Bruce, whose partner I have been at Covington & Burling for three decades. It was through Ed that I have received some of my most interesting practice opportunities. Ed's friend and classmate, Ray Clevenger, has been a much valued friend in Washington, D.C., throughout my career. Ray is presently a senior judge on the U.S. Court of Appeals for the Federal Circuit and is married to my old friend, Leslie Renchard. Finally, there is Benno Schmidt—too seldom seen. Benno was part of the "delegation" at Wolf's Head that tapped me in my junior year. He went on to sparkle academically at Yale Law School. He, Ed Bruce, and Ray Clevenger all served as Clerks to Justices of the Supreme Court upon graduation. Benno went on to be Dean of Columbia Law School and subsequently the President of Yale.

In my second year of Law School, Benno asked me to join him working as a "Pre-Law" Advisor in the Yale College Dean's Office. Our responsibilities were to counsel Yale undergraduates on the merits of various law schools and to host visits by admissions deans from law schools to Yale College. The pay was modest, but the post provided opportunities to interact with a broad array of students and with interesting admissions deans from around the country. Not the least benefit was a regular weekly doubles squash game in which Benno and I played Richard Carroll, Dean of Yale College, and Sam Chauncey, Special Assistant to Yale President Kingman Brewster.

Law School was preoccupying. However, especially after my first year, the larger world intruded. In 1965, the United States escalated its involvement in Vietnam. The only professor that I can remember expressing real concern at the time was Charlie Reich, soon to be the bard of the counter-culture. When I was home for vacations, Washington was abuzz with the Vietnam conflict. Secretary of Defense McNamara lived across from my parents on Tracy Place in D.C. I can recall being home for a long weekend at the end of exams in January 1966. There was a blizzard and by Sunday morning deep drifts covered Tracy Place. While my parents and I sat by the fire, I was sent down to answer the doorbell and found myself facing a red-cheeked Secretary of Defense. He had just returned from Vietnam the previous day but, with his usual vigor, had trekked a half a mile through snowdrifts to the nearest place one could buy a Sunday *New York Times.* Making light of his prior disagreements with my father about the MLF, McNamara handed me a copy of the *Times* stating that he wouldn't want my father to be "misinformed." To reciprocate, I was dispatched through snow drifts with a bottle of brandy for the Secretary.

On another weekend home from law school, my parents asked me to accompany them to a dinner party at the home of Hugh D. Auchincloss (whose wife was the mother of Jackie Kennedy). Apparently, I had been asked to provide companionship to Jackie Kennedy's half-sister, Janet

Auchincloss, my contemporary and slight acquaintance. The main order of business was post-dinner bridge played by the "adults." Janet and I were relegated to roles as spectators, or in the parlance of bridge, "kibitzers." My father and a partner were assigned to play against the formidable Averell Harriman, senior Democratic statesman of great wealth and accomplishment. Harriman had been Governor of the State of New York and U.S. Ambassador to Russia during the Second World War. He was about to serve as chief U.S. negotiator in peace negotiations with the North Vietnamese. To my horror, I witnessed my father "renege," that is he failed to play a card of the proper suit led by his partner. In bridge, this misplay normally carries severe penalties. Governor Harriman gave no notice to my father's mistake. I have occasionally speculated whether Harriman's oversight of my father's misplay was the product of impaired facilities (Harriman was 76 years old at the time) or whether it reflected high courtesy. In any event, both my father and Governor Harriman had much more important concerns than the outcome of a bridge game.

That same winter brought news that a Yale classmate and fellow member of Wolf's Head, Bruce Warner, while serving as a Marine tank officer in Vietnam, had been drastically wounded in the abdomen. Bruce was flown back to the United States. This once vigorous Yale hockey defenseman wasted away and died a month later. Accordingly, in March 1966, other classmates and I attended Bruce's funeral in Farmington, Connecticut, where on a bright June weekend in 1964, we had attended Bruce's wedding. The stark military honors on a cold March day 22 months later reminded us of the seriousness of Vietnam endeavors. Bruce was the first of too many of my personal friends to die unfairly young.

Two years later another friend from Yale, Dick Pershing, was killed serving in Vietnam. Dick was a brave and charismatic individual, engaged to be married to Shirley Gay, a close friend of mine from Southampton. He was the grandson of General of the Armies, John J. ("Black Jack") Pershing, who led the U.S. forces during World War I. Another victim of the Vietnam War was my childhood playmate, Edward Ayers.

In the spring of 1966, I received a notice from my D.C. draft board that I was to be drafted. As a full-time student at Yale Law School, I was entitled to a deferment, which was obtained upon a commitment that I would do military service upon graduation. To this end, I followed in the footsteps of my housemate and friend Alfred Rankin, who had obtained access to a program conducted jointly by the CIA and the U.S. Air Force. Through this program one could discharge a foreshortened military service obligation on the way to becoming a "career trainee" of the Agency. In due course, after graduation and taking the D.C. Bar examination, I went to work at the Agency.

After my second year at Law School I worked as a summer associate at the Wall Street law firm of Winthrop, Stimson, Putnam and Roberts. I owed my employment, at least in part, to a close friend of my father's, Peter Kaminer. Kaminer was the senior litigation partner at the firm. He had graduated from Yale Law School a year after my father in 1939. Given his German descent and German accent, Kaminer had difficulty, notwithstanding sterling law school grades, finding a job at a major law firm. My father found him a place on the General Motors legal staff. Eventually, Kaminer became one of the most highly regarded lawyers in New York. My summer at Winthrop, Stimson reinforced my instinct to pursue public service rather than corporate law. But it gave me a useful insight into the flavor of life in a large law firm. As was common practice, summer associates rotated assignments and office locations, moving from office to office when more senior lawyers would be away on trial or vacation. I spent one week in a "ceremonial" office at the magnificent desk of revered former partner Henry Stimson who had twice served as Secretary of War. He is reputed to have opposed code-breaking in 1929 with the line, "Gentlemen don't read each other's mail."[109] When I worked subsequently at the CIA, I reflected on the irony of having sat at Stimson's desk.

9

Romance, Marriage, and Military Service

I first met Linda Carol Kridel during my second year in Law School. The preceding summer, my friend and housemate, Alan McFarland, while visiting in Southampton, had met and fallen in love with Nell Michel. Nell was a couple of years younger and not a close friend of mine. Linda and Nell had been friends for years, growing up on the East Side of Manhattan and attending Madeira School in McLean, Virginia.

Linda and I began "dating" during the summer of 1966 and, by my senior year in law school, we were spending most weekends together. Linda was immensely bright, having graduated Phi Beta Kappa from Smith College in 1966. She was attractive and vivacious, and we shared a large range of interests. The marriage of our respective friends, Nell Michel and Alan McFarland, in August 1966 provided, if any were needed, further "glue" to our relationship. All was not easy. Linda came from a secular Jewish background, with proud and successful parents and grandparents, at a time when social (e.g., Jewish versus Catholic) distinctions had a great deal more force than they do today. Linda's and my respective families were wary of our growing bond. Matters were not eased by the fact that our two mothers (both of whom had attended Smith College) were smart, demanding, and protective.

After graduating from Smith, Linda had gone to work in New York at the Book Division of Time, Inc., and subsequently at a public relations firm. In the summer of 1967 after taking my bar examinations, I began work at the CIA, pending a slot opening at Air Force Officer Training School. As my military service commitment approached, in late 1967, I asked Linda to marry me. She agreed, but asked that our engagement be kept secret since the news "would kill her grandmother," who was then ill. (This formidable woman lived more than two decades longer.) This set of generational reflections is not the place for excessive personal detail. Suffice it to say that my relationship with John and Will's mother took some unusual turns. After I completed Air Force Officer Training School in May 1968 and moved to my duty station in California, we announced our engagement and prepared for a small wedding in Santa Barbara. The rigors of planning this event brought sufficient stress to Linda, her mother, and my mother that the wedding was canceled a week before its planned date and our engagement was broken. Nevertheless, our mutual attraction proved sufficiently strong that we eloped 18 months later in the spring of 1970.

Eager to conduct ourselves in a manner that would validate our behavior in the eyes of at least my parents, Linda obtained instruction in the Catholic faith (a prerequisite for marriage by a Catholic priest), and we were married in a Catholic church with only two witnesses, my brother Gerry and Linda's friend, Stephanie Jay. We retired to my apartment and called friends and family with our news (reinforced by a bottle of Dom Pérignon Champagne). Linda's family did not happily embrace the news. In contrast, mine showered us with flowers, and my parents insisted that Linda and I join them at a White House "prayer breakfast" the following morning. Accordingly, my father and mother picked us up in a government sedan (my father then serving as the Director of the Arms Control and Disarmament Agency) and we proceeded to the White House. Former President Lyndon Johnson was visiting, and, as we went through the receiving line, Linda and I met both Johnson and Nixon. Three and a half years later I would be centrally involved in events that would lead to Nixon's resignation in disgrace.

* * * * *

Reflection—A Digression on "Sex"

Having earlier included a digression regarding religion, I here digress more briefly on the subject of sex. (In 1990 when I was taking French lessons in Brussels, my instructor told me that the only three topics that were inappropriate for discussion at dinner parties were "religion, sex, and politics." I was left to wonder what there was left that would be worth talking about.) I achieved physical maturity at a relatively young age, before my 11th birthday. I found myself "falling for" young women who were my contemporaries or a bit older. That said, I had scant idea of the true physical, much less emotional and psychological contours of male and female relations. But my "romantic" inclinations gave me strong incentive to try to learn more.

In the well regulated environment in which I lived, "experiential learning" opportunities were scarce. It was for this reason, I became an avid reader, tackling Tolstoy, Zola, and Stendhal in my mid-teens, hoping to extract practical wisdom regarding the mysteries that fascinated me. For my children and grandchildren, it will be hard to imagine a world in which there was no *Playboy* magazine, much less explicit internet material. Movies then deemed "racy" would probably be rated PG in today's world. I remember my father warning me against seeing a particular Brigitte Bardot movie. But he was too late; I had already seen it. Even in the early 1960s, when I was in college, it was exceptional for dating couples to "go all the way." This world of restraint and mystery provided impetus to earlier marriages and more memorable and dramatic honeymoons.

The Catholic Church has long been preoccupied with human sexuality. Then as now, it taught that the only sexual congress not sinful was directed toward the possibility of conception of children within the structure of marriage. Hence all sex outside of marriage was sinful. And sex within marriage using artificial means of birth control was sinful as well. American Catholics have long abandoned the Church's teaching on birth control, but the balance of Catholic doctrine on the subject of sex remains in place. It may strike some in my and future generations as quaint—although the doctrine is also ascribed to by other, conservative Christian churches.

I remain ambivalent about the vast liberalization of sexual norms that has occurred in my lifetime. I rejoice in the elimination of social tyranny, guilt, and ignorance that characterized the 1950s and early 1960s. Similarly, I support the nation's move toward recognition of full social and legal status for gays. Under the influence of my wife, Mary, I am "pro-choice" on the question of a woman's access to abortion—although I harbor a residual horror at the use of abortion as a form of birth control.

It remains my hope that my children and grandchildren will somehow, in a coarsened world, occasionally experience the mysterious excitement that accompanied exploration and ultimate fulfillment of sexual curiosity in my generation. A superb description of the excitement that my generation experienced in unconsummated exploration of mutual sexual attraction appears in Giussepe di Lampedusa's novel *The Leopard*. His characters recall "days when desire was always present because it was always overcome, when many beds had been offered and refused, when the sensual urge, because restrained, had for one second been sublimated in renunciation, that is into real love."[110]

In Plato's *Symposium* a group of notable Athenians, including Socrates, spend an evening discoursing on the topic of erotic love. While the focus of many is, to a striking degree, on homosexual love, Socrates states that erotic love is a ladder by which one can strive for understanding of the mysteries of true virtue and beauty.[111] In a minor, unknowing way, my juvenile exploration of sophisticated literature in search of understanding of Eros, may have been proof of Socrates' sagacity. Constraining erotic pursuit to the sole purpose of reproduction likewise may inhibit human understanding and potential.

* * * * *

Military Service

As previously noted, I fulfilled my military service obligation under the auspices of the CIA. During a four-year period, I spent a year and three months in the Air Force and nearly three years working for the Agency. Though these commitments did not draw in direct measure on my Yale Law School education, they were not without interesting moments.

Beginning in the summer of 1967, until I began Officer Training School in February 1968, I filled a temporary position at the Agency's headquarters in Langley, Virginia. My only previous visit to this campus had occurred during my vetting for a position as an Agency career trainee—consisting of a lie detector test and an interview with a psychologist. Home from Law School in the early winter of 1967 for the purpose of this Agency visit, I was driven to Langley by my parents' chauffeur in their dark green Bentley. On arrival at the Agency, the guards assumed I was an important foreign visitor and directed us to a VIP parking lot adjacent to the front door.

For my temporary duty, I was assigned to the Polish branch in Clandestine Services. There I was given responsibility for a defector from the Polish diplomatic service. My duties included debriefing him on his knowledge of personalities in the Polish diplomatic and intelligence services. His descriptions gave me interesting insight into a dysfunctional Communist society.

This complex man had left his wife and children and fled to the West. As I was single, the Branch relied upon me to entertain this defector on weekends. He was in the prime of life and enjoyed theater, good meals, and aspired to female company. A product of his culture, he assumed that

U.S. intelligence officers enjoyed special privileges. At his urging, I once took him to a popular night spot in the Dupont Circle area of Washington, D.C. A long line extended from the entrance. As I took an orderly place at the end of the line, the defector kept elbowing me and urging me to "tell them who I was," assuming that as an intelligence officer I could jump to the head of the queue. I heard later of a misadventure that this gentleman had after he had been moved from a safe house and furnished with his own car and apartment. He was stopped by Virginia police driving erratically on his way home one evening. Although he spoke English quite well, he tried the gambit of saying he didn't understand the policeman, reciting that "he was a Polish man." His case officer received a call at 2 a.m. advising that the defector had been arrested for "impersonating a policeman."

Air Force Officer Training School of three months' duration presented its own challenges. Unlike the Marines or the Army, the Air Force deemphasized raw physical endurance and stressed instead mental durability. Sleep was short—five to six hours a night; class and course work was substantial, and we trainees remained accountable to have our uniforms neat, shoes and buckles shined. The instructors discovered that I had a repertoire of jokes, and they would call upon me at the beginning of classes to stand and recite a joke. Reflecting ineptitude at tempo that still afflicts my golf game, I found orderly marching to be difficult. Fortunately, I achieved the rank of Officer Trainee Major and Honor Council Representative, which status relieved me of some of the more pedestrian aspects of being an Officer Trainee.

I expressed a preference for assignment to California and found myself assigned to Vandenberg Air Force Base outside Lompoc, just west of Santa Barbara on California's foggy central coast. There, for one year, I served as the administrative officer of an aircraft maintenance squadron that was responsible for the helicopters and planes used to support missile test and training exercises that were the central mission of Vandenberg. Though not directly involved with missile activities, it is ironic that I found myself in proximity to the weapons delivery systems that had been and were soon again to become a central part of my father's professional endeavors. Periodically, the ground would rumble during test launch of Atlas or Minuteman missiles, and the occasional night-time launch was spectacular.

My year at Vandenberg was marred by the breakup of my engagement to Linda, a foggy climate, cold ocean water filled with kelp, and tarry beaches— even before the Santa Barbara blowout in the winter of 1969. However, as had my work on the pipeline, service as the administrative officer to a squadron of enlisted men from varying ethnic and social backgrounds broadened my understanding of human nature and of the diversity of this nation. The monotony of the Central Coast was relieved by occasional trips to Big Sur, Los Angeles, and San Francisco. But California never held the same allure for me as it did for my father and grandfather. Lompoc was also the site of a federal penitentiary. When Watergate defendants were sentenced to time at Lompoc, I quipped that I had "done a year" at Lompoc.

I made two strong friends. Glen Davidson, a JAG officer, rose to become a well regarded federal district judge in Mississippi (and honored me by attending my wedding to Mary Tydings, Ben's mother), in October 1985. Paul Bruun trained junior officers at launch control procedures for nuclear missiles. He was both a journalist and an outdoorsman. He remains both. Living in Jackson Hole, Wyoming, he is a prominent local fishing guide, an "ambassador" for the Patagonia Company and a weekly columnist in the local paper. He took Mary, John, Will, and me on a fishing trip in the summer of 1986. He and I also went on a terrific fishing weekend in Baja California, in February 1969.

10

G . C . S .   a n d   S t r a t e g i c
A r m s   L i m i t a t i o n s

As I was completing my "uniformed" military service in Lompoc in 1969, newly elected President Nixon appointed my father to be the Director of the Arms Control and Disarmament Agency (ACDA) and to assume the Chairmanship of the U.S. delegation to prospective talks with the Soviet Union to limit strategic arms—the so-called Strategic Arms Limitation Talks ("SALT").

ACDA, a quasi-independent agency, affiliated with the Department of State, occupied offices in the "old" State Department building at 21st and E Streets, NW. My father was tickled to occupy the office that had previously been that of Secretaries of State, including Dean Acheson, John Foster Dulles, and Chris Herter. At the age of 54, my father was highly suited to this appointment. He had studied Russian periodically since 1948. For nearly 20 years he had been involved with a wide spectrum of nuclear weapons issues, in the AEC, the State Department, and as a consultant. And, from prior endeavor, he had wide and deep acquaintanceship with important military officers, including the then serving Chairman of the Joint Chiefs of Staff, Earl Wheeler, and Admiral Rickover, father of the Nuclear Navy. He obtained White House approval to designate his old colleague, Phil Farley, as his Deputy after fending off a White House effort to place Bill Casey, later Reagan's CIA Director, in this job. His close friend and colleague from the MLF days, Admiral John Marshall ("Squidge") Lee became an Assistant Director of ACDA.

The proposed delegation to the SALT talks comprised a formidable array of talent. It included Paul Nitze, Dad's predecessor as Director of Policy

Planning at the State Department, as the representative of the Secretary of Defense. Tommy Thompson, a former Ambassador to the Soviet Union and deeply knowledgeable foreign service officer, provided Soviet expertise. Harold Brown, President of Caltech and later Secretary of Defense, provided technical depth. Royall Allison, a highly regarded Air Force officer, represented the Joint Chiefs of Staff.

At my father's insistence, the White House authorized spouses to accompany the principals on the delegation during protracted negotiating sessions in Helsinki, Finland, and Vienna, Austria. Accordingly, in the period between the fall of 1969 and the spring of 1972, my mother spent long months with my father at the negotiations. This short memoir doesn't try to tackle the story of these complex negotiations. The story, from my father's perspective, is detailed in his book, *Doubletalk*, and summarized in his memoir, *Disarming Diplomat*. Much further "granular" detail appears in a recent compilation of previously classified documents, as well as transcripts of White House conversations, published by the office of the Historian of the U.S. Department of State.[112]

This extraordinary 1,000-page document offers striking insights into the personalities of Kissinger, Nixon, Kissinger's deputy Al Haig, and Leonid Brezhnev, the leader of the Soviet Union. And, not incidentally, it records my father's personal interchanges with President Nixon and Henry Kissinger. A thorough reading of this invaluable compilation confirms and gives color to the story told in this short chapter, as well as my father's two books.

During my parents' extensive time in Finland and Austria, my father maintained his practice of dictating letters to his four "youngsters." A missive of April 27, 1971, from Vienna gives good flavor of the life of an arms negotiator and his wife during a second negotiating session in Austria:

> The second time around is never as good as the first and that goes for Vienna, too. . . . I don't care if I never have another Weinerschnitzel. . . . Waiting, in diplomacy like in soldiering, seems a necessary part of getting through. Waiting for the Soviets to make a move, waiting for translation of a statement, waiting for Washington to send necessary cables, waiting for staff to draft papers, waiting for spring to really come—snow in the Tyrol yesterday above 1,000 meters. . . . Your mother is becoming the greatest crossword puzzle and solitaire expert in Eastern Europe.

Dad wrote this letter just a few days before learning that National Security Advisor, Henry Kissinger, had been pursuing a "back-channel" parallel negotiation with Soviet U.S. Ambassador Dobrynin—a cause for the delays that Dad is lamenting.

Achieving agreement on limitation of strategic arms was a task fraught with complexity. First, the United States had to decide whether arms limitation should be pursued as an end in itself or whether progress on this front should be "linked" to evidence of Soviet goodwill in other arenas, including the level of its support for the North Vietnamese in the ongoing Southeast Asian conflict. Secondly, there was the problem of how, if at all, to account for nuclear weapons delivery systems in the hands of U.S. allies, such as England and France, as well as forward-based systems deployed in Europe by the United States. Then there was the issue of the interdependence of offensive and defensive weapons. If the two sides were to pursue deployment of antiballistic missiles (ABMs), it would make it more difficult to agree on limitation of offensive systems, the efficacy of which might be negated by robust defense. Further, there was the perennial question of how to "verify" each side's compliance with any agreed limitations. There was the complex question of whether to restrain technological advances in offensive weaponry and in particular the deployment of multiple independently targetable reentry vehicles (MIRVs). Finally, there was the vexatious issue whether limits on ABM technology should extend to "exotic" or futuristic systems not yet under development.

As is often the case with complex international negotiations, there had to be internal negotiations among different agencies of the executive branch and between the executive branch and Congress, with many conflicting perceptions and interests in play. In the Nixon Administration these internal negotiations were subject to supervision by the National Security Adviser, Henry Kissinger. Given Kissinger's historical prominence, it is worth noting the description that he accords my father in his memoirs:

> Dedicated, indefatigable, and shrewd, Smith was one of those talented executives who serve successive administrations and epitomize the ideal of public service. It was easy to underestimate him because of his occasionally ponderous manner. But he knew his way around Washington; he was no novice at the bureaucratic game. Considering that he had no power base of his own, he was able to generate astonishing pressures. He was agile in drafting instructions for himself that permitted his nominal superiors only a minimum influence over his discretionary powers. . . . Withal, he was always cheerful and honorable, a stolid warrior for a good cause. This cause was the control of arms; it was the assignment of

his agency to keep that objective alive within our government; he did it with irrepressible persistence.[113]

Notwithstanding the generally generous tone of Kissinger's memoir toward Dad, the former's behavior during the ensuring two and one-half year negotiation was often not so gracious.

At the outset of his new duties, Dad had no anticipation for the vainglory and paranoia that would come to characterize the behavior of the Nixon White House. Zealous to control what they viewed as an unruly bureaucracy and eager to claim exclusive credit for any progress, Nixon and Kissinger embarked upon secretive, back-channel negotiations with the Russians through Anatoly Dobrynin, the Soviet Ambassador in Washington. The latter would keep his principals in the Soviet leadership apprised, and they, in turn, would inform Dad's negotiating counterpart, Deputy Foreign Minister Vladimir Semenov, Chair of the Soviet delegation to the SALT talks. There were times when Semenov knew more about the U.S. position than did my father. This dysfunctional and unhealthy mode of proceeding resulted in a politically flawed agreement and an utterly cynical "purge" of worthy public servants who had labored for three years to enable strategic arms limitations.

Bizarrely, in his memoir, Kissinger repeatedly claims that his actions in opening and pursuing a parallel channel of negotiation were driven by President Nixon's fear that "Gerard Smith, rather than he, would get credit" for progress in arms limitation talks.[114] The thought that Dad, a disciplined and dedicated public servant, would try to grab glory from the President he served is entirely implausible. Nevertheless, the now publicly available official record, amply documents that Kissinger repeatedly advised Nixon that my father's substantive stances, were motivated by vanity and an effort to steal glory from the President.[115]

During the first year, November 1969 until the end of 1970, the talks meandered without serious progress, with the two sides each exploring the other's position. At the outset, one major issue was whether any agreements would constrain offensive systems, as well as ABMs. Beginning in late 1970, the chief Soviet delegate, Semenov, signaled Moscow's acceptance of the notion of constraints on offensive systems, once the outlines of an ABM agreement were at hand. Dad duly reported this information to Washington and to Kissinger. Nevertheless, Kissinger, in early 1971 began discussing SALT issues directly with the Soviet Ambassador in Washington, Anatoly Dobrynin, without informing anyone in the interested bureaucracies or the delegation negotiating with the Russians that he was doing so. The result was a White House announcement in May 1971 that agreement had been reached on a path forward that would entail restraints on both ABMs and upon offensive arms. As my father notes in his memoir, Kissinger's success in this parallel channel in 1971 was not surprising, for he had "been pushing on an open door" in light of what the Soviet delegation to the formal talks had already signaled on this issue.[116] But the precedent of the National Security Advisor negotiating separately with the Russians on behalf of the President and himself, while keeping affected national security agencies and the delegation in the dark, was not a salutary one.

Like the United States, the Soviet Union deployed offensive missiles, both on land and on submarines. Kissinger, in his "breakthrough" in May 1971, omitted inclusion of restraints on submarine launched ballistic missiles (SLBMs). The United States had a much more sophisticated submarine and SLBM force and much easier access to the world's oceans. For their part, the Russians had or were building a larger number of submarines and had plans to deploy a larger number of SLBMs. A similar "asymmetry" affected limits on land-based missiles. The United States had mastered solid fuel technology and had a much more capable missile force. The Soviets, for their part, had larger, less accurate missiles with more ponderous launch procedures. In light of these asymmetries and difficulties, it was agreed that any limitation of offensive weapons would be for a temporary period, subject to further negotiation. This "interim agreement" would take the form of an executive agreement rather than a treaty of permanent force and effect, such as the one that was to govern ABMs. When it was determined that SLBMs as well as land-based ballistic missiles should be covered (after Kissinger's probably inadvertent omission of SLBMs from his May 1971 understanding), these asymmetries deserved the close attention of experts such as those on the delegation.

Nixon had scheduled a Summit Meeting with Soviet leader Brezhnev for May 1972. The centerpiece of this meeting was to be announcement of a treaty to limit ABMs and an executive agreement to place controls on offensive weapons systems (but not MIRVs), pending further negotiation toward a final treaty. As Kissinger and Nixon prepared for this Summit, Kissinger, again behind the back of the delegation and other technical experts in the U.S. government, went to Moscow and discussed arms limitations directly with the Soviet leadership, including Leonid Brezhnev, the General Secretary of the Communist Party. There, he agreed with the Soviet Union on limits on submarine launchers and ballistic missiles in a formula presented him directly by Brezhnev. Out of his depth, technically, Kissinger allowed the Russians to keep a numerically larger number of submarine-based launchers than deployed by the United States. While the result was not strategically significant, it went against the advice of the SALT delegation, as it would be perceived by the U.S. Senate as ceding an advantage to the Soviet Union.

My father and the experts on his delegation, when apprised of Kissinger's separate negotiations on submarines, tried to warn President Nixon that the tentatively agreed approach could cause a political backlash. For his troubles, my father was told by President Nixon that his position was "bullshit." While the official State Department history does not contain a transcript of this particular exchange, it does contain a record of a conversation among Nixon, Kissinger, and Haig immediately following the one in which Nixon angrily confronted my father. Nixon appears somewhat remorseful regarding his behavior toward my father. Haig chimes in sycophantically stating his belief that the President "had the right term" for my father's position. The conversation ends with Kissinger arguing to Nixon that there is no real substantive problem but rather an effort by Dad and Secretary of State Rodgers to preempt the historical credit that will redound to Nixon for a successful SALT outcome.[117]

My father and his delegation were directed to remain in Helsinki as the Moscow Summit began in May 1972. In Moscow Kissinger continued to iron out highly technical details of the pending arms limitations agreement with only perfunctory recourse to the technical experts in Helsinki. At the last minute, my father, Paul Nitze, and Royal Allison were told to fly to Moscow for the signing ceremony. On arrival, they found no one to meet their plane and received confused instructions as to where they were to go. They barely made it to the U.S. Embassy with the official, final copy of the ABM Treaty after first being misdirected. My exhausted and peeved father, confused by certain last-minute agreements achieved by Kissinger on SLBMs and other matters, was asked to conduct a press conference. Kissinger, nonplussed by my father's confusion, terminated the press briefing. He later conducted an extensive press briefing at 1:00 a.m. from which my father was excluded. I remember my father arriving home several days later, apparently depressed by what should have been the high point of his professional career. Kissinger, in his memoirs, had this to say about the logistical confusion in Moscow:

Family photos of young William G. Maguire, entrepreneur and pipeline pioneer.

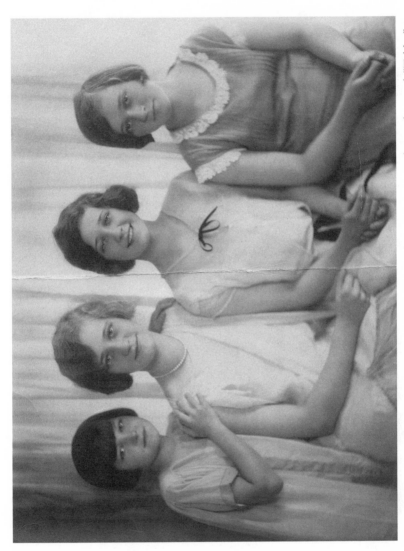

The four Maguire sisters in St. Louis in 1926. My mother, Bernice Latrobe, nicknamed "Tubby," is on the right.

John Thomas Smith at 20, graduating from Creighton College.

J.T. as earnest young lawyer in 1911.

The mature John Thomas Smith as Executive Vice President and General Counsel of General Motors, circa 1933.

Future arms controller, Gerard C. Smith, in 1917.

Mary Agnes Smith at the Jersey Shore in 1920 with sons Gregory (left) and Gerard (right).

Carefree young Gerard Smith at Mt. Tremblant, Quebec, in the winter of 1941.

The *Innisfail* on a calm sea in 1940—owned by John Thomas and son, Gerard Smith.

The *Welkin* in a 1947 photo
romantically inscribed
"Remember these days."

The oceanside "Ark" in Southampton, Long Island, family summer home 1949–1979.

A growing family interfered with yachting. In Southampton in the summer of 1949, the author, Gerry, and Sheila.

Mother and Dad at a reception for the SALT delegation given by the President of Finland in 1970. At the right are Paul Nitze and his wife, Phyllis.

Glasses raised at the signing of the first SALT agreements at Moscow Summit Meeting, May 1972, with Kissinger and Nixon in the foreground. Dad appears tired and somewhat disgruntled by chaotic events leading to this historical moment.

The author (right) and his close friend Dick Darman at the Department of Defense in 1973.

(U)   -   Existing Forrestal and later class aircraft carriers - 9 (see
          separate sheet)

(S)   -   Navy is programmed to reduce aircraft carriers from current 15
          to 12 by Fiscal Year 1976.

      -   By 1976, three additional large modern carriers will come into
          the active Naval fleet.

          -   CVA-68   USS Nimitz

          -   CVA-69   USS Eisenhower

          -   CVA-70   Unnamed   *Nixon*
                                 Tricia
                                 Seventh Crisis
                                 Bonhomme Richard
                                 Spirit of Peking
                                 Total Force
                                 Projection of Power
                                 Public Welfare
                                 Generation of Peace
                                 The Julie & Tricia
                                 The Spiro of '76
                                 Constitution
                                 Melvin R. Laird
                                 Stennis

Elliot Richardson's playful annotation of a memo in April 1973 regarding naming of
a new aircraft carrier. His suggestions include "Nixon," "Bonhomme Richard," "The
Julie and Tricia," "The Spiro of '76," "Constitution," and "Stennis." He was unaware
of his imminent appointment to be Attorney General that would involve him in the
prosecution of Spiro Agnew and the Watergate constitutional crisis.

The author's mother with Elliot Richardson at the author's wedding to Mary Tydings in 1985 at St. John's Church (designed by Benjamin Henry Latrobe).

The author with brothers Hugh Maguire and Gerard Lawrence Smith at family wedding in London in July 1996.

Ratcliffe Manor, the family's center of gravity, 1945–1995, on an early spring day.

[Smith] was the victim of honest bungling, though it must be admitted that the administrative practices of the Nixon Administration tended to inflict this sort of indignity on decent and able men, usually by accident, occasionally by design. There is no question but that Smith deserved better.[118]

One of Kissinger and Nixon's complaints about the "professional" arms controllers was that they "leaked" to the press.[119] Kissinger, of course, spent a significant portion of his public career manipulating the press, who were flattered by the attention of this charming and extraordinarily intelligent man. In 1973, my friend, John Newhouse, published the first, comprehensive popular history of the SALTs, called *Cold Dawn: The Story of SALT*. At the time Newhouse was conducting his research, he asked to interview my father, then in Helsinki. "Good soldier" that my father was, he cabled the White House seeking guidance as to whether to talk with Newhouse. He received a prompt response directing that under no circumstances was he to talk with Newhouse. The resulting book was viewed as quite favorable to Kissinger. My father's annotations of the book show that he found a number of inaccuracies. At the time Kissinger was pending Senate confirmation to be Secretary of State in the summer of 1973, the question was raised whether he had leaked classified information to Newhouse. He denied it.

Kissinger was also questioned about certain wiretaps placed on members of his office staff by the FBI allegedly at the request of Kissinger. At the time, I was serving as Executive Assistant to Attorney General Elliot Richardson, who had custody of the wiretap authorization records. I drew the uncomfortable duty of assisting Kissinger's dealings with the Senate Foreign Relations Committee on this front. When the related "national security" issue of Kissinger's purported leaks to Newhouse arose, I was dispatched to meet with Kissinger's assistant, Peter Rodman, on this subject. Rodman assured me that the only involvement by Kissinger or his staff with composition of the Newhouse book had been reviewing a draft to ensure no material inaccuracies. A later, thorough examination of this subject by investigative journalist Seymour Hersh records a somewhat more encompassing involvement of Kissinger's staff. According to Hersh, beginning in 1971, Kissinger tasked various members of his staff to brief Newhouse on progress at the SALTs with an aim of making Kissinger look good. On at least one occasion, in May 1972, Kissinger authorized a staff member to release sensitive information. As a result, *Cold Dawn*, while accurate to a high degree regarding internal governmental debates on SALT negotiation policy, reflected the views of Kissinger and the White House.[120]

Notwithstanding the confusion and insult that attended the Moscow summit, Dad, ever the good soldier, did his duty to defend the SALT agreements before Congress. As he had feared, conservatives, especially Scoop Jackson, expressed anxiety regarding "advantages" apparently accorded the Russians, especially in respect of SLBMs. Jackson introduced legislative language demanding that any future SALT agreements achieve numerical equality—a requirement that was to unnecessarily limit the prospects for future arms control agreements. Since the SLBM limitations were not a significant factor in the strategic balance, and indeed the Soviets never built up to the limits allowed them under the interim agreement, Kissinger's single-handed negotiation of SLBM limits was counterproductive. Again, in his memoir, Kissinger is gracious to my father stating:

> I also owe it here to Gerry Smith to stress that after the understandable flair-up in Moscow, he fought for the ratification of the SALT agreements with tenacity and skill.[121]

By the fall of 1972, my father realized that he did not enjoy the confidence of President Nixon (unknown to my father, Nixon had other things on his mind—the looming Watergate investigation). My father tendered his resignation by writing Secretary of State Rogers in October 1972. He thereupon agreed to remain in service through a pending negotiating session to begin "SALT II" in Geneva in the late fall of 1972. At the beginning of January 1973, my father's resignation became effective. To his great distress, shortly thereafter, the White House agreed to a "purge" of his agency to mollify Scoop Jackson. Even though Kissinger is gracious to my father in his memoir, his robust survival instincts allowed him without scruple to have the blame for the imperfections of the SALT agreements fall upon dedicated public servants in preference to himself or President Nixon. Of the 17 people in ACDA's top positions in 1972, only three remained in 1974. Also, in 1973, the Administration cut ACDA's budget by 33 percent.[122]

My brief tour of duty with Elliot Richardson in the Defense Department in 1973 gave me an opportunity to witness one aspect of this "purge." At Jackson's behest, the Joint Chiefs of Staff were to replace the exceptional Air Force General, Royal Allison, who had been an important part of the SALT effort. The Chiefs nominated a highly knowledgeable Navy Admiral,

Mike Michaelis, to take Allison's place. Jackson vetoed this appointment and insisted that a hard-line Army General, Ed Rowney, be made the Joint Chiefs representative on the SALT delegation. In my presence, Chairman of the Joint Chiefs of Staff, Admiral Thomas Moorer, lamented that it was a sad precedent when an individual senator would be allowed by the White House to make a general officer assignment.

Dad's immediate hurt from Kissinger's treatment of him and his delegation was moderated slightly by receipt of an honorary degree from Yale in June 1972. Other 1972 honorees included the author, Saul Bellow, Dad's Southampton acquaintance, Henry Ford II, and his Washington friend, Kay Graham, publisher of *The Washington Post*.

J.T.S. II,
Initial Public Service

The CIA

As my father was embarking upon the daunting challenge of negotiating SALT agreements, I returned to the East Coast and began training to be a CIA officer. The training consisted of interesting class work, as well as a several-week session at "The Farm," an Agency facility in Southern Virginia that gave one an introduction to the mission and techniques of the under-cover "Clandestine Services," whose "case officers" recruit foreign agents to provide intelligence about foreign government intentions. The instructors there, perhaps compulsive practitioners of their art, tried hard to recruit me to become a clandestine service officer. While this was the "glamorous" part of the Agency, and I was well suited by my personal background and foreign travel to pursue such a career, I resisted. I was uncertain that I wanted a long-term Agency career, as distinct from an expedient means to complete my military service. Second, I was uncomfortable with the notion of spend-ing a lifetime pretending to be one thing, while actually being another. Also, the more prudent part of me looked with misgiving on the paramilitary training in Panamanian jungles—a required part of the curriculum during the ongoing Vietnam conflict.

As an alternative, I followed in the footsteps of my law school friend, Al Rankin, who introduced me to John Clarke, Director of the Agency's Office of Planning, Programming and Budgeting. There I took Al's place as the budget analyst for the Agency's Research and Development programs. Although the job sounds prosaic, it gave me a broad purview, since all major divisions of the Agency had R&D programs supporting their missions. There was little need for my legal training, although I was called upon to review major research contracts. I instead learned something of the language of business and finance—as well as government budgeting. Moreover, the substance of the Agency's R&D programs was intrinsically fascinating. These programs ranged from overhead satellite reconnaissance—a necessary part of any scheme of verification for strategic arms limitation—to more traditional programs involving communications with foreign agents in codes and secret inks. A significant part of the Agency's R&D was directed to finding better means for interception of communications. I was struck by the sheer overlap of communications interception programs of the Agency and those of the National Security Administration (NSA), the Defense Intelligence Agency, and those of the individual military services.

I recall being deeply conscious of my father's strategic arms endeavors. I argued against a nascent program to employ microtechnology to create jamming devices that could be clandestinely scattered near Soviet ABM radars. Whatever the benefits of missile defense, I thought conduct of clandestine programs to neutralize missile defense radars could be viewed as a hostile and destabilizing action. Another classified program sought to link microtechnology to drone, bird-like platforms that could be used in a highly defended environment to collect intelligence. This research program long anteceded the widespread current use of drone vehicles in South Asia.

In the course of my training and work at the Agency I made two close friends. The first, Chuck Goldmark, had graduated from Yale Law School shortly after me. As a student, he had participated in the National Student Association, which had been revealed in 1967 to be a "front" for the CIA in dealing with international student congresses. Chuck went on to found a law firm in Seattle, do serious mountain climbing, and engage in political activities for the Democratic party in the State of Washington. Tragically, on Christmas Eve in 1986, he and his entire family were bludgeoned to death by a right-wing maniac who broke into their home. He apparently associated Chuck with the activities of his father, a political activist who had been falsely accused of being a Communist decades previous.[123] Chuck's murder made national news, although none reported the irony that he had been involved with the CIA combatting Communism.

My other friend, introduced to me by Al Rankin, was a young expert on the Soviet Union—Robert Gates—who became one of the greatest public servants of our generation, serving as Deputy Director of the CIA, then Director of the CIA, and eventually Secretary of Defense in both the George

W. Bush and Obama Administrations. Bob was then, as he is now, a man of great intelligence, integrity, humor, patience, balance, and perceptiveness. On March 14, 2012, I had the honor of participating in the award to Gates of the Elliot L. Richardson Prize for Excellence in Public Service. In a public discussion at the award event, Gates amply displayed great acuity regarding means to effective public administration.

In the course of my service in the Agency's budget office, my father suggested that I explore the possibility of employment at the National Security Council which, under Kissinger, was perceived as the center of "action" for ambitious young people in Washington. My father, although a highly experienced public servant wise to the ways of Washington, had not yet realized the degree to which Kissinger was undercutting him. Dad offered to obtain an interview for me, for possible employment on Kissinger's staff. I was interviewed "pro forma" by Kissinger's Chief of Staff, but not offered a job. In retrospect, it is apparent that, whatever my qualifications, the last person Kissinger wanted in his office was Gerard Smith's son. At the time, Gates, conscious of my privileges of birth and the connections of my father, commented, without resentment, that I had a chance to "really go places" in Washington, whereas he would resign himself to being a first-rate intelligence analyst. Little did he or I know what large opportunities for accomplishment would be his. (In his book about the Agency and Director Bill Casey, *Veil*, Bob Woodward, based on a discussion with me, described this episode erroneously. He stated that Gates was always fiercely ambitious. I had told Woodward the story simply to highlight the irony that Gates had advanced on sheer excellence rather than connections or ambition. Woodward, as the unofficial chronicler of current events, especially in the national security field, sometimes misses important nuance. In any event, Gates has never held Woodward's mischaracterization against me.)

In the spring of 1971, Richard Helms, the Director of CIA, learned that his Executive Assistant, Bob Kiley, planned to leave. Through my family, I was fortunate to know Helms then and later. He was an exemplary and admirable man and a great public servant. He asked various Agency offices to nominate likely young officers for Kiley's post. My boss nominated me. When Kiley took me to lunch and began to tell me sensitive information about his duties, I was given to believe that the job was mine. Nevertheless, I was not selected, apparently because Helms felt his friendship with my family would give my selection the aspect of favoritism. Although I have profited much in life from the attributes and ties of my family, in this instance they provided a useful handicap. Within 18 months, Helms was no longer the Director of the CIA, and I was working for Elliot Richardson in an extraordinary series of challenging posts.

Years later I had an illuminating conversation with Helms about an unrelated matter while walking on the Ratcliffe Manor lane during one of his visits to my father. I told him of my admiration for the espionage novels of British author, John le Carré. Helms responded that he hated these books, as they presented a much too cynical and bleak picture of the important work of clandestine espionage.

Department of Health, Education and Welfare

In the late spring of 1971, as I was completing my fourth year of Air Force/CIA service, Russell Byers, a friend from Yale, asked me if I would be interested in a job at the Department of Health, Education and Welfare (HEW). Russell was serving as the Executive Assistant to the Under Secretary, Jack Veneman, and was seeking a replacement for himself in anticipation of a promotion at a different government agency. He explained that, for a young person, HEW was then a very appealing place to work. A year previously, President Nixon had appointed Elliot Richardson, one of the most brilliant individuals of his generation, to be Secretary. The Department, under Richardson's leadership, was wrestling with a wide array of fundamental domestic policy issues, including a national health care initiative, welfare reform, and refinement of the federal role in education. Due to the substance of this agenda and Richardson's drawing power, a significant number of very bright individuals, including former "systems analysts" from the Department of Defense, were taking staff positions at HEW.

At Russell's initiative, I interviewed with several of the senior officers of HEW. When Russell did not leave his job working for Under Secretary Veneman, I received an offer of employment from Bruce Cardwell, the Assistant Secretary, Comptroller. Bruce was the senior career civil servant at HEW and presided over the development and implementation of the largest single budget in the federal government (when Social Security was taken into account). I was drawn to Bruce by his quick mind, broad perspective, and gentle demeanor. I appealed to Bruce, not only because of my background in budgeting at the CIA, but, more importantly, because Bruce saw me as having a personal and educational background similar to that of the immediate staff in Secretary Richardson's office.

My duties as Cardwell's Special Assistant were not onerous. He asked me to help with writing of speeches and undertaking special projects. Also,

I would participate in all his meetings to take notes and assure appropriate follow-up. On occasion, I would field telephone calls from angry members of Congress. And, I would represent the Comptroller's Office in so-called management meetings that Secretary Richardson would convene to discuss policy objectives across the broad range of HEW programs. As I had been at the CIA, I was impressed by the dedication and intelligence of the career public servants that served as Cardwell's staff and throughout the constituent agencies of HEW.

In the fourteen months that I worked for Cardwell, I gained insights into the special challenges posed for federal executive branch administrators by the activities and interests of members of Congress. Beginning in the middle of the 1960s, the federal government had been funding a promising program called "Head Start," designed to furnish early childhood education to economically disadvantaged children. Efforts to evaluate the efficacy of various local Head Start programs revealed good results in some places and disappointing outcomes in others. But Congress always wanted to expand Head Start as a source of federal funding in Congressional districts. The staff of HEW applied rigorous evaluation criteria and ranked Head Start programs nationwide.

The chairman of the Congressional subcommittee with jurisdiction over the Head Start Program was a colorful and powerful congressman from Johnstown, Pennsylvania, Dan Flood (a memorable and ironic name in light of the famous Johnstown flood). I was with Cardwell when he met with Congressman Flood to discuss the Head Start program evaluations and to propose a funding cutoff that would deny funds to those determined to be the least effective. Flood scanned the list of programs and noted that the Johnstown program was well down in the rank order. He endorsed the idea of denying funds to less effective programs as a means to fiscal probity, but insisted that the line be drawn, not at the 50th percentile, but at the 20th percentile, just below the Johnstown program.

On another occasion, I recall being in Cardwell's office when he learned that Congress was adding access to kidney dialysis for all who needed it under the Medicare program. Bruce commented that this was a "disaster." Cardwell was not hard hearted. Rather, he recognized that, as technology advanced and became more expensive, adding entitlements to such health care technologies would drive costs to potentially unsustainable levels. In 2008, on a luxury golf trip, I was seated with a successful health care entrepreneur from Massachusetts. Like so many of his economic echelon, he was conservative in political outlook and decried the overreach of federal programs. In the course of our discussion I learned that much of his fortune derived from provision of kidney dialysis services reimbursed by Medicare. I noted that I had been in the Office of the Comptroller of HEW when access to these services, funded by the federal government, had been passed into law. The conservative entrepreneur, without any sense of shame or recognition of irony, commented proudly that he had been a central part of the successful lobbying effort that achieved this result.

In the spring of 1972, Cardwell sent me on a trip organized by the so-called Educational Staff Seminar. This organization brought together Congressional staff, HEW employees, and consultants for trips to learn about research efforts receiving federal funds. As seems often the case with federally funded travel, I found myself in San Francisco. The program took place at the Stanford Research Institute (SRI) in Palo Alto. On my return, Cardwell asked me to prepare a short memorandum describing what I had seen and learned. I did so and included a tongue-in-cheek description of one of the SRI programs designed to stimulate student interest in science by applying an electric wire attached to a hand-crank generator to light a small bulb. In my memo I portrayed the delight on the face of a powerful Hill staff member, Harley Dirks, when his bulb lighted. Cardwell forwarded my memo as an information item to Secretary Richardson's office. There it was reviewed by Richardson's executive assistant, a brilliant young lawyer named Marshall Moriarty, and by Richardson. The humor, if not the substance of my memorandum, caught their attention.

Elliot Richardson

As a direct consequence, Marshall tapped me to accompany Secretary Richardson on a trip he was making in May 1972 to deliver a speech at Northwestern University outside Chicago. My role was mundane—making sure that the Secretary made it on time to his flights (not always easy), that he was met by appropriate contacts in Chicago and that, upon return, appropriate thank-you notes were sent to all who had assisted with the event in Evanston. These were duties that were well within the competence of a Yale Law School graduate and former Air Force officer. This trip provided me with my first one-on-one exposure to Secretary Richardson. At the time, I did not imagine that this brilliant man was to become my mentor and friend, with whom, within a year and a half, I was to experience some of the most exciting days of my professional life. In any event, on the flight back from Chicago on that May evening, we shared martinis in a first class cabin and spoke about a broad array of topics. Richardson noted then, as he would on other occasions, that civilization may have reached its apogee by enabling one to witness sunsets flying miles above the earth, while enjoying a martini.

I was exceptionally fortunate to be appointed Richardson's Executive Assistant to replace Marshall Moriarty, when he determined in 1972 to return to Boston and the private practice of law. Marshall might not have given up his job if he had been able to foresee the adventures that lay in Richardson's immediate future as Secretary of Defense and then Attorney General.

Richardson made a compelling mentor. Born into a distinguished Boston family of lawyers and doctors, Richardson had graduated from Harvard in 1941. He became an officer in a combat medical battalion and distinguished himself, landing at D-Day and being injured by a mine as U.S. troops advanced through France. After the war he attended Harvard Law School and was elected President of the *Harvard Law Review.* Subsequently he clerked for two of the most renowned judges of the 20th century, Learned Hand of the Second Circuit and Justice Felix Frankfurter of the Supreme Court. Unsatisfied by private law practice, Richardson went to Washington. After working for Leverett Saltonstall, his Massachusetts Senator, he became, at the age of 37, an Assistant Secretary of HEW for legislation. He was then appointed U.S. Attorney for the Commonwealth of Massachusetts, and later was elected its Lieutenant Governor and its Attorney General. He served as Under Secretary of State for the first year of the Nixon Administration, where he worked with my father on SALT issues, before his appointment as Secretary of HEW. He was profoundly intelligent, unfailingly kind and polite, intellectually curious, and a moderate, internationalist Republican of a sort now virtually extinct. Moreover, he respected and supported the critical roles played by career civil servants, making them an important part of his management team in each of the cabinet departments where he served.

In September 1972, I began sharing Marshall's office with him and learning my role by watching Marshall in action and duplicating his tasks. These were exciting days in other respects. Linda was about to give birth to John. I recall Richardson being amused when I declined an invitation to accompany him and his wife in the Presidential Box at the Kennedy Center. I advised I had a commitment to attend a childbirth class. John arrived on my birthday, October 22, 1972. While I had not intended to impose my rather plain name on any of my children, a sense of mischief in me compelled me to name him John Thomas Smith III. With the identical birthday (but for the year), I felt the two of us could present challenges to government paperwork. John proved "athletic" from the start. When he was four months old he managed to roll himself off a changing table. I was in a meeting with Richardson, who was then Secretary of Defense, when I was given an emergency message to go home as quickly as possible because of John's athletic adventure. I did so and was relieved to find the young acrobat no worse for the wear.

In joining Richardson's immediate staff, I was made part of a "family" of extraordinary caliber and energy. Moriarty had been a Supreme Court clerk and later was a distinguished partner of the law firm of Ropes and Gray. Richardson's senior-most assistant was Jonathan More. Jonathan had aided Richardson in Massachusetts political campaigns and at the State Department. He was whip smart and had huge tactical sense. He had a broad grasp of policy as well as politics, and a gregarious personality. By the same token, he was fiercely protective of his senior relationship to Richardson, a fact that I took as being within the natural order of things. Also on Richardson's staff was a colorful "pol" from Massachusetts, Dick Mastrangelo. Dick helped tend Richardson's political home fires in Massachusetts and worried more broadly about relationship politics. Dick was a friendly, kind, down-to-earth individual with a distinct Massachusetts voice. Also, part of the family was Wil Hastings, the Department's General Counsel and a Richardson colleague from Massachusetts. Wil went on to a distinguished legal career and can be proud of his son who founded NetFlix. Concetta or "Cetta" Leonardi was Richardson's Executive Secretary, again a loyalist from Massachusetts. Cetta was so smart that she had no difficulty keeping up with the highly cerebral Richardson and the band that surrounded him. Then there was Richardson's actual family. Once you worked directly for Richardson, you became a de facto part of his personal family, warmly entertained by his wife Anne and acquainted by his three children, Henry, Nancy, and Michael.

Somewhat on the edge of this group was a luminously intelligent Deputy Assistant Secretary of HEW for Policy, Richard G. Darman. Dick's sheer intelligence, bureaucratic acumen, and ambition commended him to Richardson. (Dick was also a citizen of Massachusetts.) In these days, Dick and I formed a bond. We became closest personal friends and cross godparents of each other's children. I had the privilege of working with Dick for Richardson in four additional cabinet departments. More about this friend, without parallel, appears later in these reflections.

No longer a civil servant, but a political appointee, I accompanied Richardson on at least one campaign trip in the lead-up to Nixon's reelection in November 1972. Although Richardson viewed himself as a man of the people, the White House targeted him at potential voters among the East Coast elite. Therefore, the campaign trip that I participated in took Secretary Richardson to Yale University and then to Princeton, where he spoke to faculty and students. I have a crystalline memory of walking with Richardson around the Princeton campus on a glorious fall morning. The school had recently become co-ed. Looking at the attractive female students, I commented to Richardson that I wished I could begin my college career over again. Richardson responded forcefully that he had never wanted to repeat a single day of his life. On reflection, this episode told me a lot about Richardson. He was relentlessly optimistic and forward-looking. And, he was not inclined to reflect long on past mistakes or misadventures (granting that they were few).

Election night of 1972 found me and other Richardson staff with tickets to attend an election party at the Shoreham Hotel. Not being a particularly political creature, I felt somewhat out of place. To my great good fortune, I found myself in a long conversation with Ann Morton, the wife of the Secretary of Interior, Rogers Morton, and the mother of contemporaries of mine growing up in Easton, Maryland. She was then and remained for another four decades later a woman of great spirit, intelligence and charm. She died in September 2011 after a very full life.

Shortly after the election, Nixon announced his intention to shuffle his Cabinet and rid his Administration of "burnt out volcanoes." (He apparently found this metaphor reading a biography of the British 19th-century statesman, Benjamin Disraeli, furnished him by Pat Moynihan.) The relatively young and dynamic Elliot Richardson was definitely not burnt out, and he was selected by Nixon to become Secretary of Defense. His replacement at HEW was to be Cap Weinberger, who would later serve as Secretary of Defense in the Reagan Administration. I was gratified that I was tapped—along with Jonathan Moore, Dick Mastrangelo, Cetta Leonardi, and Dick Darman—to accompany Richardson to the Pentagon.

Department of Defense

I had some interesting adventures as the Secretary prepared for the transition to DOD. First, I accompanied Richardson to the series of briefings at the Pentagon conducted by the civilian and military leaders of each service. Having recently been discharged as a very junior Air Force officer, I remember especially the Air Force briefing. I was seated next to the Air Force

Chief of Staff, a tough looking, swarthy Irishman and four-star general, John Ryan. With appropriate deference to an incoming civilian official, Ryan turned and offered me a cigarette. I told him thank you but that I didn't smoke. Then, nervously (and idiotically) I said, "But I don't mind if you do." Before that same meeting, as we passed through the Office of the Secretary of the Air Force, Robert Seamans, I admired a large black-and-white photograph of the surface of the moon. I recall Seamans telling me that Henry Kissinger, on seeing the same photograph, had quipped that he assumed that it was a picture of North Vietnam (after U.S. bombing).

I also accompanied Richardson in a DOD jet to make courtesy calls upon the Chairman of the House and Senate Armed Services Committees. It being December, with Congress not in session, Richardson met with these estimable gentlemen near their hometowns. In the case of the House Chair, Edward Hebert, we landed at the Edward Hebert Air Station in Louisiana. From there we proceeded to Meridian, Mississippi, to meet with Senate Armed Services Chairman John Stennis at the Stennis Naval Air Station. (Ten months later, Senator Stennis would figure in the events leading up to the so-called Saturday Night Massacre.)

Richardson's actual service as Secretary of Defense began in January 1973 and ended in May of that same year, with his appointment to serve as Attorney General. Four decades later, I retain vivid memories of these few months. Only a year and a half after my departure from the CIA, as a relatively junior officer, I was occupying a desk outside the door to the office of the Secretary of Defense, privy to all matters that came to his attention. These included not only the final wind-down of the U.S. military presence in Vietnam, but also issues of nuclear weapons policy that had been a primary focus of my father's public service career. (My father's resignation as Director of ACDA had taken place simultaneously with Richardson's assumption of his duties as Secretary of Defense.)

In the Defense Department, there was no position for a civilian executive assistant. The functions of managing the Secretary's schedule, ensuring that speeches were prepared in a coherent and timely fashion, screening all documents on their way to and from the Secretary and attending meetings as a note taker to ensure a clear record and timely follow-up were all functions conducted by two "military assistants" assigned to the Secretary. Nevertheless, Richardson, on the advice of Jonathan Moore, decided to have me carry out these duties in tandem with the military assistants. Accordingly, I was assigned a desk adjacent to that of Admiral Dan Murphy, the senior military assistant. This arrangement could have proved awkward but for two factors. First, Murphy was naturally a gracious, intelligent and secure person. Second, the outgoing Secretary of Defense, Mel Laird, had submitted Murphy's nomination to become the Commander of U.S. Naval Forces in the Mediterranean, and Murphy's future was in no way affected by having to share his responsibilities with a young civilian. (Dan served with distinction in the Mediterranean and later became Chief of Staff to George H. W. Bush while the latter served as Vice President.)

In the first week of Richardson's tenure as Secretary of Defense, Dick Helms, the Director of the CIA, whose Executive Assistant I had almost become 18 months earlier, arrived at Richardson's office without an appointment seeking to impart important intelligence information to the Secretary. Richardson, conscious of my background in intelligence, invited me to join his discussion with Helms. The latter's sole purpose was to make sure that the Secretary of Defense knew that the United States had reliable information that Israel had developed a nuclear weapons capacity. This remains a subject of considerable sensitivity, but little doubt, 37 years later. It remained a topic of great concern to my father, who believed that Israel's maintenance of nuclear weapons provided incentive and pretext for Islamic states to develop nuclear weapons capacity. He so stated in an article published in *Foreign Affairs* in 1989.[124] Present day, paramount concern regarding Pakistan's nuclear weapons and Iran's drive to develop nuclear weapons capacity amply validate my father's concerns.

On a lighter note, I became the object of efforts by senior officials in the Pentagon to befriend and cultivate the civilian staff of the new Secretary. Promptly, John Warner, the Secretary of the Navy invited me to play squash. (The Pentagon has a set of squash courts located underneath the Mall in front of the building where military ceremonies are conducted.) The Secretary, who appeared in good physical condition, arrived with the fanciest array of high technology racquets and shoes that I had ever seen. Nevertheless, I was able to defeat him handily. Whether because of this fact or because he determined that I was insufficiently senior in the pecking order, he did not invite me to play again. Shortly thereafter, I was included as a guest at a dinner given for Secretary Richardson by Admiral Thomas Moorer, the Chairman of the Joint Chiefs of Staff. I recall that my wife and I were the only guests to arrive by personal transportation (a Chevrolet station wagon), whereas the others all had government cars and drivers.

From my vantage point at the door of the office of the Secretary of Defense, I gleaned some firsthand insights into the methods of operation employed by Henry Kissinger as National Security Advisor. He would seek to exclude from White House meetings to plan for SALT Pentagon representatives who had earned his disfavor—in one instance Paul Nitze, who still served as the Representative of Secretary of Defense—in preference for less knowledgeable representatives, including the newly appointed Texas oilman, Deputy Secretary of Defense, Bill Clements. (Clements, while ignorant of military affairs, was a fairly quick study, a man who combined genuine personal warmth with deeply conservative viewpoints. He later was elected Governor of Texas.) Continuing a practice instituted by Mel Laird as Secretary of Defense, any time Kissinger would call Secretary Richardson by phone, Admiral Murphy would listen on a "deadkey." Murphy, while a dedicated officer, had scant patience for Kissinger's antics. I recall him becoming visibly angry when he heard Kissinger mildly disparage Lawrence Eagleburger, who was under consideration by Richardson for appointment as an Assistant Secretary of Defense. Eagleburger, who had previously suffered a nervous collapse serving on the NSC staff for Kissinger, was later to serve as Secretary of State. Kissinger condescendingly described this exceptional public servant to Richardson as a "first class, second-class intellect." Kissinger's real purpose in denigrating this individual may have been to dissuade Richardson from appointing him insofar as his large capacities, as well as his knowledge of Kissinger's foibles, would have enhanced the Defense Department's bureaucratic capital in policy deliberations, thereby impinging upon Kissinger's supremacy.

Workdays at the Pentagon began early and ended late. I remember in the winter of 1973 consistently going to work in the dark and coming home in the dark. One dark morning as Admiral Murphy and I scanned the overnight cable traffic for matters worthy of Richardson's attention, I came across a cable referring to the then obscure Persian Gulf principality of Abu Dhabi. At this somewhat innocent time, before the first Arab oil embargo later in 1973, I had never heard of Abu Dhabi. Facetiously I turned to Admiral Murphy and said, "Dan, what the hell is Abu Dhabi?" The soon to be Commander of the Navy's Sixth Fleet replied, "Beats me." The intervening decades have put Abu Dhabi and other Persian Gulf principalities very much on the map.

As already described, my function at the Pentagon was, in large measure, redundant with that of the military assistants. As a result, Richardson increasingly assigned me to a variety of special projects. One was to deal with growing Congressional pressures to reduce perquisites traditionally accorded high-ranking military officers. Congress's biggest target was the assignment to general officers of "enlisted aides." Such aides had been spotted doing household chores, walking dogs, and retrieving dry cleaning. Depending on the number of stars worn by a general officer, he or she might be entitled to as many as three enlisted aides. Richardson correctly felt the need to respond to Congressional concern on this score. At the same time, as a new Secretary of Defense determined to work constructively with the military brass, he did not wish unduly to upset long-established military culture, whatever its merits. He assigned me to explore the feasibility of some reasonable accommodation of Congressional concern. I visited each of the military chiefs of staff, explained the Secretary's desire to find some reasonable middle ground and invited suggestions as a way to preserve military aides, albeit on a reduced scale.

Responses varied. Air Force Chief of Staff, Jack Ryan, chief of the "newest" uniformed service saw the merit in political compromise and promptly offered a generous curtailment of the scale of the enlisted aide program in the Air Force. At the other extreme, Admiral Elmo Zumwalt, the somewhat fierce Chief of Naval Operations, suggested that his Congressional critics could go do something unprintable to themselves. Creighton Abrams, Chief of Staff of the Army, offered some cuts, but was not as forthcoming as his Air Force counterpart. I reported the fruits of my conversations to the Secretary, with recommendations for a moderate middle course. I believe these changes were adopted and, together with an elevated sensitivity on the part of general officers regarding the proper use of enlisted aides, the program continued. Again, two years previous as an Air Force First Lieutenant, I could not have imagined that I would soon be negotiating perquisites with the highest ranking military officers of the nation.

A somewhat more serious project involved vetting of proposals for base closure and realignment. (This perennially vexatious topic was not, in 1973, subject to the unbiased recommendations of the present-day Base Realignment and Closure Commission, and hence was the subject of lively political controversy.) At issue in the winter of 1973 was a proposal by the Army to consolidate its basic training function at a single location in Louisiana. It proposed closure of its venerable training facility at Fort Dix, New Jersey, which it claimed was subject to urban encroachment. Less controversial was a proposal by the Navy to close certain Rhode Island facilities that had been used to support World War II era aircraft carriers, with resulting consolidation in Jacksonville, Florida. The Governor of New Jersey, with whom Richardson and I had stayed during his fall of 1972 campaign trip to Princeton, lobbied strenuously for retention of Fort Dix. I recommended to Richardson that he overrule the Army and keep Fort Dix in service.

Having driven through the "Pine Barrens" of south central New Jersey, I did not find the Army's complaints of urban encroachment to be plausible. Undoubtedly, also, I was influenced by the effective lobbying of a moderate Republican New Jersey Governor.

In recognition of the fact that I was my father's son, Richardson and Jonathan Moore also gave me the "informal portfolio" for staffing the Secretary with respect to issues of nuclear weapons acquisition and strategy. Early in Richardson's tenure, I arranged a quiet luncheon meeting in his office with my father's deputy, Phil Farley, and another arms control expert, Ron Spiers, of the State Department. I wanted to ensure that Richardson had the benefit of their perspective on nuclear weapons issues and not the unalloyed views of the Defense Department. Within the Defense Department, as will be shown, there were civilian planners who were quite bullish on the utility of nuclear weapons as part of a "spectrum," a force that could be deployed in interest of the nation's security. However, among the uniformed military, there was a healthy skepticism about the usability of such weapons.

As previously noted, I accompanied Richardson, on an orientation trip to the Headquarters of the Strategic Air Command outside Omaha, Nebraska. (I recalled the family roots in Omaha. John Thomas Smith had attended Creighton College and my sister Sheila had received the sacrament of Confirmation at Strategic Air Command Headquarters.) During extensive briefings on the Single Integrated Operational Plan (SIOP) governing potential use of nuclear weapons, the Air Force briefer cast doubt on the utility of the redundant megatons of nuclear weapons the United States was capable of raining upon Soviet targets.

This trip not only gave insights into the nation's tremendous capacities, but also offered me an opportunity to exercise "civilian control" over the military—on an admittedly minor matter. As we prepared to return to Washington, I was advised by Richardson's more junior military assistant, Air Force Colonel Bob Taylor, that we would be traveling back to Washington on a prototype airborne warning and command (AWAC) plane. On questioning, I learned that this plane was still owned by its manufacturer, Boeing. The Pentagon had not yet made a final decision on the scale of procurement of such planes, and I feared that the effort by Boeing and the Air Force to lobby the Secretary could give an appearance of lack of objectivity in any final decision. Without conferring with Richardson, I directed that the Air Force arrange a different plane to return us to Washington. In retrospect, I was probably too zealous about protecting appearances on the Secretary's behalf. In any event, I regret not having had a chance to witness the capabilities of one of these remarkable high-tech flying command centers.

When we arrived at the Pentagon in January 1973, a major staff exercise was underway to rethink the acquisition, deployment, and use of nuclear weapons. This ongoing work, under the leadership of Dr. John Foster, Director of Defense Research and Engineering (DDRE), was given life when the Pentagon received word from Kissinger that President Nixon had determined that, in the event of a limited nuclear attack, the United States needed options short of an all-out nuclear strike with which to respond. The Pentagon's civilian planners used the President's request as an opportunity to package the thinking of the Foster Panel into a draft National Security Study Memorandum (NSSM). The draft NSSM spun out scenarios in which there could be limited and controlled use of nuclear weapons.

Frustration by planners regarding the apparent uselessness of such weapons had long vexed the Defense establishment, and the White House request stimulated dangerous thoughts. Recall that my father had advised against a contemplated limited nuclear strike in the Quemoy-Matsu crisis in 1958. And in the various Berlin crises and in the case of the Cuban Missile Crisis, potential cataclysm had been avoided by decision makers who realized that the planet would be in jeopardy if nuclear weapons were ever to be used again. Jonathan Moore instinctively knew that the draft NSSM might cause Richardson trouble and asked me to write a candid memorandum pointing out the flaws and dangers of the plans being spun out by the Foster Panel.

In an April 1973 "eyes-only" memorandum, I pointed out that a fundamental flaw of any scheme of limited use of nuclear weapons was that both parties to any such exchange would need to maintain "national command authority" sufficient to order cessation of escalation. However, one could never be sure that the other side would foreswear targeting of "national command authority." Loss of such authority could eliminate any chance of controlling the exchange. This risk of world cataclysm was above and beyond the questions of massive civilian casualties and environmental damage from even the most limited nuclear exchange.

I concluded that the Foster Panel's recommendations were, "in large measure," a rehash of schemes that had been proposed throughout the nuclear era by civilian planners. I pointed out that "technological momentum, human ingenuity, and planners' impatience about apparent inutility of tactical nuclear weapons, have continually converged to propound 'more rational' schemes for the employment of nuclear weapons." I reminded that

Presidents, Secretaries of Defense, and Secretaries of State had in the past opted against moving to schemes entailing limited use of nuclear weapons, and I urged that it "would be a shame if Elliot Richardson were to be an instrument of this historical reversal." I concluded that:

> Logic can urge that nuclear weapons, large or small, are simply weapons, to be used as necessary to deter, or failing deterrence, to limit the scope of international conflict. To date, decision-makers in the U.S. and the U.S.S.R. have chosen not to take this "logical view." They have treated nuclear weapons as extraordinary. . . . As a consequence of their special treatment, nuclear weapons have had a special deterrent value. They have made conventional conflict between major powers impossible. Discussion of usefulness of tactical nuclear weapons, controlled escalation and the like carry a doctrinal admission that use is possible, even desirable under certain circumstances. This, in turn, erodes the extraordinary status these weapons have been accorded.

I shared my memorandum with Admiral Murphy, who stated that he concurred completely in my analysis. So did Jonathan Moore. Richardson signaled that he had no answers for some of the questions I had raised, and it was my impression that he was of a mind to curtail the work of the Foster Panel. However, before he could do so, events intervened. On the weekend of April 28, Richardson was notified that, as a consequence of the growing Watergate political scandal, the President was accepting the resignations of his two top staffers, Bob Haldeman and John Ehrlichman, as well as that of Attorney General Richard Kleindeinst, and that he was nominating Richardson to become Attorney General. Richardson was disappointed by this development. He had told his staff that Attorney General was a job he had already done (in Massachusetts), and he was delighted to serve as Secretary of Defense, able to play a major role in defense and international affairs. Nevertheless, he necessarily did the President's bidding and accepted his nomination as Attorney General.

On the following Monday, before Richardson's appointment as Attorney General had been made public, Richardson's schedule included a monthly meeting of the Defense Policy Review Council. This meeting was statutorily required. It brought together the most senior uniformed and civilian leaders of the Defense Department, supposedly to discuss policy. Previous meetings had been devoid of substantive policy discussion. The leaders of the uniformed services much preferred to make their policy desires known to the Secretary unilaterally. They did not, in any event, debate policy as a group in front of civilian leadership. It happened that the agenda for this particular meeting included a briefing by Foster on the work of his panel. As Foster described a scenario in which there could be limited use of nuclear warheads on a hypothetical European battlefield, the usually reticent Army Chief of Staff, Creighton Abrams, looked Foster in the eye. It would be his soldiers, not airmen or naval personnel, who would be most directly in harm's way. He articulated simply and unmistakably a central truth of the nuclear era. He said: "Bullshit. One mushroom cloud will be reported as a hundred and it will be the beginning of the end of the world." Abrams's statement was the only substantive exchange that I remember in a Defense Policy Review Council meeting during our four months at the Defense Department. But his point was a telling one.

* * * * *

Reflection—A Digression by a Member of the First Nuclear Weapons Generation

The first nuclear weapons were tested and then used on Japan before my second birthday. By my 66th birthday the President of the United States was calling for policies that would lead to the eventual elimination of nuclear weapons from the planet.[125] Significantly, beginning in 2007, a surprising, bipartisan coalition of statesmen, including Henry Kissinger, George Shultz, William Perry, and Senator Sam Nunn has urged this policy objective in a series of articles in the *Wall Street Journal*. The efforts of this group and the broader history of the nuclear arms race are deftly chronicled in a recent book by Philip Taubman, a veteran national security journalist.[126]

Logically, the first step toward this goal will be further reduction by the United States, Russia, and other nuclear powers in the scale of their nuclear arsenals as well as redoubled efforts to stem the dreadful risks of proliferation of nuclear weapons capacity to additional nations and potentially to nonstate actors such as terrorist networks. Unless the United States leads by example toward achievement of this goal, there will be zero prospect of success in generations to come. In the last chapter of my father's memoir, he reminds that United States and Russia have long been legally obliged under Article VI of the Non-Proliferation Treaty of 1968 to achieve meaningful reductions of their nuclear arsenals. This commitment, imperfectly honored, was the quid pro quo for other signatory nations foregoing development of nuclear weapons capacities.[127]

There remain serious obstacles to significant reduction, much less elimination, of nuclear weapons capacity. Although the nation does not like to recognize its own culpability, one must confront the fact that we released the nuclear genie from its bottle, and we are the only nation ever to use a nuclear weapon in wartime; we have led the world in development of increasingly sophisticated and numerous nuclear warheads and have pursued policies of relying on a nuclear arsenal as a "cost-effective" method of national defense; and unlike Russia, we have not been willing to adopt a "declaratory" policy that we would never be the first to use nuclear weapons, as distinct from maintaining the capacity to use them in retaliation.

From my vantage point as a member of the first generation in a nuclear armed world, as my father's son, and as a short-time official in the Department of Defense, I am aware of numerous, complex factors that have caused us to set such an imperfect example with respect to this potentially world-ending technology.

Our brief monopoly of nuclear weapons at the end of the Second World War led us to consider a system of international trusteeship for nuclear technology as early as 1947 under the auspices of the newly created United Nations. Promptly, justified suspicion of the Soviet Union under Stalin doomed any such effort and fed the political paranoia of McCarthyism. The Oppenheimer case had the impact of imposing a standard of political correctness that probably inhibited scientists who had the greatest appreciation of the terrors posed by these weapons from full participation in the councils of government. In the ensuing decade of the 50s, the United States found it economically expedient to rely on its "nuclear deterrent" in lieu of less cost-effective investment in expanded conventional military capacity with which to assure Western Europe that it would not be overrun by hoards of Soviet soldiers. The Kennedy Administration accomplished a treaty that limited testing of nuclear weapons in the atmosphere. This treaty, ironically, had the effect of moving such weapons tests underground and placing their terror "out of sight, out of mind."

Although "primitives" like Air Force General Curtis Lemay believed deeply in the efficacy of nuclear weapons, by the time I served in the Pentagon in 1973, the top officers in the military were, as already noted, skeptical of the efficacy of these weapons. Notwithstanding this skepticism by the uniformed military, the United States continued to build more sophisticated nuclear warheads and delivery systems throughout the 1970s and 1980s.

Civilian defense intellectuals gave major impetus to these investments. In the 1970s, they discerned a "window of vulnerability." As previously discussed, the Soviet Union, given its limited access to the oceans and its vast expanse of Eurasian land, had centered its nuclear deterrent on a large number of heavy ICBMs. The first strategic arms limitation agreements did not limit either side in deployment of MIRVs, and, by the late 1970s, conservative theorists posited that a disabling first strike on the U.S. land-based missile force by Russian MIRVs could eliminate our land-based deterrent. In this event, a U.S. President would either have to capitulate to the Soviet Union or use our submarine ballistic missile force to strike Russian cities, which would then create the risk of a Russian retaliatory strike on our own cities. While these intellectuals argued that it was inconceivable that any rational Russian leadership would undertake such risks, they posited that perception by others in the world that the United States was at this "disadvantage" would reduce our geostrategic leverage. Their articulation of this exquisitely intellectual hypothesis was curious. By calling on other nations to perceive a weakness in U.S. nuclear capacity, which was far from self-evident, its authors were potentially issuing a self-fulfilling prophecy. Moreover, this hypothesis became a driving force behind investment in a new generation of mobile, land-based ballistic missiles—the "Peacekeeper"—and in the serious attention given by the Reagan Administration to the pursuit of a Strategic Defense Initiative (SDI).

Throughout the nuclear era, there have been insufficient opportunities for robust public debate of the U.S. posture. There has also been a tendency by those expert in nuclear weapons matters to act as a kind of "priesthood" intolerant of commonsense intervention by the uninitiated. Nonetheless, much healthy demystification has occurred by publication of detailed and thoughtful studies of nuclear weapons development, arms control negotiations, and the like.[128] One pernicious aspect of the priesthood phenomenon has been the necessity for American policy experts to appear "tough" so as to remain in the larger political game. Dad's colleague, Paul Nitze, was a case in point. He was one of the "discoverers" of the "window of vulnerability." Although he had negotiated the ABM Treaty and written a letter to the Senate saying that it barred deployment of "exotic" defensive systems, he recanted this position in order to endorse Reagan's SDI and thereby remain in the game. However, at the end of his career in 1999, five years before his death, Nitze joined the chorus saying that the paramount objective of the United States should be the abolition of nuclear weapons.[129]

Even though the Cold War has now been over for two decades and United States and Russia have both agreed to reduce their strategic nuclear warheads down to approximately fifteen hundred per side, both nations still maintain arsenals disproportionate to any conceivable military need. Moreover, together the two nations still maintain numerous "tactical" nuclear weapons in Europe. As Creighton Abrams pointed out in my presence nearly 40 years ago, these weapons have dubious practical utility.

Although most knowledgeable statesmen and the current President of the United States fervently believe that the nation's interest would be served by further reductions in its nuclear arsenal with an eye toward achieving the ultimate goal of abolition of nuclear weapons, the country's political process appears hostile to this objective. This political hostility remains even though, as already noted, some of the nation's most experienced statesmen have endorsed the objective of abolition of nuclear weapons. Recent Senate advice and consent to ratification of a modest new arms reduction treaty repeated a process whereby the cost of agreements with Russia to reduce nuclear weapons has been expensive commitments to upgrade the technology of the remaining systems.[130]

Nonetheless, the greatest danger of continued political impasse in the United States is erosion of the example that we must set if we are to exercise leadership in persuading other countries to prevent proliferation of nuclear weapons capacities. For the first six decades of the nuclear era, these weapons of mass destruction have been under the control of rational actors (including the Soviet submarine officers who, as previously recounted, determined not to use a nuclear torpedo at the height of the Cuban Missile Crisis). The pursuit of a nuclear weapons capacity by North Korea and Iran raises the specter that this technology is now and will soon be in the hands of actors who may not be entirely rational.

Some believe that the solution to the problem of a nuclear armed world lies in defensive technology. Ever since President Reagan, relying upon a science fiction movie-making experience—and urged on by Edmund Teller, the father and proponent of the H-Bomb—endorsed a strategic-defense initiative, conservatives in the United States have placed faith in defensive technology. More conventional arms controllers have consistently pointed out that investment in defense drives investment in countervailing offensive systems, and that the latter are inexpensive compared to the former. Moreover, defensive systems that rely upon or will trigger nuclear explosions are hardly a solution. However, at least one serious physicist/philosopher, Freeman Dyson, has eloquently pointed out the essential morality of investment in non-nuclear defensive systems.[131] Presently the United States, with its allies, is investing in theater defensive systems meant to counter the potential development of a nuclear missile capacity by Iran. But, ultimately, the only sensible way to rid the planet of the risks of nuclear weapons is to get rid of the capacity by anyone to possess or use such weapons.

Any effort to eliminate nuclear weapons will have to take into account legitimate global demand for electricity generated with nuclear power. North Korea, Iran, and others have claimed that construction of nuclear reactors has been for peaceful electrical generation. But nuclear fuels can be diverted for weapons purposes. At present, as we confront global climate change, nuclear power is gaining new respectability as a source of electricity that minimizes release of greenhouse gases that contribute to climate change. Yet without adequate safeguards and transparency, such technology can be diverted to weapons programs. Especially problematic is power generation using plutonium derived from breeder reactors. While this recycling technology abates the supposed problem of long-term disposition of spent nuclear fuels, it risks widespread availability of bomb-grade material.[132] The risks are serious. During the Ford Administration in 1976, Henry Kissinger's staff endorsed the idea of setting up "regional" reprocessing centers to limit national proliferation of the technology. I remember a proposal to locate one such center inside the borders of Iran.

It is my hope that future generations will find a way to surmount these difficulties and achieve a world without nuclear weapons. Doing so may require internationalization of existing nuclear weapons and their destruction under international supervision. A skeptic may readily say that a world that seems unable to come meaningfully to grips with the evident risks of global climate change is not a world that will readily cede such a vital topic as nuclear weapons capacity to international jurisdiction. Indeed, there will need to be a profound change in the U.S. political climate before our Senate would begin to contemplate such an arrangement. I fear that the world will have to suffer the shock of actual use of a nuclear weapon before it will come to its senses. The "good news" is that the use of a nuclear weapon will probably not occur in any exchange between the United States and Russia, but more plausibly in the Middle East, South Asia, or the Far East. This is scant comfort.

12

J . T . S . I I ,
Six Months of Justice

In mid-April 1973, I accompanied Richardson on a trip to California, where Jack Veneman, his former number two at the Department of Health, Education and Welfare, was running (unsuccessfully) for Governor. During our flight across the United States in a Defense Department jet, Richardson read and annotated my memorandum to Jonathan Moore regarding nuclear weapons policy. He also read a paper from the Navy, regarding Navy force structure. The paper noted that three new aircraft carriers were to become active in 1976. Two had been named, the *USS Nimitz* and the *USS Eisenhower*, but one remained to be named. Richardson, somewhat playfully, annotated the Navy memorandum with possible names for this nameless vessel. His list included *Nixon, Bonhomme Richard, the Julie and Tricia, the Spiro of '76, Constitution,* and last but not least, *Stennis*. The first three of these proposed names reflected at least a subconscious preoccupation with the President, the fourth made sparing fun of the Vice President, Spiro Agnew. The final two unwittingly presaged a constitutional crisis in which both Senator Stennis and Elliot Richardson were to play major parts a few months hence.

With the announcement of Richardson's nomination to be Attorney General, as the only lawyer on Richardson's immediate staff, my attention turned increasingly to preparation for the Secretary's new responsibilities. Before his nomination, Richardson had paid scant attention to the emerging Watergate scandal. Suddenly, he was being thrust into its middle, and he was to learn that Watergate was potentially a much more far-reaching problem than a simple burglarization of an opponent's campaign office.

During the first week of May, Richardson and I participated in a set of extraordinary meetings in which various parties, including the chief of the Watergate prosecution, Assistant Attorney General Henry Peterson, and representatives of the White House, including Len Garment, the President's Special Counsel, sought to brief the new attorney general on the tortured events that had led up to the resignation of the President's principal staff officers. The day after his nomination, at the request of President Nixon, Richardson met with Egil (Bud) Krogh. Since February Krogh had been serving as the number two officer of the Department of Transportation. Before then he had been a White House staffer working for John Ehrlichman, in whose law office in Seattle he had worked briefly before Nixon's election. Krogh had a story to tell regarding White House behavior that made my hair stand on end. He had been deputized by Ehrlichman to work with an informal White House investigative group, the soon-to-be famous "Plumbers," tasked with finding sources of leaks of classified information. The "Plumbers" included former CIA operatives Howard Hunt and Gordon Liddy.

The catalyst for the establishment of the Plumbers had been the famous leak of the so-called Pentagon Papers by a former government employee, Daniel Ellsberg. This several thousand-page analysis of archival materials about the involvement of the United States in Vietnam had been commissioned by Secretary McNamara during the Johnson Administration. It contained much material embarrassing to the United States by showing that political leaders had dissembled regarding actions in Vietnam. But release of the Pentagon Papers had scant if any impact upon the conduct of defense policy by the Nixon Administration in Southeast Asia or elsewhere. Nonetheless, Nixon and Kissinger saw the leak as a damaging precedent that threatened their control of foreign policy. At Ehrlichman's direction, but allegedly without approval of the President, the Plumbers had burglarized the office of a psychiatrist whom Ellsberg was seeing in Los Angeles. The burglary was designed to find medical records with which to discredit Ellsberg. It did not succeed. Krogh had been persuaded that national security justified this effort.

Krogh's problem on April 30 appeared to be that he felt himself under a direct order from the President not to reveal the facts of this burglary. The President claimed that the whole matter was one of vital national security. Krogh correctly felt he had a obligation to share this information with federal district judge, William Byrne, who was currently conducting a trial in Los Angeles of Daniel Ellsberg for alleged violations of federal law in furnishing the Pentagon papers to the news media.

Richardson was in no position to resolve the matter during his first business day as Attorney General designate, without a better understanding of what exactly was transpiring. Follow-up meetings during the next two days with Leonard Garment created a strong inference that the President himself had ordered the burglary of Ellsberg's office. If true, such an action by the President could make the facts of the Watergate eavesdropping, and subsequent cover-up, appear relatively mild. The inference took on an even more lurid cast as it was revealed that the White House had met with Judge Byrne and explored his willingness to become the Director of the FBI. Failing this desperate effort by the White House to deal with the "Ellsberg" problem, Nixon, through John Ehrlichman, authorized Krogh to file an affidavit with Judge Byrne, demonstrating government misconduct, which led to dismissal of charges against Ellsberg on May 11, 1973. These sordid details have long been subordinated to larger historical events but, in May 1973, they loomed large. For the first time in my life, I felt paranoia. As I drove home in the evening from my Pentagon office that week, I would check my rearview mirror to assure that I was not being followed by some agent of the Nixon White House.

There was a feeling of both disappointment and relief as it emerged that the Senate, as a condition of confirming Richardson's nomination, would insist upon appointment of a Special Prosecutor to be accorded a large measure of independence in investigation of Watergate and related matters. Richardson drafted Wil Hastings, his HEW general counsel, to conduct the search for a Special Prosecutor.

The search by Richardson and his staff for a Special Prosecutor became subject to intense media and political scrutiny. Casting a broad net, Richardson received recommendations of a significant number of the "pillars" of the American Bar, including that of Leon Jaworski (considered by Richardson as too much of a "wheeler-dealer" and not offered the job), who ultimately did serve with distinction as Special Prosecutor. Some of those approached turned down the job, based upon family and professional commitments. One prominent lawyer, Warren Christopher, who later served with distinction as Deputy Secretary of State under President Carter and Secretary of State under President Clinton, appeared an ideal candidate. (He had previously been Deputy Attorney General under President Johnson.) Nonetheless, he advised Richardson that his family and professional commitments in California precluded him from accepting the job. We were disconcerted when reporters caught up with Christopher at the airport as he was departing for California. There, he was quoted as saying he had turned down the job because he did not believe that as Special Prosecutor he would enjoy sufficient independence—a concern that Richardson did not recall him having mentioned.

Ultimately, Richardson approached Harvard law professor, Archibald Cox. Cox had taught Richardson when the latter was a student at Harvard Law School. In 1949 Richardson had sought his advice whether to take a job offered him by Secretary of State Dean Acheson. Cox advised Richardson that before taking a Washington job it was good to "come from somewhere." On the strength of this solid advice, Richardson turned Acheson down.[133]

Cox had served with distinction in the Kennedy Administration as Solicitor General. Although he lacked prosecutorial experience, Cox radiated probity, balance, and integrity. Following some negotiations with the Senate Judiciary Committee regarding the details of a "charter" articulating the role of the Special Prosecutor and insulating Cox from political interference by the Nixon Administration, Richardson was confirmed. After an elaborate White House swearing-in ceremony, he took up his responsibilities as Attorney General on May 26, 1973. The Special Prosecutor's charter was in a sense a compact between Richardson and the Senate. It also was made a regulation of the Department of Justice. In it the Attorney General agreed that he could not remove the Special Prosecutor from office except for "extraordinary improprieties."

The charter, as negotiated among Richardson, Cox, and the staff of the Senate Judiciary Committee, did not limit the Special Prosecutor's jurisdiction to matters directly linked to the Watergate break-in. It gave Cox jurisdiction to investigate all allegations of criminal conduct by White House assistants or presidential aides. Hence Cox's jurisdiction would extend to White House involvement in burglarization of Ellsberg's psychiatrist's office; solicitation of potentially illegal corporate contributions; unlawful wiretapping; and other abuses of governmental powers. The breadth of Cox's jurisdiction was to become a constant irritant to the White House, and it would drag Richardson back into "Watergate" notwithstanding Cox's appointment as an independent Special Prosecutor. It deserves note that, at the time of Cox's appointment and Richardson's confirmation, there was no inkling that Nixon had been tape recording his White House conversations, creating a potentially vital source of evidence of criminal wrongdoing.

Richardson had not consulted the White House on the selection of Cox to be Special Prosecutor. Nixon and his staff, already paranoid, took immediate offense when they read newspaper reports of Cox's swearing in at the Justice Department. In attendance were Cox's friends, Senator Ted Kennedy and Bobby Kennedy's widow, Ethel Kennedy. As Cox's investigation proceeded and the noose tightened around Nixon's neck, Richardson would receive incessant complaints that Cox was on a partisan crusade, acting as a puppet of the Kennedys. These claims were an insult to a man of impeccable integrity and objectivity. Nevertheless, hindsight suggests that it would have been better if the Kennedy family had not attended Cox's swearing in.

Jonathan Moore, Dick Darman, Dick Mastrangelo, Cetta Leonardi, and I all accompanied Richardson to the Department of Justice. There I resumed my role as Executive Assistant, no longer sharing responsibility with any "military assistant." I was ensconced in a small library directly connected to the Attorney General's private office. I retain lucid memories of my few months at Justice, for they proved to be the most exciting and demanding months of my adult professional career.

Although divested of direct responsibility for the Watergate investigation, Richardson soon encountered a different historical challenge. In June of 1973, he learned that the U.S. Attorney for Maryland had uncovered evidence that Vice President Spiro Agnew may have received bribes from contractors in his former post as Governor of Maryland. At the same time, the Attorney General came under increasing pressure from President Nixon and his Chief of Staff, Al Haig, to constrain the activities of Archie Cox as Special Prosecutor, even though the latter's charter confirmed his independence. These extraordinary matters came to a head, almost simultaneously, in October 1973, with Agnew's forced resignation and plea of "no contest" to a charge of tax fraud, and in the "Saturday Night Massacre" in which Richardson resigned rather than carry out a White House directive to fire Cox. Cox, in turn, was dismissed by acting Attorney General Robert Bork. This event, which triggered a national outcry, is generally acknowledged as the "beginning of the end" for President Nixon, who was forced to resign less than 10 months later in August 1974.

It fell to me as Richardson's Executive Assistant to be the principal point of liaison between the Attorney General and both Cox and the U.S. Attorney in Baltimore investigating Agnew. These momentous events are exhaustively covered elsewhere, and I would achieve little purpose in a redundant recounting. The best treatment of the Agnew investigation and resignation appears in *A Heartbeat Away*, by Jules Witcover and Richard Cohen.[134] The most thorough discussion and explanation of the events of the Saturday Night Massacre appears in Ken Gormley's masterful biography of Archibald Cox.[135] After leaving government in October 1973 and free from the normal constraints that cause public servants to speak either on "background" or "off the record" to journalist/historians, I served as an on-the-record source for these authors. Accordingly, their accounts of these momentous events set forth my more contemporaneous understanding of these matters. This chapter seeks to provide a summary and a retrospective understanding. It does not attempt the detail that can be found in cited sources.

One of my duties as Executive Assistant was to control the Attorney General's calendar. In this capacity, I inadvertently prevented Richardson from learning about the portentous investigation of Agnew by George Beall, the U.S. Attorney for Maryland. Beall had alerted Richardson's predecessor, Richard Kleindienst, that the Vice President might be implicated in an ongoing investigation of kickbacks in state contracts. Kleindienst had not seen fit to flag the matter for Richardson. Shortly after we moved to Justice, Beall turned up, without an appointment, to brief the Attorney General on his Maryland corruption investigation. Richardson was quite busy, and I asked one of the career secretaries whether it was traditional for U.S. Attorneys to meet with the Attorney General without first securing an appointment. She responded that an appointment was normally required. Accordingly, I sent Beall back to Baltimore, urging him to make an appointment. Beall returned on June 12 and gave Richardson a long but cautious briefing without sounding alarms regarding the Vice President's potential culpability. On July 3 after some misstarts, Beall and three assistants met Richardson and briefed him on the unfolding investigation that, by this time, showed unambiguous jeopardy for the Vice President.

Richardson, who had served as U.S. Attorney for Massachusetts, had a clear appreciation of the contours of state level corruption and of the large discretion accorded U.S. Attorneys in exercising prosecutorial powers. He immediately grasped the significance of Beall's disclosures. He called me into his office and expressed alarm at what he had just been told. At the same time that President Nixon was under investigation by a Special Prosecutor, his putative successor, the Vice President of the United States, was in jeopardy of criminal prosecution for corruption.

The importance of Beall's July 3 revelations was amplified by other events the same day. Richardson had to interrupt Beall's briefing to take calls from the White House. First Haig, and then Nixon himself, expressed angry concern regarding (erroneous) news reports that Cox was investigating public expenditures on Nixon's San Clemente, California, home. Thus began a series of requests from the Haig and White House Counsel J. Fred Buzhardt to Richardson to curtail Cox's activities—something that Richardson could not readily do given his commitment to Cox and the Senate as recorded in Cox's charter. The situation became more dire when a White House aide, Alexander Butterfield, revealed to Congressional investigators on July 16, 1973, that Nixon had routinely recorded his conversations in the oval office. To do his job, Cox needed to seek access to portions of these recordings that potentially pertained to the Watergate break-in and any possible, subsequent cover-up. The White House exhibited strong determination to deny the Special Prosecutor any access to these recordings, citing the doctrine of Executive Privilege and invoking (fabricated) concerns about national security.

Another controversy about electronic interception of conversations by the Nixon White House had preceded the July disclosure of Nixon's taping system.

Wiretaps

In May 1973, William Ruckelshaus, as acting Director of the FBI, discovered that in the period 1969–1971, the FBI, at the request of the White House, had conducted a series of unusual wiretaps, without court warrant, on the home telephones of 4 reporters and 12 White House staffers, and on the office phone of General Robert Pursely, the military assistant to Secretary of Defense Laird. Ruckelshaus announced his discovery at a press conference on May 14, 1973. The initial significance of this discovery pertained to the trial of Daniel Ellsberg, who, as described, had been earlier prosecuted for leaking the Pentagon Papers. He had been overheard on a wiretap of the home phone of Kissinger staffer, Morton Halperin, a fact that was conveyed to the court along with information about the break-in to the office of Ellsberg's psychiatrist. In the perturbed environment of Watergate Washington, these taps took on wide significance. The White House contended that previous administrations had engaged in comparable conduct. Critics contended the taps were unprecedented and reprehensible.[136] This was a topic on which I had some preparation. As previously noted, nine years before, I had written a paper in my Constitutional Law seminar under Charles Reich on the subject of whether warrantless electronic surveillance of U.S. citizens violated the Fourth Amendment. I argued that it did. My view was vindicated by the

Supreme Court in the *Keith* decision of 1972—after the wiretaps at issue had ceased.[137]

It turned out that a safe in a back closet of the Attorney General's suite contained sensitive records of such wiretaps dating back to the Kennedy Administration. That Administration had tapped the phones of journalists Bernard Fall, an expert on Southeast Asia, and Lloyd Norman and Harrison Baldwin, who reported on the Pentagon; as well as that of Robert Amory, a senior officer of the CIA. The Kennedy wiretaps occurred in a different legal context before the Supreme Court ruled in 1967 that wiretapping constituted a search subject to the Fourth Amendment's strictures on unreasonable search and seizure. White House Chief of Staff Al Haig pressed hard for disclosure of these previous taps to provide context for the controversial Nixon wiretaps. The FBI pushed back, arguing that it was a bad precedent to publicly disclose sensitive wiretaps and to implicitly tarnish the character of the targets of these wiretaps.[138]

FBI records regarding the taps of the Nixon Administration suggested that, in a number of instances, the requests had originated with National Security Adviser Henry Kissinger. The question of Kissinger's role in the wiretapping became prominent when Nixon nominated Kissinger for the post of Secretary of State in July 1973. The FBI prepared a special, highly sensitive report regarding 17 extraordinary wiretaps during the first Nixon Administration. The Administration negotiated an arrangement with the Senate Foreign Relations Committee whereby this report could be reviewed, but not copied or disseminated, by a specially designated two-member subpanel of the Committee. On behalf of the Committee, this subpanel was to satisfy itself as to Kissinger's role in this wiretapping. I was charged with the task of being the "courier" who took this report up to the Capitol. There, I met with Senators John Sparkman and Clifford Case, as well as Henry Kissinger. I remained in the room while the Senators read the report and had an opportunity to question Kissinger.

Kissinger did not deny that some of the taps had been initiated at his request. He took the position that these events had transpired when he was relatively new to Washington and unpolished in the ways of bureaucracy. There had been great pressure in the White House to discover the source of leaks of national security information, and Kissinger had supported the institution of these taps. He stated that upon mature reflection, looking back from 1973, he was no longer so naïve as to contend that such conduct would be justified in the future.[139] I was fascinated to watch this powerful figure squirm in front of these senior Senators, and I held no affection for

Kissinger, given his ill treatment of my father. In any event, Kissinger satisfied the Senate Foreign Relations Committee that his conduct with respect to the wiretaps was not a disqualification. I returned with the sensitive wiretap report and locked it in the Attorney General's safe.

As a result of post-Watergate reforms, as well as the Supreme Court's *Keith* decision in June 1972, warrantless electronic surveillance of American citizens, even for national security purposes, became a clear violation of law.[140] Although Haig was correct that there was precedent for the Nixon White House's behavior, the scale of the Nixon Administration wiretaps exceeded that of any previous administration, as far as Justice Department records could show. Also, the timing and scale of this behavior, in conjunction with the establishment of the "Plumbers Group" were early signs of the rot that would lead to Watergate and the eventual resignation of President Nixon in disgrace.

In July and August 1973, Richardson's attentions increasingly focused on the Agnew investigation. Beginning with a meeting on July 11, Richardson asked me to join him in meetings with U.S. Attorney George Beall and his staff. The latter were initially suspicious, wondering whether I could be trusted with the vital secrets they were imparting. At the same time, the case against the Vice President tightened based upon the agreement of Allan Green to testify that he had paid off Agnew for state business to the tune of $50,000, with payment continuing after the former governor had become Vice President. Green had handed envelopes of cash to Agnew as late as 1972 in the Old Executive Office Building. Green was represented by Brendan Sullivan, an up-and-coming young lawyer. (Sullivan today is without peer in the white collar defense bar and a national personality from his representation of Oliver North in the Iran-Contra hearings. He is also a personal friend.)

In August, articles began to appear in the *New York Times* and elsewhere regarding the possibility that the Vice President was under criminal investigation. Using a time honored tactic, the Vice President contended that the leaks constituted prosecutorial misconduct. (In fact, subsequent discussions with members of the press indicated to me that their principal sources of information were in the Vice President's own office.) The Vice President and his lawyers demanded an investigation of the Justice Department to determine the source of the leaks and in September sought to subpoena newsmen to disclose their sources.

At no time in the summer of 1973 did I or, to the best of my knowledge, any other member of the Attorney General's staff speak with the press regarding the highly sensitive Agnew investigation. But, we were under siege by the press once articles began to appear reporting on the prospect of prosecution of the Vice President. Also, as tensions between the White House and the Office of the Special Prosecutor became more apparent, representatives of the press would call the Attorney General's office and his immediate staff seeking to glean insights to aid reporting. I found myself, for the first time, subject to high interest by the press. I received guidance from Jonathan Moore on the unwritten rules that govern the curiously symbiotic relationship between the national media and federal officials.

Under principles originally worked out by a Christian Science Monitor reporter, Ernest Lindley—the so-called Lindley Rule—a source within the government would agree to speak "off the record." In this case a reporter could use any information gleaned in pursuit of other sources of information, but could not use the information directly and under no circumstances could identify the off-the-record source. Sometimes this method of dialog was also characterized as "deep background." A source could also speak to a representative of the press on "background." Here, the press could use the information directly, but could not name the source. The press could cite unnamed sources such as "a senior official." "On-the-record" questions with the press were just that. The information could be quoted and the source could be identified. Such on-the-record conversations normally occurred between the press and official spokespeople for Cabinet Departments. The latter would normally be insulated from truly sensitive matters. Those who have been most successful in high profile public service have been adept cultivators of the press. Henry Kissinger was a highly skilled and deliberate leaker. Jim Baker apparently used his leverage as a source to demand a right of prior review of any news article in which the reporter planned to use information from Baker, even if it was to be used "without attribution."

To a large extent the interplay between the government and the press led to the Watergate Scandal, as well as aided in its resolution. White House concern with leaks led to a pattern of questionable wiretaps, then to the actual burglarization of Daniel Ellsberg's psychiatrist's office. The same employees used in this extraordinary venture later conducted the break-in and attempted bugging of the offices of the Democratic National Committee in the Watergate Office Complex. The artful and relentless pursuit of information from inside government sources by investigative reporters such as Bob

Woodward and Carl Bernstein, contributed importantly to the unraveling and downfall of the Nixon Administration.

In September and October 1973, Woodward and Bernstein began calling me in the Attorney General's office. I refused to take their calls. They then began to call me at home on Saturday evening. I continued to refuse to talk with them. As already noted, I did talk with them and other reporters after my resignation from government service in late October on the heels of Richardson's resignation in the Saturday Night Massacre.

From this experience I grew to realize that the attention of the national media can be flattering—dangerously so for political figures with loose tongues or insufficient understanding of the rules of the game. I also learned from this and subsequent experiences that the interplay between government and the press has been an important means by which individuals in government advance their political and policy agendas. And, even inappropriate leakage of sensitive information, generally advances the public good by making government more open and by limiting opportunities for government abuse.

Although vexatious at the time, the leaks of sensitive information about the pending Agnew prosecution probably increased pressures for prompt resolution. This outcome was ironic if, as I suppose, the principal source of leaks was the Vice President's office itself in an attempt to build a claim of prosecutorial abuse. In actuality, the tactic backfired.

The other, more substantial facet of the Agnew matter was the question whether a sitting Vice President could be subjected to criminal prosecution. Initially, the White House was ambivalent. Given Nixon's potential jeopardy under Watergate, the White House was wary of an argument that the Vice President could be prosecuted. The concern was that if a Vice President could be prosecuted criminally, so might a sitting President be amenable to criminal process. Contrariwise, successful argument by the Vice President that he was subject only to Congressional impeachment had its downside. If impeachment proceedings were successfully launched by Congress against the Vice President, such proceedings might accelerate against the President himself. Eventually, the White House agreed to Richardson's position that criminal prosecution of a Vice President would not debilitate the nation. In contrast, a sitting President should be subject only to impeachment proceedings.

Accordingly, when the Vice President's lawyers filed a motion for a determination by a federal district court that the Vice President was immune from criminal process, the Justice Department responded with a powerful brief, written principally by Solicitor General Robert Bork, contending that the Vice President, as distinct from the President, was subject to criminal process. In the lead-up to this pleading, the Attorney General asked the Assistant Attorney General in charge of the Office of Legal Counsel for a formal "opinion" on the topic. It was a close enough question that the law professor serving in that post called me one evening at home to inquire quietly as to which way the Attorney General wanted the opinion to come out. I assured him that the Attorney General hoped the opinion would support criminal prosecution of the Vice President, which it did.

In September 1973, serious plea bargaining by the Vice President began. The outlines of a deal emerged under which Agnew would agree to the extraordinary step of resigning the Office of Vice President in return for a plea of *nolo contendere*, or "no contest," to a single charge of failing to pay taxes on certain sums and a recommendation by the Attorney General of no jail time. Richardson sagely insisted that such a deal would only be feasible if accompanied by a detailed filing by the Department of Justice of the information developed by the U.S. Attorney in Baltimore regarding the broad pattern of corruption he was prepared to prove if the matter had gone to trial. In this way the American public would be informed fully of the reasons for the Vice President's disgrace.

To achieve the "bargain" Richardson had not only to obtain the concurrence of the Vice President and his counsel, he also needed the support of the U.S. Attorney's office. The bright and ambitious young prosecutors who had developed the case against Agnew were eager to see him suffer the full consequences of his apparently corrupt actions. Richardson artfully included the young prosecutors in decision-making and negotiations. He treated them as close confidants. In so doing, he obtained their support and loyalty. Even the most senior and aggressive of the Assistant U.S. Attorneys, Barney Skolnick, became an enthusiastic supporter of the outcome. The entire process was a good example of Richardson's instinctive respect for public servants and political virtuosity.

On October 11, 1973, I accompanied the Attorney General to federal district court in Baltimore. A mob of press waited on the courthouse steps. They assumed that the proceedings would address the enforceability of the subpoenas sought by the Vice President to examine the press on sources of leaks, an issue of immense interest to the press. However, to the surprise of the press, the Vice President of the United States appeared, entered a plea of *nolo contendere*, and announced his resignation of the Vice President of the United States. Attorney General Richardson made his recommendation to the court that Agnew be spared a prison sentence. Richardson's words are worth quoting:

> Out of compassion for the man, out of respect for the office he has held, and out of appreciation for the fact that by his resignation he has spared the nation the prolonged agony that would have attended upon his trial, I urge that the sentence imposed on the defendant by this Court not include confinement.[141]

After a statement by Agnew, Federal District Judge Hoffman, by prearrangement, reluctantly noted his acquiescence in the plea agreement and his determination not to impose a jail sentence.

As a 29-year old, I was dazzled to witness the appearance of the Attorney General and the Vice President of the United States in court and by the dreadful humiliation that Agnew had brought upon himself. Initially, there was some criticism by commentators regarding the absence of a jail sentence for the Vice President. However, the weight of historical opinion has sided with Richardson's courageous and compassionate decision that the national interest was best served by the prompt bargain struck with the Vice President.

The day following the Vice President's resignation and plea, Richardson treated Jonathan Moore, Dick Darman, and me to lunch at a favorite restaurant, Jean Pierre, in downtown Washington. Richardson's satisfaction at the successful outcome of the Agnew matter was tempered by the fact that another, potentially larger problem loomed. The Attorney General pointed to a painting on the wall of the restaurant of a bullfight and mentioned that he had avoided one bull but that another was fast approaching. Richardson was adverting to a discussion he had had with President Nixon on September 25 regarding the status of the Agnew matter. Nixon had commented in an off-hand way that once the Agnew situation was resolved, it would be time to deal with Special Prosecutor Cox. It soon proved that the President had not been speaking in jest. Al Haig called Richardson on Sunday, October 14, and asked to meet with him on Monday morning, the 15th. At this meeting, Haig unveiled a plan that was to end five days later in the so-called Saturday Night Massacre.

The historical context of the week of October 15 was exceptional. Not only was the United States without a Vice President, a genuine national security crisis existed. On October 6, Egypt and Syria had attacked Israel, and the latter was in retreat. The Soviet Union was asserting its support for the Arab nations. The United States countered with moral and then massive, logistical support for Israel. In addition, the White House tapes issue had come to a head.

After Alexander Butterfield revealed in July the existence of White House tapes, Special Prosecutor Cox had moved ahead to seek access to a limited number of tapes that testimony from former White House Counsel John Dean and others suggested contained information pertaining to the Watergate break-in. The President's lawyers strenuously resisted access to the tapes on grounds of Executive Privilege. Cox moved to compel disclosure before Judge Sirica in federal district court and obtained an order compelling production. Sirica stayed his order to allow an opportunity for appeal to the U.S. Court of Appeals for the D.C. Circuit. On Friday, October 12, while we were lunching at Jean Pierre, the Court of Appeals upheld Sirica's order and gave the White House until close of business Friday, October 19, to seek Supreme Court review if it so chose.

When Richardson arrived at the White House on Monday, October 15, Haig began with a lengthy discussion of the dangerous situation in the Middle East. Richardson briefly indulged the illusion that the White House wanted to send him—as former Under Secretary of State and Secretary of Defense—on a peacemaking mission to the Middle East. Then, Haig got down to business. He stated that the President had formulated a plan regarding the White House tapes. Under this plan, the President himself would prepare a summary of what was contained in the subpoenaed tapes. This summary would be provided to Judge Sirica, and then the President would fire Cox. Ironically, this "brainstorm" on the part of the President had been stimulated by two of my law professors, Alex Bickel and Robert Bork. The former had published an article in the summer of 1973 in *The New Republic*. As a proponent of judicial restraint, Bickel had long taught that courts should not address issues in the absence of a genuine "case or controversy." Since Cox was an appointee of the Executive Branch, he was, according to Bickel, subject to dismissal by the President. Accordingly, the courts of the land could not appropriately resolve any "dispute" between Cox and the President. It seems certain that Solicitor General, Bork, a close friend of Bickel's and a supporter of Bickel's position, had brought this theory to the attention of the White House.

Asked by Haig what he thought of the President's plan, Richardson stated without hesitation that, if the President pursued this plan, Richardson would have to resign. Richardson returned to the Justice Department, a visibly shaken man. Haig called later to say that he had persuaded the President to endorse an alternative approach. Under this approach, the White House would ask Senator John Stennis to prepare a summary of the subpoenaed tapes to be furnished both to Cox and to Judge Sirica. Haig stated that he had obtained Nixon's reluctant approval of this approach on the condition that, after provision of the tape summaries authenticated by Stennis, Cox was to have no further access to any presidential materials.

There thus began a week of high stakes negotiation between and among the White House, the Attorney General's Office, and Special Prosecutor Cox. The events of this week are exhaustively recounted in the Gormley biography of Cox.[142] They are also addressed in Richardson's book, *The Creative Balance*.[143] Further, the events of this week are the subject of a case study prepared at the Kennedy School of Government at Harvard based on interviews of me, Jonathan Moore, and members of Cox's staff in the spring of 1974. (A review of the transcript of my interview for this case study at Harvard reveals that my most vigorous interlocutor was a somewhat abrasive graduate student named Charles Schumer. Chuck Schumer is now a senior and powerful Democratic Senator from New York. The evening following this interview, I accompanied my brother Gerry, then attending Harvard Business School, to a dinner party hosted by my Yale contemporary, John Kerry, also now a powerful Senator.)

In retrospect, my understanding of certain events of the week of the "Saturday Night Massacre" is clearer than it was at the time and it may be useful to record my perceptions here.

First, the initial condition laid down by the President that the fruits of the Stennis compromise be the last White House materials furnished to the Special Prosecutor was an impossible condition. In the course of the week's discussions, this condition receded only to emerge again at the end of the week as an obvious deal breaker. It appears that Richardson had hoped that by ignoring this condition, he could make it go away. He couldn't.

Second, it is clear in retrospect that the White House was striving for an outcome in which Richardson would be willing to continue as Attorney General and Cox would resign. While the historical record accurately records the bravery and integrity of both men in standing up to the President of the United States, the White House came closer to obtaining its preferred outcome than most historians understand. Richardson did not presume guilt on the part of the President. He respected the President's claim to privilege for recordings of the inner workings of the White House. He did not think that the Stennis compromise was unreasonable on its face, except for the prospective prohibition against seeking further evidence from the White House. He was also deeply conscious of the national security crisis that provided the backdrop for the White House's claim that the President could not be seen as weak, as he would be if he gave in to the Special Prosecutor.

Because of the conflicts Richardson felt (including his consciousness of national security and his gratitude toward Nixon for appointing him to three cabinet posts), he probably gave Al Haig a misimpression regarding his willingness to support the Stennis compromise, even if it were to be rejected by Cox. In any event, Cox did reject the compromise, and, contrary to the White House's hopes, did not resign. Instead, he forced the White House's hand to make it fire him. Richardson could not fire Cox without breach of his commitment to Cox and the Senate as recorded in Cox's charter, and Deputy Attorney General Ruckelshaus readily followed Richardson's lead in resigning rather than doing the White House's bidding.

Third, while Robert Bork, who became Acting Attorney General when Richardson and Ruckelshaus resigned, suffered obloquy for firing Cox, he had the support of Richardson and Ruckelshaus in doing so. Although Bork, like his friend Alex Bickel, felt that the White House could and should seek the dismissal of Cox, he worried, properly, that his role in this historic vortex would harm his reputation and inhibit his performance of his duties as Solicitor General of the United States. He could not have forecast that it would also emerge as one of the factors that would feed Democratic opposition to his nomination to serve on the Supreme Court 14 years later.

Fourth, Al Haig and the White House, either by deliberation or incompetence, sewed confusion throughout the week. It turned out, for instance, that Senator Stennis, a very honorable man, had been given the impression that he was to vet the White House tapes only for the purpose of disclosure to the Senate Watergate Investigating Committee under Senator Sam Irwin. Stennis had never intended to interpose himself between the Special Prosecutor and Federal District Judge John Sirica.

In any event, I had the "good fortune" to be a witness and participant to these extraordinary events and to watch, and occasionally advise, while great men, such as Richardson, Ruckelshaus, and Cox struggled to find an honorable outcome to a clear constitutional crisis. On Saturday night, October 20, two days before my 30th birthday, Richardson and Ruckelshaus had resigned and Cox had been fired. On Al Haig's ill-considered order, FBI officers sealed off the Office of the Attorney General and the Office of the Special Prosecutor. I, nevertheless, gathered my most sensitive files reflecting my knowledge and involvement in Watergate events and the work of the Special Prosecutor, placed them in my briefcase, and went home unimpeded by the FBI. I took these files and hid them in the attic of my house in Georgetown. Richardson's irreverent April 1973 doodling regarding the possible names for a new aircraft carrier, including *The Bonhomme Richard, Constitution, the Spiro of 76,* and *Stennis* had been alarmingly prescient.

It turned out that Nixon had not solved his Watergate problem. The nation erupted and the White House, as well as the Attorney General and Special Prosecutor's Offices, were deluged with citizens' letters and telegrams. In a matter of days, Leon Jaworski was appointed to replace Archibald Cox as Special Prosecutor, with fresh guarantees of independence from White House interference. The White House turned over the tapes that had been the catalyst for Cox's dismissal. Jaworski subsequently sought large quantities of additional White House materials.

Jaworski's demand for additional tapes was litigated to the Supreme Court. Contrary to Professor Bickel's theory, the Court ruled that the matter was justiciable. It reasoned that the Special Prosecutor's charter, which had been made into a regulation under the Administrative Procedure Act, insulated the Special Prosecutor from dismissal in the absence of "extraordinary impropriety." Unless or until the regulation was withdrawn in accordance with the Administrative Procedure Act, the Special Prosecutor had standing to litigate access to White House materials. The Court also went on to say that Executive Privilege could not bar access to White House tapes to provide evidence in a criminal proceeding. See *United States v. Nixon,* 418 U.S. 683 (1974).

* * * * *

Reflection—A Digression on Drinking

A particularly "smarmy" aspect of the events surrounding the Saturday Night Massacre was Al Haig's effort to tarnish Richardson's integrity by deliberately suggesting that he was acting under the influence of alcohol. The facts are quite simple. On the Friday night of Saturday Night Massacre week, Haig called Richardson in his office and read him the draft of a letter directing Richardson to order Cox to accept the Stennis compromise and to cease and desist from seeking further White House materials. Richardson let Haig know that he felt that he was being treated "shabbily" and that he could not conceivably give Cox the order the White House was requesting. Later that evening, Haig called Richardson at home. By then the Attorney General had had a cocktail to relax from an extraordinarily pressured week. In trying to calm troubled waters, Richardson told Haig that "after a cocktail" he regretted the harsh words he had spoken earlier in the office about shabby treatment. (In any event, the White House never sent the letter that Haig had read to Richardson over the phone directing him to order Cox to accept the Stennis approach.)

Haig later told the press that some of the confusion in the events leading up to the Saturday Night Massacre may have resulted from the fact that the Attorney General was "drinking." In fact, rumors of a "drinking problem" had pursued Richardson throughout his career. While he was a student at Harvard, he had been in an automobile accident, and drinking had been an issue. (It may not have been the proximate cause of the accident, since Richardson was a terrible driver, even under the best of circumstances.) When Richardson ran for office in Massachusetts, his opponents discovered the record of this accident and put it about that Richardson "was a drinker." Regrettably, this tarnishing rumor has recently been given fresh impetus in an otherwise fascinating novel by Thomas Mallon entitled *Watergate*.[144]

Like the majority of individuals of his generation, including my own parents, Richardson doubtless enjoyed cocktails as a social lubricant and as a relaxant. Richardson was always quite deliberate of manner. He would choose his words slowly and carefully, almost as if he were trying to ensure that everything he said came out in coherent, grammatical paragraphs. After he had a cocktail, his natural manner would be slowed, not accelerated, and he could give the impression that he was impaired by drink, when such was not the case. One of my jobs as his Executive Assistant was to manage two briefcases of material that he would typically take home each evening. Usually, he would return these materials the next morning, and they would have been closely reviewed and annotated, with directions for follow-up action. He often reviewed 200 pages or more in an evening. On occasion, acquaintances would tell me that they had seen Richardson the evening before at some reception and that he was inebriated. I would reply that the supposedly inebriated Secretary had done more work that evening than most mortals would complete in a 12-hour day.

The matter of Richardson's alleged "drinking problem," magnified by Haig's desperate maneuver, took on added importance in the months and years following the Saturday Night Massacre when a number of prominent people urged Richardson to run for President. (He never did, but along with Bill Ruckelshaus, was rumored to be on a "short list" of potential Vice Presidential candidates considered by President Ford in 1976.) In this context, his staff became concerned that the rumors of Richardson's supposed drinking problem would undermine his national political prospects. Somehow, I drew the "short straw" and was designated to speak to Richardson about the matter. We went to lunch one day and, as was Richardson's normal practice, he ordered a glass of wine. I cleared my throat and asked Richardson whether it was prudent for him to be seen "drinking at midday" in light of the unfair rumors that surrounded him. Perhaps, I suggested, so long as his national political ambitions were alive, he should foreswear this practice. Richardson took no offense. Rather, he thanked me for my concern but pointed out that if he changed his ways, people would notice and take this change as confirmation that he had a problem that he didn't have. End of discussion.

In the following years, and in the preparation of this memoir, I have had occasion to give some thought to alcoholic beverages. As already noted, John Thomas Smith started as a non-drinker but began to take a cocktail in the evening as a protest in principle against the intrusiveness of prohibition. William G. Maguire appeared to enjoy a stiff bourbon. To neither of these highly accomplished men did alcohol appear to be a handicap. My mother's mother was a strict Christian Scientist and, consistent with the tenants of her faith, was quite hostile to drinking. My parents, typical of their generation, enjoyed cocktails and wine. My father could "hold his liquor" admirably. I don't remember him ever uttering an angry or foolish word while imbibing. Alcohol did not treat my mother as kindly. In the last year before her death, she foreswore all alcohol while battling cancer. Poignantly, this change of behavior allowed my mother consistently to radiate her high intelligence and personal charm that had sometimes been masked by alcohol.

In my generation, for better or for worse, we have emulated our parents' drinking behavior. However, to his immense credit, Hugh gave up drinking a few years ago. Gerry, Sheila, and I still enjoy a drink or two. Whether any of us holds liquor as well as our father is open to question. On occasion, I detect in myself a tendency to be gratuitously argumentative under the influence of wine, a trait that reminds me of my mother rather than my father.

The good news is that the weight of medical evidence shows that drinking in moderation may actually contribute to heart health. Achieving and maintaining this moderation is always a challenge. My advice to future generations is to drink only in moderation, and if you find that moderation is not easy to achieve, give up drinking altogether. I readily confess that I have lost many hours of a lifetime by making myself drowsy with alcohol in the evening, when the hours after dinner could have been used for productive endeavor. Ironically, I came across a diary entry by my father complaining of this same phenomenon when he was still a young man.

13

G.C.S. in the 1970s

In the fall of 1972, as he prepared to resign his duties as the nation's chief arms control negotiator, Dad received an interesting invitation from David Rockefeller. Rockefeller, a banker and philanthropist, proposed the creation of a Trilateral Commission to convene business, academic, and political leaders from North America, Europe, and Japan to study and discuss issues of common concern. Each of the three geographic areas comprising this trilateral structure was to have a chairman. Rockefeller invited Dad to become the first North American Chairman of the Trilateral Commission. (The suggestion to Rockefeller of Dad to fill this post originated with Dad's ever-loyal friend, Henry Owen). After consulting several people (including Henry Kissinger), Dad accepted this relatively prestigious (but unpaid) post. Taking no offense, he later learned that he was Rockefeller's second choice. The first choice, former Pennsylvania Governor William Scranton, had declined.

From his State Department responsibilities in the 1950s, his publication of *Interplay* magazine in the 1960s, as well as his need to coordinate arms control issues with European governments, Dad had long been a student and proponent of broad cooperation between the United States and Western Europe. The chance to widen the dialog to include the rising economic power—Japan—made good sense and added appeal and challenge to the proposed undertaking. Dad's new duties provided opportunities for him and my mother to travel to the Far East, as well as to Europe, for meetings of the commissioners, who included many of the most establishment figures in the host regions. Among the rising politicians named as U.S. commissioners, was Jimmy Carter, Governor of Georgia. As Executive Director of the Trilateral Commission, Rockefeller hired Zbigniew Brzezinski. The latter was assisted by a former rising star of the British foreign ministry and son of former British Ambassador to the United States Christopher Makins.

In 1977, when Jimmy Carter became President, he appointed Brzezinski to be his "Kissinger," serving as a dynamic and powerful national security advisor. Carter and Brzezinski soon asked my father to become part of the new administration. They first sought to appoint him United States Ambassador to the Soviet Union. After three years of living in hotels in Helsinki and Vienna during the SALT talks, my father was not eager for a renewed stint of dealing with Russians in a cold, dark climate. More significantly, at the time, news reports had appeared stating that the Russians were irradiating the U.S. Embassy with microwaves in an attempt to gather intelligence. My mother had undergone surgery for breast cancer in 1969, and my parents did not think it was prudent to expose her on a full-time basis to what was deemed a potential initiator of further cancer. Accordingly, my father declined the post. Subsequently, the White House approached Dad with an offer he couldn't refuse. The President asked him to become an "Ambassador at Large" with chief responsibility for diplomacy to limit the proliferation of nuclear weapons. He was to report not only to Secretary of State Cyrus Vance, but also on a direct line to Brzezinski in the White House.

In this role, my father was the nation's chief delegate to the International Atomic Energy Agency in Vienna. He had been "present at the creation" of this Agency pursuant to the Eisenhower Administration's "Atoms for Peace" initiative in 1953–1954. He embarked, with my mother as usual at his side, on a series of challenging trips to countries that were actively considering development of nuclear weapons. Their travels took them to South America to attempt to dissuade Brazil and Argentina from pursuing a nuclear option. They also visited South Africa (in my mother's opinion the most beautiful place she had ever been). That nation, still suffering under apartheid, was actively engaged in the covert development of nuclear weapons, but lied to Dad regarding this endeavor. Later, South Africa became the only country to actually develop a nuclear weapon and then relinquish this capacity. My parents also traveled to India and Pakistan. Here my father's endeavors met with no success.

Soon after my father undertook his duties as Ambassador at Large for Nuclear Nonproliferation, a serious dispute arose between the United States and Japan about the latter's ability to conduct "reprocessing" of nuclear fuel at a pilot plant. At the time, the United States' policy was to prevent or discourage such reprocessing, as it involved recovery of plutonium for use as nuclear fuel. Dad chaired a delegation that went to Tokyo in late 1977 and worked out arrangements that abated the tensions between the two countries by allowing the pilot plant to operate but obtaining in return promises by Japan to become an active participant in international and bilateral nonproliferation efforts. Several years later, the Japanese government recognized Dad's role in these events by awarding him the "Grand Cordon of the Order of the Sacred Treasure."[145] Dad, while glad of the honor, was somewhat bemused by the elaborate decoration that accompanied it.

In 1989, I made a business trip to Tokyo with colleagues from Covington & Burling. In a discussion with a representative of Japan's foreign ministry, I had occasion to "boast" that my father had been awarded this decoration. I inquired as to its significance in comparison to another Japanese decoration, "The Order of the Rising Sun." With Japanese tact, my contact replied that, "Both awards are very important."

After leaving the Carter Administration, Dad rejoined the Trilateral Commission, but no longer as North American Chairman. By this time, the Commission had become the focus of conspiracy theorists on both left and right. Redoubtable left-wing academic Noam Chomsky saw it as an international cabal of capitalists designed to bend global affairs to their will. More potently, the right-wing saw the Commission as a conspiracy of wealthy internationalists who were acting to undermine the national interest. In the early Reagan Administration, membership in the Trilateral Commission would disqualify one from political appointment. Reagan, great political artist that he was, indulged conspiracy theorists, while buying none of the theory himself. In his second Administration, he actually invited the U.S. members of the Trilateral Commission to a reception at the White House.

Dad was always amused that conspiracy theorists accorded the Trilateral Commission consequence way beyond actuality.

Family Life in the 1970s

Dad's role as North American Chairman of the Trilateral Commission was only a part-time job. He accepted an offer from his friend, Lloyd Cutler, to become Of Counsel at the law firm of Wilmer, Cutler & Pickering. After a quarter century away from the private practice of law, Dad had little zeal for legal practice. He spent most of his time working on his memoir of the first round of SALT, entitled *Doubletalk*, as a reflection on Kissinger's pursuit of a separate, parallel channel of negotiation. Dad completed this book in the mid-70s and submitted it for governmental review to ensure no untoward revelation of classified information. By the time this review was complete, he had accepted his post in the Carter Administration, and prudence dictated that publication of *Doubletalk* be placed on hold while my father remained in public service. The existence of my father's book and its provocative title became widely known. When I traveled to Moscow on government business in May 1977, a Russian "academic" at a reception made clear that he knew me to be my father's son and that his yet to be published SALT narrative was titled *Doubletalk*.

Doubletalk did not appear in print until 1981, after publication of the first, self-justifying volume of Kissinger's memoirs. It is possible that Kissinger's mostly generous words about my father in his memoir (quoted earlier) are a preemptive response to my father's description of Kissinger's double dealing.

In this period, Sheila, Gerry, and I and our spouses were all raising young families: Gerry in New York and subsequently in Paris, Sheila and I in Washington. Younger brother Hugh, who turned 18 and graduated from Canterbury School in 1972, began a series of college adventures, but his schedule allowed him opportunities to travel with my parents to Japan and to Europe on Trilateral Commission business.

When not traveling, my parents' lives continued as in the past. They resided at Tracy Place in Washington, but spent most weekends at Ratcliffe Manor. Summers took them to the Ark in Southampton, although my father's travel schedule, as well as the fact that the "nest" was largely empty, except for visits from children and grandchildren, led my parents to use the Southampton house less and less. Sadly, they sold "the Ark" in 1979, ending decades of summer delight. (During the economic "malaise" of the late 1970s, my father was content to sell the Ark, unfurnished, for a price in non-inflation-adjusted dollars approximately 10 times its purchase price (fully furnished) in the late 1940s. During the prosperity of recent decades houses like the Ark would sell for 25 or even 50 times the amount my father received. Subsequent owners of this wonderful house included Woody Allen; Freddie Gershon, the manager of the British rock group; The Bee Gees; and ultimately Howard Stein, the founder of the Dreyfus Fund. In a spectacular fire in the winter of 2003, the Ark burned to the ground.)

During this period, my parents initiated the practice of celebrating my mother's birthday on New Year's Eve with a black-tie dinner, followed by parlor games to fill the time until the start of the New Year. The core of the guests would be houseguests down to Ratcliffe Manor for the weekend, as well as those from a parallel house party hosted by Ella Burling, an extraordinarily smart and vivacious neighbor with a vast circle of acquaintances. I recall raucous charades involving luminaries such as Secretary of Defense Harold Brown, Lloyd Cutler, and former Supreme Court Justice Potter Stewart. On at least one occasion, Elliot Richardson and his wife, Anne, attended these revels as houseguests of their Talbot County friends Russell and Aileen Train.

Also, during the Carter Administration, Zbigniew Brzezinski, his wife, and three children would make weekend visits. Brzezinski's wife, a talented sculptress, embarked on making molds of old trees on the Ratcliffe Manor lane. I was deputized to take members of the Brzezinski family fishing— excursions on which no fish were caught. Among the three children was a gangly adolescent named Mika. She has grown into a talented news personality whom I watch frequently on early-morning television.

End of Government Service

Reagan's defeat of Jimmy Carter in the 1980 election signaled the end of my father's government service, but not, as will be seen, his involvement in issues of nuclear arms control. The end was marked with a singular honor when President Carter bestowed upon Dad the National Medal of Freedom—the nation's highest civilian award. In the citation accompanying the award, Carter gave recognition to my father for "helping us all to perceive that in this nuclear age security and peace are indivisible." The President went on to remark that Dad had been involved from "the very beginning of our nation's policy on nonproliferation" and that he had been "a teacher of leaders in this country and around the world." Referring to Dad's tutelage of Carter on national security and arms control issues in the Trilateral Commission, President Carter concluded with the remark that he was "personally indebted" to Dad.[146]

I attended the awards ceremony in the White House accompanied by my son, John. The latter, having just turned eight, appeared bored by the proceeding (or tired by the rigors of school work), and yawned loudly throughout. Others receiving the Medal of Freedom that day included Zbignew Brzezinski, Harold Brown, Warren Christopher, Edmund Muskie, Earl Warren, and actor Kirk Douglas. In retrospect, it is fitting that this award was bestowed upon my father, a lifelong Republican, by a Democratic President. (Similarly, it was President Clinton who 17 years later bestowed the Medal of Freedom on another lifelong Republican: my mentor, Elliot Richardson.) Both my father and Richardson were exemplars of a brand of moderate, Eastern, internationalist, Republicanism that is now almost extinct.

The evening of the White House awards ceremony, sister Sheila hosted a dinner in honor of the event. In addition to the family, attendees included my father's close collaborators and friends, Robert Bowie, Henry Owen, and Sarge Shriver. Lloyd Cutler was also present, but left early to deal with Iranian hostage negotiations on the eve of change of administrations. Doubtless, it was Cutler who recommended my father for the award. Skilled operator that he was, Lloyd never disabused us of this notion and, indeed, separately gave both me and my mother the impression that he had been acting upon suggestions originating with each of us. In any event, Dad indisputably deserved the award.

Sheila had the foresight to record the toasts that evening. Reviewing the transcript 30 years later, I discover that I picked up on President Carter's reference to Dad as a "teacher." I toasted Dad as an "effective, wonderful teacher," never stern but one "whose lesson was compelled simply by example." I stand by these words and I have tried, imperfectly, to lead my sons by example.

14

J.T.S. II, 1973–1978

The five years following my abrupt departure from the Department of Justice, while not as eventful as my five months at Justice, proved highly important. Contrary to prior plans, I entered the private practice of law. My second son, William Gerard Smith, arrived in June 1975. In January 1976 I seized the chance to return to public service after Elliot Richardson was made Secretary of Commerce by President Ford and asked me to become General Counsel of the Commerce Department. A year later, I joined Richardson as a Deputy when he became the head of the U.S. Delegation to a highly important international negotiation regarding Law of the Sea. After returning to the practice of law in the fall of 1977, I had the great good fortune to be made a partner in Covington & Burling at the end of September 1978.

In law school I had no intention of entering the private practice of law. Instead, I planned to emulate my father and pursue public service. The precipitous termination of my Justice Department service compelled me to reevaluate career alternatives. With son John age one, and Linda in her first year at law school, I could not for long "lick my wounds" from the Saturday Night Massacre. I began a somewhat desultory search for law firm employment. One day, when I was visiting him in McLean, Virginia, Richardson responded to a call from Dan Gribbon, Chairman of Covington & Burling's Management Committee. Gribbon had been pursuing Elliot to join Covington as a partner. (They had the common bond of having both clerked for Court of Appeals Judge Learned Hand.) Richardson had decided to decline Covington's offer, but he spontaneously told Gribbon that the firm should hire me. I was invited to interview and found myself greatly more drawn to Covington than to other firms with which I had spoken. On February 1, 1974, I began an association with Covington & Burling, which was to last the balance of my professional career but for one more stint of public service.

At the time I began work at Covington, I knew that the firm had provided my father tax and business counsel. I was not aware that it had worked for John Thomas Smith as Tax Counsel to General Motors. Nor was I aware of the firm's long-time role as counsel to DuPont Corporation, including representation of DuPont in momentous antitrust litigation requiring it to divest its controlling share of GM gained in the early days of GM's existence.

Although employment as an associate at Covington & Burling did not seem as momentous as sitting at the elbow of Elliot Richardson in three Cabinet posts, the work was demanding, and the intellectual caliber of my colleagues and superiors was superb. Recognizing that at that point I was nearly seven years out of law school and had skipped the normal apprenticeship that law firm associates undergo to develop skills as litigators or tax lawyers, I sought assignment in fields that were relatively new, where the learning path would be less steep. I naturally gravitated toward environmental law—a somewhat new field that presented some of the same public policy trade-offs as I had thought about in government. I also worked with Alfred Moses, who had a widely diverse practice and highly colorful clients. Alfred Moses later served in the Carter White House and as U.S. Ambassador to Romania during the Clinton Administration. Last but not least, I did extensive pro-bono work with a legendary senior Partner Howard Westwood.[147]

At the time, Covington & Burling was Washington's largest and most prestigious law firm, with approximately 160 lawyers. It was an extraordinarily collegial place in which it was possible to become well acquainted with a large cross-section of one's colleagues and their spouses. Notwithstanding my exciting government experience, I was humbled by the qualifications of my colleagues and superiors, a significant number of whom had clerked on the U.S. Supreme Court or had been Rhodes Scholars. Long hours were expected, but represented no real hardship given the long days and weeks I had experienced working with Richardson. Travel was part of the job, and comfortable travel it was. In those days, even relatively junior associates traveled first class. I soon found myself making routine trips to Seattle on a Clean Water Act case with a young partner named Allan Topol. I accompanied Al Moses to New Orleans and to Dallas.

The firm had only a modest number of women lawyers and had not yet benefited from their civilizing influence. In June 1975, when Linda was in the hospital giving birth to our son Will, Al Moses called me in her hospital room to discuss a legal matter. Linda admired Al and was not immune to his charm. Nevertheless, even after she became a successful lawyer herself, Linda would recall Al's presumption in calling an associate lawyer at such a time. Today, in more civilized times, both female and male lawyers are accorded maternity/paternity leave of several weeks. In 1975, this concept did not exist.

In November 1975, when I was in Seattle working on a Clean Water Act matter, I received a call from Dick Darman, who informed me that President Ford had asked Richardson to return from London, where he was serving as U.S. Ambassador, to fill yet another Cabinet post, as Secretary of Commerce. Darman had agreed to accompany Richardson and to serve as Assistant Secretary for Policy. He wanted to know if I would be interested in becoming the Department's General Counsel.

I did not hesitate in signaling my interest in rejoining Richardson and Darman in the public sphere. At the same time, as I learned more about the offered post, I had occasion to doubt my qualifications. Technically, the General Counsel was the third-ranking official of the Commerce Department, preceded by only the Secretary and the Under Secretary. I would have supervisory responsibility for a staff of approximately 100 lawyers, covering areas such as export administration, science and technology, patent and trademark, economic development, maritime subsidies, and ocean, climate and fisheries issues. In addition, the staff of the General Counsel was responsible for advising the Secretary on a wide range of legislative issues affecting business and commerce. With only two years of actual practice experience, I had no illusions regarding my substantive qualifications. My principal qualification was quite simply my preexisting relationships with Richardson and Darman formed in previous cabinet offices and especially in the Department of Justice. Upon my ready acceptance, Richardson arranged for me to be nominated by President Ford. Routine confirmation by the Senate Commerce Committee followed, as did a congratulatory phone call from the Committee Chairman, Strom Thurman. On February 1, 1976, I formally began my new responsibilities.

When I told Howard Westwood at Covington & Burling that I was to take this post, he swore (as was his practice) and proceeded to advise me that "nothing interesting had happened at the Commerce Department since the days of Herbert Hoover." Westwood was correct in his perception that the

Commerce Department was not then a "front line" Cabinet Department. Nevertheless, Richardson, Darman, and I found some interesting issues with which to engage.

When we arrived at the Department, the Under Secretary was a smart, politically adept Texas lawyer named James A. Baker III. Several months after our arrival, Baker was tapped by President Ford to move to the White House and help direct the President's campaign for election in 1976, but it was a privilege to work with Baker for a short period of time. (Upon Baker's departure, as the third ranking officer of the Department, for a time I briefly served as Under Secretary, and, when Richardson embarked on a 10-day trip to the Far East, I briefly was Acting Secretary of Commerce—with the perquisites and responsibilities of a second-tier Cabinet Officer.)

Baker went on to prove to be, like Richardson, one of the truly extraordinary public servant/politicians of the last 50 years. He served as President Reagan's White House Chief of Staff and subsequently Reagan's Secretary of the Treasury. He then served as Secretary of State for President George H.W. Bush and then again as White House Chief of Staff. In November 2010, I was delighted to participate in a ceremony in which Baker was honored with the Elliot L. Richardson Prize for Excellence in Public Service.

In my first weeks at Commerce, I felt overwhelmed by the scope of my duties. Fortunately, my law school classmate and Covington colleague, Homer Moyer, signaled an interest in coming to the Department as the Deputy General Counsel. His Republican credentials were somewhat suspect, and Richardson and I had to tussle with the White House to obtain clearance for Moyer's appointment. Once on the job, he proved invaluable. Moyer managed to stay on at the Commerce Department after Carter's election and subsequently enjoyed large prominence in private practice and as a cofounder of an important effort by U.S. lawyers to help newly independent Eastern European nations adapt to the rule of law in the 1990s.

In the spring of 1976, business representatives approached the White House and urged the Ford Administration to undertake a searching review of the adverse economic effects of product liability litigation. In such litigation, manufacturers are sued for alleged injuries caused by their products, often by large "classes" of plaintiffs organized by lawyers retained on a contingent-fee basis. It fell my lot to chair an interagency committee to study the problem and to propose federal legislation, if appropriate. My instinct then, as it remains now, is that product liability, in our federal system, is a topic appropriately left to the laws and courts of individual states, even if this is not the most efficient way to proceed. I soon divested myself of practical responsibility in this topic area when a well-regarded law professor, Victor Schwartz, wrote to Secretary Richardson volunteering his services. I interviewed Schwartz, and Richardson and I promptly hired him. More than three decades later he remains one of Washington's principal experts on this topic, which has yet to become the subject of federal legislation. After several years at the Commerce Department, he migrated into private practice and has done well indeed. (Schwartz is a talented and very funny public speaker. He would often describe the challenges of obtaining completed staff work in the "bowels" of the Commerce Department. Once when he chastised a career civil servant for delay by stating, "J.T. Smith is waiting for this memorandum," the subordinate responded, "Who the f— is J.T. Smith?")

An issue of greater political moment emerged from the imposition of an economic boycott on Israel by Arab countries. Richardson found the Arab practices to be abhorrent and also saw practical advantage to President Ford, in a national election year, if he could fashion sensible legislation in response to the Arab boycott. This boycott was especially pernicious, in that it didn't simply involve refusal by Arab countries to allow direct trade by their nationals with Israel. Rather it involved a "secondary boycott" whereby Arab countries would refuse to do business with foreign companies that had any economic relations with Israel—a so-called blacklist. At a time of growing reliance by the United States and its allies on petroleum supplies from Arab nations, the matter was both sensitive and urgent.

We devised amendments to export control legislation that would require American companies receiving requests to participate in this boycott to report the requests, as well as their proposed responses, to the Commerce Department. The State Department under Secretary Kissinger strenuously opposed any such legislative initiative, arguing that it would be offensive to important leaders in Saudi Arabia. The result was an impasse at the White House, and the Administration did not advance such legislation. An argument can be made that, had it done so, it might have influenced important votes at the margin in states like New York and, in so doing, brought about a different electoral outcome in 1976, when Jimmy Carter narrowly defeated Ford. In any event, the new Carter Administration, with the involvement of my former colleague, Al Moses, then serving on the White House staff, promptly achieved adoption of legislation along the lines the Richardson Commerce Department had proposed.

The Department of Commerce played a broad advocacy role in regard to federal legislation and regulations affecting business interests. One of my responsibilities as General Counsel was to execute letters responding to the Office of Management and Budget, which would routinely seek departmental views as to whether the President should sign particular pieces of legislation. Although I have no memory of the event, I apparently signed a letter stating that the Department of Commerce had no objection to the proposed Resource Conservation and Recovery Act (RCRA), a set of amendments to the Solid Waste Disposal Act. This 1976 enactment provided the legal framework for an extensive set of federal regulations adopted in the 1980s to govern the management and clean-up of hazardous wastes. This area of environmental regulation would become one in which I would obtain a deep specialization after returning to the private practice of law.

My single largest involvement during my year as General Counsel was with respect to "questionable payments" by U.S. corporations in international commerce. In the mid-70s, it became apparent that international corporations were bribing, and sometimes being extorted by, foreign officials as the price of obtaining contracts or other foreign business access. The White House asked Richardson, as Secretary of Commerce, to conduct a "cabinet level" review of the situation and to propose, as appropriate, remedial law or regulations. Richardson asked Darman and me to carry out this mission. We met tirelessly with representatives of other government departments, including the Department of State, the Securities Exchange Commission, and the Department of Justice. We learned that U.S. law already carried potential consequence for companies making such payments. Publicly traded companies were under increased pressure to disclose such payments in financial statements made to the SEC. Moreover, they had to be lawfully accounted for in tax filings. We also learned that developed world competitors of U.S. companies were not under any legal constraint in making such corrupt payments. In some countries such payments were encouraged and rewarded with tax deductions.

Richardson was determined to propose a disclosure requirement whereby all U.S. companies making such payments would have to do so in "sunlight," with the payments being fully disclosed to their shareholders, the U.S. government, and the broader public. For this purpose, we recommended a reporting regime, analogous to that which we were seeking with respect to Arab boycott compliance requests. We argued against a set of criminal penalties for such corrupt payments, reasoning that jurisdictional and other barriers would make such penalties difficult and uneven of enforcement. The SEC opposed the effort, reasoning that its existing disclosure requirements were adequate. The State Department opposed, worrying about abrasion in our relations with other countries. And, again, the White House was unwilling to proceed with a controversial initiative in an election year. The Carter campaign made the matter a political issue and, upon election, promptly sought and enacted legislation—the Foreign Corrupt Practices Act (FCPA)—prescribing criminal penalties for a wide range of corrupt payments in international commerce.

More than three decades later, other developed nations are increasingly coming around to the U.S. point of view. Moreover, under the FCPA, the Justice Department has brought an increasing number of investigations and prosecutions of U.S. companies, as well as foreign corporations with shares publicly traded in the United States.[148]

It will always be difficult for the United States to find the right balance between morality and pragmatism as it and its businesses operate in the world. At the time Darman and I were working on this issue, we were conscious that corruption was a widespread facet of dealings between businesses and government at home in the United States—especially at the state level. We had in mind the rather recent example of a corrupt governor of Maryland, who became Vice President and eventually had to resign.

We encountered a "real case" of corrupt payments securing a valuable commercial franchise, when the Department was called upon to provide financial subsidies for the construction of liquefied natural gas (LNG) tankers at a General Dynamics Shipyard in Quincy, Massachusetts. In this case the corrupt payments had been made by a British oil company to certain officials in Indonesia, and not by a U.S. concern. The tankers were to be used to carry LNG from Indonesia to Japan. However, there was an obvious tension between our policy prescriptions designed to limit corrupt payments in international commerce, on the one hand, and the Department's desire to subsidize employment and an important new technology at a major U.S. shipyard. The matter was still pending after Carter's election, and before his inauguration. Representatives of the Carter transition received a full briefing and decided to leave the matter to Richardson's discretion. In the final week of his tenure as Secretary of Commerce in January 1977, Richardson approved the subsidies. For his troubles, he was excoriated by the *New York Times*. However, he never regretted his decision.

When Richardson unsuccessfully sought the Republication nomination for Senate in Massachusetts in 1984 the matter was brought up by his primary opponent, a conservative businessman named Ray Shamey. At

Elliot's request, I prepared a memorandum detailing the justification for his decision, and this memorandum put the matter to rest. In any event, Richardson did not receive the nomination, and Shamey was trounced by my Yale and Fence Club colleague, John Kerry.

As the Ford Administration wound down, I received expressions of interest from a handful of law firms, willing to make me a partner. (One, unseemly offer came from a prestigious firm with a strong vested interest in the pending LNG subsidy issue. I turned down this offer summarily and dictated a memo to the file regarding this development. To that firm's embarrassment, this memo was unearthed in subsequent litigation regarding the subsidy matter.) Covington & Burling indicated their interest in my return, but for continued service as an associate with assurance of relatively prompt consideration for promotion to partner. Before I could make a decision, immediately after Carter's inauguration, new Secretary of State Cyrus Vance, asked Richardson to take over the chairmanship of the U.S. delegation to an ongoing UN-sponsored Conference on Law of the Sea, and Richardson invited Darman and me to join him as deputies.

Law of the Sea

As the world's greatest maritime power and largest economy, the United States has a vital interest in the legal regime for the oceans. In the late 1960s, and early 1970s, developing countries in Latin America and elsewhere had begun asserting national sovereignty over areas of the ocean beyond the traditionally recognized "three-mile limit." Their purpose was to secure exclusive right to fisheries and potentially other resources for their nationals. In so doing, these developing countries threatened traditional rights of freedom of navigation long enjoyed by maritime powers, such as the United States. Additionally, in the 1960s, it became apparent that there were large mineral resources, in the form of copper-containing manganese nodules, on the deep ocean floor well beyond claims of national jurisdiction. Idealistic internationalists declared these mineral resources to be the "Common Heritage of Mankind." The third UN Law of the Sea Conference (UNCLOS) thus sought a grand bargain under which the developed country maritime powers with the resources and technology to access these deep seabed minerals would agree to a regime that would allow developing countries to obtain part of the economic benefit of such mining. In return, it was hoped that developing countries would agree to limit their seaward claims of sovereignty.

At the time, economists predicted that the world would have sufficient economic need for these seabed minerals to justify the extraordinary costs of deep seabed mining by the mid to late 1980s. Fashioning an appropriate regime for exploitation of these resources therefore took on a sense of urgency. (Discovery of new, more readily accessible land-based minerals has belied this prediction. Also, new oceanic mineral resources have been discovered in a different form, polymetallic sulfides, closer to coasts. Accordingly, deep seabed minerals have remained unexploited, although, in 2011, China indicated that it planned to proceed to explore feasibility of deep ocean mining.)

The Conference also had to deal with other significant issues, including setting standards for resolution of disputes about maritime boundaries, a regime for access to resources on nations' continental shelves, regulation of ocean access for scientific research, improved standards to prevent ocean pollution from navigational and other activities, and regularization of practices for marine fisheries beyond limits of national jurisdiction. In most of these matters, the developing countries formed their strategy as part of the "Group of Seventy-Seven."[149] Certain major maritime powers coordinated with each other in a "Group of Five" consisting of the United States, Russia, Japan, England, and France—all countries with large commercial and military interests in freedom of the seas.

Richardson charged Darman and me with lead responsibility for negotiations regarding the regime for access to deep seabed minerals, deemed at the time to be the chief obstacle to a comprehensive treaty. After a few weeks at the Department of State familiarizing ourselves with the negotiating record, we set out on a series of trips to try to develop support for the U.S. position among other participants in the Conference. The broad outlines of the U.S. position, announced by the delegation at the previous session of the conference and endorsed by Secretary of State Kissinger, was to favor a "parallel system." Each site on the ocean floor determined to contain recoverable quantities of minerals would be cut in half. One-half would be available for exploitation by mining companies from developed countries. The other half was to be available for exploitation by developing countries. Many issues remained regarding how developing countries would achieve access to the necessary deep-sea mining technology, what entity would set rules and regulations for the conduct of mining, how the two halves would be allocated between developing country representatives and developed country mining companies, and so forth. The ensuing negotiations have been deftly chronicled elsewhere,[150] and any further discussions here would overburden this short memoir.

In February 1977, Darman and I accompanied Richardson to a "preparatory session" conducted in Geneva, Switzerland. There we met some of our negotiating counterparts and received exposure to the culture and method of multinational negotiation. After two weeks in Geneva, we set forth in a series of trips on our own. First, we visited Africa, stopping in Senegal, Cameroon, Nigeria, Kenya, and Egypt. Then we traveled to Columbia, Peru, Brazil, and Venezuela. Finally, we visited Norway, Germany, Russia, and England. These trips were both exhausting and invigorating, marred only by the fact that during long plane rides, Darman consistently slaughtered me in games of gin rummy. In each country we would meet with senior representatives of foreign ministries, often the legal adviser, and in the case of Brazil, the actual Minister of Foreign Affairs. In Cameroon we met with Paul Engo, a charismatic international diplomat who served as chairman of the Committee of the Law of the Sea Conference, tasked with development of the regime for seabed mining.

In June and July 1977, the full Conference (with delegations from 150 nations) met at the UN in New York City. Darman and I shared an apartment a short walk from the UN and commuted home to our families on weekends. Progress was excruciatingly slow, involving negotiation among countries and blocs with widely heterogeneous interests. Memorably, during the New York session, there was a widespread power outage on the East Coast. In our travels in Africa and South America, Darman and I had experienced outages of water and electricity. Ironically, we found ourselves without water or electricity in New York City—cause for humility, as well as a terrific candlelit party in the offices of the U.S. delegation. Subsequent looting in New York City during the blackout provided a useful reminder that the greatest power of the "First World," was in other respects not that far removed from the "Third."

At the session's end, our position suffered a serious setback. Chairman Engo took it upon himself to add language to a draft negotiating text that had not been discussed openly. The language appeared to compel technology transfer from wealthy countries to poor countries for seabed mining purposes and in other ways contravened the negotiating position and expectations of the United States and its allies. Engo's high-handed behavior, as much as the substance of this text, revealed that a long road lay ahead for the United States before a politically acceptable treaty could be achieved. Consequently, both Darman and I decided to resign our State Department posts. As great was the privilege of working with and for Elliot Richardson, we were both approaching our mid-30s and knew it was time to pursue independent careers.

As I prepared to leave the State Department I was flattered when the Legal Adviser, Herb Hansell, asked whether I would be willing to become his principal deputy. I doubted that I had the substantive qualifications for this job, but the matter became moot when the White House advised that my Republican background would be an insurmountable obstacle to an appointment for this job. (Apparently, House Speaker Tip O'Neill had taken offense at appointment of Richardson, a prominent Massachusetts Republican, to head the Law of the Sea delegation.) I also was approached by Lloyd Cutler who invited me to work as his deputy on a special project he had undertaken to negotiate resolution of fisheries disputes between the United States and Canada. On reflection, I accepted an invitation to return to Covington & Burling—as an associate, with assurance of being considered for partnership relatively promptly. I was gratified to be elevated to partnership a year later.

In the following years, I kept up with developments in Law of the Sea, serving on the State Department's Law of the Sea Advisory Committee and, with Darman, preparing a series of analyses for the Law of the Sea Committee of the American Branch of International Law Association. In these contexts, and in an article I published in the *University of Virginia Journal of International Law*,[151] I expressed pessimism regarding the prospects for achievement of a global bargain including terms of access to seabed minerals that would be satisfactory to both the developed and the developing world.

Negotiations on the Convention continued until 1981. The Reagan Administration deemed the resulting seabed minerals regime unacceptable. Richardson and others, in informal international discussions extending over several years, subsequently achieved a package of amendments that overcame each of the objections made by the Reagan Administration. Consequently, in October 1994, the Clinton Administration sought the Senate's advice and consent to ratify the Law of the Sea Convention. The Congressional elections the following month led to Republican control of Congress. The new Chairman of Senate Foreign Relations, Jesse Helms, would not even hold a hearing on the matter. Richardson nonetheless continued to attempt to build political support for the Convention, but he died in 1999 without having persuaded the United States to ratify. Thirteen years later, notwithstanding the broad support by the Department of Defense, the Department of State, representatives of American industry, the White House, and the Senate Foreign Relations Committee, the United States continues to spite its own interest and withhold ratification of this important treaty. The only obstacle is the ill-informed objections of a handful of Republican Senators.

A "Special Report" prepared by the Council on Foreign Relations in 2009 summarizes how U.S. national interest should compel prompt ratification of the treaty. It cites a broad range of self-evident national security, economic, and environmental interest, including economic resource and environmental concerns in the Arctic Ocean, the need for a coherent response to piracy in the Indian Ocean, potential boundary and resource disputes in the South China Sea, and efficacious means to expand international efforts to counter nuclear proliferation. An additional concern emerged in 2011 when China appealed to the UN Seabed Authority for a license to begin potential exploration of deep seabed minerals. The United States lacks the "legal" means to pursue such minerals. In short, our nation's interest in the Law of the Sea Convention remains compelling.[152]

Our constitutional and legislative practice of allowing a handful of U.S. Senators to countermand cogent national interest is alarming in an increasingly interdependent world. This blocking action has implications beyond Law of the Sea. In recent years, the world has been trying to come to grips with the risks of global climate change. Efforts to craft an enforceable global regime addressing these risks have encountered some of the same political obstacles in the United States as the Law of the Sea Convention. In 1992, I published a short article pointing out the similarity of the two challenges and recommended against continued efforts to obtain a global bargain.[153] On mature reflection, two decades later and in the absence of any progress to address potential climate change, I regret the pessimistic caste of my 1992 article. The United States should lead a reinvigorated global effort on this front. But again, the political obstacles are daunting. As the comic strip character Pogo famously said, "we have met the enemy and he is us."

Although my father spent much of his professional career at the State Department, my nine months there did not allow me any overlap with him. He commenced his duties as Carter's Ambassador at Large for Nuclear Nonproliferation, just as I was leaving the Department in the fall of 1977. My very short State Department career was an indiscernibly pale reflection of his. If I had qualified politically for the Deputy Legal Adviser job, I might have had a real opportunity for professional collaboration with my father.

* * * * *

Reflection—A Digression on Family and Friends

The 1970s, in retrospect, were a golden decade. There was the first enthusiasm of true adulthood, marriage, and the arrival of young children. Linda and I additionally enjoyed an expanding and relatively glamorous social life with new and old friends—all taking place in the context of interesting governmental and political developments that are the lifeblood of Washington, D.C.

As already mentioned, Linda and I eloped in April 1970. Within a year, we bought a house in Georgetown on 34th Street and Reservoir Road. In my parents' absence at the SALT negotiations we made extensive use of Ratcliffe Manor. We also purchased a 27-foot sailboat, christened *Osprey* (a reflection, however modest, of the *Innisfail* or *Welkin*), and spent weekend afternoons picnic sailing on the Choptank River and the Chesapeake Bay. With the arrival of John, our first son, on October 22, 1972, our weekend sailing diminished, and I sold the *Osprey* in 1974. From September 1973 until May 1976, Linda was a full-time law student at George Washington. She and I were able to time our second son Will's arrival on June 20, 1975, so as not to interfere with the academic calendar. Even with two young children, because we could afford to employ a reliable "live-in" housekeeper, we were able to pursue an active social life with an expanding circle of friends with similar interests and outlook.

My Yale friend, Russell Byers, was a bachelor, who lived in a fine house with a swimming pool near the National Cathedral. He entertained generously and enjoyably. (His wide circle of friends included certain young White House aides such as Jeb Magruder who later became "famous" in Watergate.) As previously described, it was Russell who, in 1971, suggested that I interview for a job at the Department of Health, Education and Welfare. It was because of this invitation that I had the extraordinary opportunities that followed, working with Elliot Richardson. Russell dated a series of smart, attractive women. (He was divorced from Connie Mellon, whom he had married twice—the first time as a Yale undergraduate.) Eventually, he met and married a second wife, Laurada. In the winter of 1972, and again in 1974, Russell and I jointly chartered a sailboat in the British Virgin Islands, where we tasted the joys of large boat sailing and consumption of imprudent amounts of Mount Gay Rum.

Russell was an individual of great personal warmth and magnanimity. Although born of considerable wealth and educated at St. Paul's and Yale,

Russell spent his life in public service and in socially constructive journalism. He was a terrific father to two children and a generous and treasured friend. In the winter of 1999, he was tragically murdered in a convenience store robbery while protecting Laurada. His name lives on with both his son, Russell, and a thriving charter school in Philadelphia nurtured by Laurada and Russell's friends.

Other friends from this era who remain valued friends include Mallory and Diana Walker, John and Symmie Newhouse, and Dane Nichols. The Walkers joined Russell and us on our first sailing charter in the Caribbean. Symmie serves as our son Will's godmother. Memorably, to celebrate their 30th birthdays in the winter of 1972, Symmie and Diana jointly gave a "1942" themed costume party. As may often be the case in a gathering of 30-somethings in costume, the party took on a raucous and flirtatious aspect. It was punctuated by the appearance of Carter Brown, later head of the National Gallery of Art, meticulously attired as a Nazi officer. Though endowed with strong visual and aesthetic sense, Carter may not have thought hard enough about the lasting but unfortunate impression he would make.

Shortly after his election to Congress in November 1971, Linda and I were introduced by the Walkers to John Heinz and his wife Teresa. We became fast friends and benefited immensely from their hospitality in Washington and Pittsburgh. When he couldn't find a better game, Jack would challenge me to a tennis match. He was always the much better player. Teresa serves as Will's godmother. Jack, a moderate Republican and potential Presidential aspirant, was elected to the U.S. Senate in 1976 and served until his death at the age of 52 in a plane accident in the spring of 1991. Once again I lost a good and deeply admired friend, unfairly young.

Other good friends in the early 1970s included Preston and Betsy Brown. They entertained us frequently and warmly in their Wesley Heights house. Preston was slightly older than us and had a sophisticated background. His father was a famous author, John Mason Brown. His friends included Jay Rockefeller and the late *New York Times* journalist, R.W. ("Johnny") Apple. Preston and Betsy were the first of our friends whose marriage unraveled. After a number of years both ended up in long and happy marriages to others. In Betsy's case, the second spouse was none other than Johnny Apple.

Importantly, Preston introduced us to Charlie Peters, a West Virginia lawyer who had come to Washington in the Kennedy Administration and who had worked with Sarge Shriver at the Peace Corps. Charlie had started a terrific "small" journal, *The Washington Monthly*. With a relatively small list of subscribers, *The Washington Monthly* consistently published incisive, irreverent, and insightful articles regarding politics and policy. It ran on a shoestring. In 1971 Preston approached me and asked if I would be willing to invest in the *Monthly* as a way of helping Charlie Peters keep the wolf away from the door. I did so ($10,000, as I recall) and Charlie's gratitude extends to this day. Charlie, now in his 80s, remains a vigorous observer and writer and, overall, one of the truly exceptional individuals I have ever been privileged to know.

In November 1974, we moved to a larger house in Georgetown on 31st Street just south of the intersection of 31st and R street. This house, which dated to the 19th century, suffered from certain deferred maintenance. But it had fine space and a large backyard. John and Will both spent much of their childhood there; John until he was nearly 13 and Will until age of 10. The house provided easy access to Montrose Park. After a neighbor, Senator John Warner, married the late Elizabeth Taylor, the famous actress would lean out of her chauffeur-driven car and say "hello beautiful children" to John and Will en route to Montrose Park with their Guatemalan caretaker (a thrill to the latter, if not the boys).

With young children, it was appropriate to take protracted summer vacations. In the summer of 1975 we rented a house for two weeks in Southampton, Long Island. Beginning in 1979, we rented a house for the entire month of August in Martha's Vineyard. Additionally, in 1976, my parents offered to "sell" us a parcel of land on Ratcliffe Manor, conditioned upon our willingness to build a weekend home. I chose a six-acre field on Dixon Creek with a nice southwest exposure. Consistent with the salary of a law firm associate and public servant we erected a prefabricated "Yankee Barn," which, given its location on Ratcliffe Manor, I dubbed "To the Manor Barn." Construction was finished at the end of May 1977, while I was involved in the Law of the Sea negotiations. In the intervening years, the original prefab has been replaced by a larger and more complex structure. Now I have the temporally bittersweet satisfaction of looking at 50-foot trees that I had planted as saplings. In the late 1970s, we enjoyed weekend visits by Russell and Laurada Byers, Mallory and Diana Walker, Jack and Teresa Heinz, as well as Congressman and later Senator Tim Wirth and his wife, Wren. Mallory initiated me to the art of catching bluefish on the Chesapeake Bay. Jack Heinz proved a threat to the dove and Canada goose population of Talbot County, and continued my schooling on the tennis court. Often, the weekend would include an old-fashioned "Sunday lunch" at Ratcliffe Manor with my parents and whomever else might be visiting.

In these times, we would frequently dine with a bachelor friend, Philip Nuttle. He had been a friend for more than 20 years, dating back to sailing class in the mid-1950s. An English major at Princeton and a local lawyer, he delighted in language and literature and, even expressed an appreciation for some of my bad puns. (Phil was a short man, 5 feet, 4 inches. He especially enjoyed a neologism that I created to describe a grumpy little man as a "curmidgeon.") He helped deepen my appreciation for life on the Eastern Shore. He was a keen tennis player, and, in a lifetime I played more sets of tennis with him than with any other man. He served as one of Will's godfathers. He did not marry until he was 40, and it was at his wedding that I first met Mary Tydings, a school friend of Phil's wife Nancy. Phil proved ill-suited to marriage. His one son, Philip Nuttle III is my godson. Phil was a smoker, and this bad habit took its toll. He died from a combination of leukemia and congestive heart failure in December 1996, still in his mid-50s.

I already have had occasion to mention Dick Darman. Our professional cooperation, beginning at HEW in 1972 and extending through the Law of the Sea negotiations up until autumn of 1977, led us to close collaboration on a number of public policy projects, as well as global travel. With our wives we saw each other socially, in addition to our professional endeavors. Dick's wife Kath is an attractive, scholarly woman of great intellectual sophistication. In the mid-1970s we took two vacation trips together—one to St. Maarten in the Caribbean and another to Cabo San Lucas on the Pacific Coast of Mexico. Dick, along with Phil Nuttle, became Will's godfather. Dick and Kath made Linda and me godparents to their first son, Will, and I am godfather also to Dick's second son, Jonathan.

Will Darman's christening celebration in 1977 was a revelation. Linda and I traveled to Martha's Vineyard for the event. After a mid-day baptism in the Episcopalian Church, we gathered at Kath Darman's mother's house for a reception. When the caterer was delayed, the Martha's Vineyard family and friends of the Darmans proceeded to remove all clothes and frolic nude in Vineyard Sound. The godparents, including not only Linda and me but Elliot Richardson as well, did not join in this immersion part of the proceedings. But the event did make quite an impression on me and may have influenced a decision in later years to spend summer vacations in Martha's Vineyard so as to participate in this admirably liberal environment. (I gather that nude bathing was the norm in 19th-century America—although probably not in its co-ed variation.)

Dick was a prodigiously smart man. When not in government, he taught a course in public policy at the Kennedy School of Government at

Harvard where he was a very popular professor. Dick was not always popular, however, with his coworkers in government. He could be prickly and quite tough as a bureaucratic operator. Some have described Dick as "not suffering fools gladly." A more accurate description would be that he did not suffer them at all. He went on to serve as Deputy White House Chief of Staff in the first Reagan Administration and then Deputy Secretary of the Treasury and a principal architect of tax reform in the second. Subsequently he served as the Director of the Office of Management and Budget (a Cabinet Office) in the George H.W. Bush Administration. Later he was a Managing Director of the successful private equity firm, the Carlyle Group; Chairman of the Board of AES, a global power generating firm; President of the Board of the American History Museum; a director of the Howard Hughes Medical Institute and of various mutual funds. He was an accomplished amateur painter, bibliophile, and a dedicated parent. He wrote a memoir, *Who's in Control*,[154] regarding his service in the Reagan and Bush Administrations, which demythologizes Republican tax policy. In a life full of encounters with exceptional people, Dick Darman stands out for me as having no equal.

Given his disproportionately high intellect and occasionally prickly demeanor, it is remarkable that Dick consistently nourished and respected our friendship. Possibly, he did so because I tolerated his idiosyncrasies better than others. Even when our political allegiances diverged, as they did with Reagan's election in 1980, we remained personally aligned and attuned to the degree that I have experienced with no other friend. Dick and I began government service as moderate Republicans. I believed in the application of sensible federal programs. I balked at Reagan's avowal that government was the "problem and not the solution." Also, I shared my father's deep concern about Reagan's initial hostility to nuclear arms restraints. Dick did not shy away from the opportunities presented him for productive government service and proudly withstood the suspicions and even outrage of right-wing purists. But our views on larger public policy issues remained the same. In 2008, had he lived, I believe Dick might well have voted for Obama.

In Book VIII of his *Nicomachean Ethics*, Aristotle discourses on the subject of friendship. He observes that friendships can fall into three overlapping categories. The first is friendship based upon mutual usefulness in which the bond is measured in terms of the practical benefits that the friends offer each other. In an era when much discussion is given the topic of "networking," this form of friendship is readily understood. The second form of friendship is one based upon the pleasure that individuals give each other. We may enjoy friendship with a beautiful woman given her beauty, and, she in return may enjoy a friend's company because of his wit or sophistication. Two men may enjoy a friendship based upon mutual enjoyment of hunting or playing golf or tennis. But for Aristotle, the highest form of friendship is based upon the meshing of character based upon the intrinsic goodness and virtue of two individuals. Aristotle comments that such friendships are rare. They require a nurture of time and familiarity and the winning of full confidence. Though I am reluctant readily to claim the kind of "virtue" that appears a prerequisite to Aristotle's ideal of the highest form of friendship, I like to indulge the illusion that my friendship with Dick approached this standard.

In November 2007, Dick was suddenly stricken by leukemia. He entered Georgetown Hospital, never to emerge before his death in January 2008. He instructed that I be asked to serve as one of three eulogists at his funeral. In my remarks I called Dick, "the friend of a lifetime," referring to both the strength and duration of our ties. I adverted to his somewhat controlling character and speculated about "the union of Dick's great mind and spirit with whatever awaits us all beyond," stating that "I expect that what is often called a 'disorderly universe' may soon exhibit signs of greater order." Alas, my expectation has yet to be realized.

Another eulogist, James Baker, generously stated that he believed that in large measure his success as White House Chief of Staff and Cabinet Officer was owed to Dick Darman. In addition to the vast benefits received from my family, my understanding and appreciation of the world has been most enhanced by my friendship with Dick.

15

The 1980s—A Fraught Decade

The 1980s proved a turbulent decade for my father and his family. Although his public service was at an end, my father remained deeply engaged in public advocacy with respect to nuclear weapons and had occasion to fight against dismantling by the Reagan Administration of the ABM Treaty that had been the centerpiece of the SALT negotiations that he had led. During this period my father co-authored important articles on nuclear policy that appeared in *Foreign Affairs*, served as the Chairman of the Arms Control Association and on the Board of the Brookings Institution. He also served as a Director of Panhandle Eastern Corporation and as a Limited Partner in the Baltimore investment firm, Alex Brown and Company. Although he turned 70 in 1984, he continued to go to work each day at the international consulting firm, Consultants Group International, which he had founded with his friend Henry Owen and others in 1981.

On the family front there were two divorces, three marriages, my mother's death from cancer in 1987, coronary bypass surgery for my father coinciding with his 75th birthday in 1989, as well as a cancer diagnosis for my father in 1988.

Arms Control Issues in the 1980s

By virtue of his Chairmanship of the Arms Control Association, as well as his reputation and friendships from long involvement in arms control, my father found himself at the center of major policy debates during the 1980s. As the decade began, the United States' relations with the Soviet Union had soured. The political backlash in the United States against Nixon and Ford era efforts at nuclear arms control as part of a policy of "détente" spearheaded by Kissinger, was part of the problem. The Soviet invasion of Afghanistan in 1979 seriously compounded the problem. The election of Ronald Reagan, a professed anti-communist hardliner, was alarming to my father and other members of the arms control community.

Reagan relatively promptly confirmed their worst fears. He was caught joking near an open microphone saying that he was going to launch a nuclear strike in "20 minutes." He also made a remark that revealed that he didn't understand that nuclear missiles, once launched, could not be recalled. Reagan's lamentable Secretary of State, Alexander Haig, publicly mused on the possibility that the United States would detonate a nuclear warhead as a demonstration to deter the Soviet Union from a prospective invasion of Western Europe. The new Administration evidenced a determination to spend substantial sums on a new generation of intercontinental ballistic missiles. Then, in 1983, with no warning to the public, or for that matter, to his national security bureaucracy, President Reagan announced his support for pursuit of a large scale "Strategic Defense Initiative" (promptly dubbed "Star Wars"). Pursuit of this initiative could contravene the terms of the ABM Treaty that my father and others viewed as the prerequisite to limiting the race to develop further offensive nuclear weapons and delivery systems.[155]

The Gang of Four

Dad's old friend Sarge Shriver shared the alarm felt by my father and others at the direction of Reagan's national security policy. Beginning in October 1981, Shriver convened a series of small, working dinners at his house to foster discussion of how to counter the untoward thrust of Reagan Administration policy. The first dinner included former Secretary of Defense Robert McNamara, George Kennan, former CIA Director William Colby, Dad, and Father Bryan Hehir, the luminously intelligent Director of Policy for the National Conference of Catholic Bishops.[156] The group decided to advance the proposition that the United States should foreswear "first use" of nuclear weapons.

The United States had for three decades extended a "nuclear umbrella" over Europe, promising to use such weapons if necessary to counter a Soviet conventional attack. A declaration by the United States of a policy of "no first use" was thus a radical shift, with broad implications for alliance relations and allocation of defense resources. Whatever the presumed deterrent value of our threat to use nuclear weapons, carrying out this threat potentially presaged global catastrophe. (Eight years earlier, the Army Chief of Staff, Creighton Abrams, had made this same point in my presence.) Shriver and the attendees at this 1981 dinner enlisted, in addition, McGeorge Bundy, former National Security Advisor under Kennedy and Johnson. The group agreed on three propositions: First, any use of nuclear weapons would incur an unacceptable risk of escalation to a disastrous nuclear war; second, while the United States should retain the option of a nuclear response to a nuclear attack, it should foreswear first use in any conflict; and third, adopting a policy of no first use would require enhancing American conventional non-nuclear, military capacities.

As a result of these discussions, and at the continued urging of Shriver, McNamara, Kennan, Bundy, and my father co-authored an article advocating the policy of "no first-use."[157] The article attracted broad attention. It could not be dismissed as the simple ranting of a group of peaceniks, for, as stated by the *New York Times*, the article had been written by four men who "had helped shape America's defense strategy for a generation."[158] The four authors were subsequently designated "peace laureates" by the Einstein Foundation for World Peace.

This article by the "Gang of Four" had significant impact on the nuclear policy debate ongoing in the United States, and there followed the development of a "pastoral letter" on nuclear policy by the National Conference of Catholic Bishops. Bryan Hehir was a principal author. The Bishops released this letter in draft in October 1983. It included the recommendation of the "Gang of Four" that the Administration renounce any first-use of nuclear weapons. My father joined Shriver in a letter to the Editor of *The Washington Post* strongly backing the effort of the Catholic Bishops and rebutting the argument, advanced by some, that the Catholic Church had no business meddling in national security policy. The Bishops formally adopted a final version of this letter on May 2, 1984. George Kennan characterized the letter as the "most profound and searching inquiry yet conducted . . . into the relations of nuclear weaponry . . . to moral philosophy, to politics, and to the conscience of the national state."[159]

While endorsing a policy of no first-use, the Bishops approved a declaration of willingness of the United States to use nuclear weapons under tightly limited conditions, including no deliberate targeting of civilian populations and commitment by the United States and the Soviet Union to continue good-faith efforts to reduce nuclear weapon systems. Although Dad welcomed and supported the initiative of Father Hehir and the Catholic Bishops, he remained troubled by the prospect of the use of nuclear weapons in any context. In his "final reflections" shortly before he died, Dad noted:

> In trying to resolve the moral conundrum posed by maintenance of a nuclear deterrent by prescribing criteria for use of nuclear weapons, the Bishops implied that limited use of such weapons for purely military purposes could be acceptable. I respectfully disagree.[160]

Star Wars and the ABM Treaty

In the negotiation of the ABM Treaty during SALT I, there had been in-depth consideration whether the Treaty should bar development of systems based only on current technology, or whether its restrictions should extend also to "exotics," that is, systems based upon new technologies such as lasers and space-based platforms. The United States wanted to preserve the right to do research into "exotics." Such research would maintain our ability to understand any work done by the Soviet Union, and to explore future avenues of defense. It was agreed that such research as could be conducted in laboratories or otherwise beyond discernment by "national technical means" of verification such as satellites, would not be barred by the Treaty. However, development and engineering activities, such as those involving testing that could be detected by satellite, would be barred.

President Reagan's sudden announcement of a "Strategic Defense Initiative"(SDI) in March 1983, was made either in ignorance or willful disregard of this binding legal restraint—assuming the President intended more than basic research into defensive systems based upon new physical principles.

It fell to members of the Reagan Administration to somehow square the circle to legally justify SDI. Under the ABM Treaty either party could withdraw after giving six-months' notice. Also, nothing would bar an attempt by the United States to renegotiate the Treaty. However, the Administration did not choose either of these approaches. Instead, in October 2005, National Security Advisor Robert "Bud" McFarlane (one of the original actors in the 1983 announcement of SDI) pronounced to the amazement of many, including members of the Administration, that the United States was adopting a "new interpretation" of the ABM Treaty that allowed testing and development of defensive systems based on "exotic" technologies.

McFarlane's announcement scandalized the foreign policy community as well as key members of the Senate. Dad held a news conference to object to the Administration's reinterpretation. He was not alone. Senator Sam Nunn immediately expressed strong concern, as did President Reagan's close ally, Margaret Thatcher of Great Britain.[161] Even Secretary of State, George Shultz, was appalled by McFarlane's statement.[162] As an immediate result of the public and political reaction to McFarlane's new and "broad" interpretation of the ABM Treaty, the Administration announced that although it believed the broad interpretation "fully justified," it would continue to honor the prior "restrictive interpretation" of the Treaty in conduct of its SDI program.

The story of how the Reagan Administration reached its new interpretation of the ABM Treaty is complex, and its details are beyond the scope of this short memoir. Central to the story are several "defense intellectuals" such as Richard Perle and Fred Iklé, long-time hardliners in dealing with the Soviet Union. They enlisted the support of a new State Department Legal Adviser, former federal district judge, Abraham Sofaer, and a young Defense Department lawyer, Philip Kunsberg, neither of whom had any prior experience with interpretation of the ABM Treaty or background knowledge in its negotiation and interpretation and application. To my father's profound disappointment, one of the "players" in the reinterpretation was his friend and former delegation member, Paul Nitze, who had been the principal negotiator of the ABM Treaty and was on record (in a letter to the Senate) affirming the traditional interpretation.

My father, together with his SALT Legal Adviser, John Rhinelander, testified before the House Committee on Foreign Affairs in October 1985 and cooperated with an in-depth study spearheaded by Sam Nunn of the Senate Armed Services Committee. Their concern was not only for preserving the integrity of the United States with respect to its existing treaty obligations, but also with respect to the potential, practical impact of the Reagan Administration's posturer on future arms control. If the United States could reinterpret its prior commitments at will, the Soviet Union would have little incentive to enter new agreements. Moreover, investment in defensive technology had always been shown to give added impetus to buildup of offensive weapons systems, which are inevitably more cost effective than defensive ones.

Initially, Reagan's tight embrace of SDI proved an obstacle to future arms control, even when an exceptional new Soviet leader, Mikhail Gorbachev, showed strong interest in pursuing arms control. Eventually, contrary to my father's expectations, the Reagan Administration and the Soviet Union reached agreement on very substantial arms reductions. They did so, however, only after Gorbachev became persuaded not to allow the United States to use SDI as a bargaining lever. According to Frances Fitzgerald, the most influential Soviet citizen in persuading Gorbachev not to worry about SDI, was Andrei Sakharov, father of the Russian hydrogen bomb. Gorbachev, as part of his liberalization policies had freed Sakharov from internal exile in December 1986. In the following year, with the help of Roald Sagdeev, Director of the Soviet Institute for Space Research, Sakharov managed to dispel Soviet fears of SDI.[163] A few years later Sagdeev married the granddaughter of President Eisenhower, Susan Eisenhower. In the early 1990s, before my father's death, Susan and Roald would visit Ratcliffe Manor on weekends.

There is a fitting symmetry to the story as laid out by Fitzgerald. Edmund Teller, a principal advocate and scientific contributor for the U.S. hydrogen bomb, was among those who influenced Reagan's decision to announce a commitment to strategic defense. A few years later, it was Teller's Russian counterpart, Andrei Sakharov, who helped persuade Gorbachev not to permit SDI to be an obstacle to arms control agreements. There are many who believe that Reagan's advancement of SDI provided no only leverage for meaningful arms control, but also the catalyst for the demise of the Soviet Union, once its leadership realized that it could no longer compete economically with the United States. Others give principal credit to years of economic dysfunction and the fortunate emergence of Gorbachev as leader of the Soviet Union. Certainly, my father would fall in the latter camp, as do I. But matters of this historical complexity can only be determined from a longer perspective. In the United States we tend toward quick judgment and strongly held opinions based upon those judgments. Others prefer a longer perspective. An often cited anecdote about Chinese Communist leader Chou En Lai is instructive. Asked by French intellectual Andre Malraux in the 1950s what he thought of the French Revolution of 1789, Chou responded "It is too early to tell."

In December 2001, the George W. Bush Administration, citing perceived risk of attack by rogue nations such as North Korea or by terrorists armed with weapons of mass destruction, formally withdrew from the ABM Treaty. It remains a mystery how large-scale investment in strategic missile defense addresses the latter threat. By this time the Soviet Union no longer existed and the prospect of investment in more offensive nuclear weapons by Russia and the United States had abated. The United States continues to pursue missile defense systems, but Reagan's dream of rendering nuclear weapons obsolete has not been realized.

* * * * *

Reflection—A Digression on My Mother

In the fall of 1985 as my father was waging combat against the "broad" interpretation of the ABM Treaty, my mother learned that she faced a more personal battle—against stomach cancer. My mother had been diagnosed with breast cancer in 1969 and had undergone a radical mastectomy, the normal response to this disease at Johns Hopkins at the time. She had made a courageous recovery from this severe surgery and lived in relatively good health for the ensuing decade and a half. The return of cancer to my 73-year-old mother was a blow to her, my father, and her children. Her diagnosis presaged a premature end to a fervent and exemplary marriage.

Although my mother had a college degree and had been a successful professional, upon marriage to my father she dedicated herself as a wife and mother. She played an integral role in encouraging my father not to succumb to the leisure opportunities that inherited wealth allowed him, but rather to pursue a career of productive public service. Her management of children and three homes, skills as a hostess and unselfish companionship to my father were vital elements in his admirable career.

In preparing these reflections, I have realized that my father did not say much about his own mother. She too was a very bright woman and a professional (school teacher) before marrying my grandfather. She too died much too young—in her 60s. To prevent a similar gap in the record, I here set down in outline form a profile of my mother.

She was born on January 1, 1912, in St. Louis, Missouri. (She chose to celebrate her birthday one day earlier, December 31, and by retaining the 1912 birth year managed to render herself a year younger.) She attended a Christian Science day school, Principia. At summer camp, one of her counselors was future Democratic Statesman, Clark Clifford. She attended Emma Willard, a girls' boarding school in New York State, until expulsion for smoking. Later, she was admitted to Smith College and graduated in 1933. She moved to depression era New York City, where she worked first at *Time Magazine* and subsequently at the department store, Lord and Taylor. There she rose to be Director of Publicity. After a blind date with my father in the fall of 1940, they fell in love and were married in August 1941. We children followed: Sheila in July 1942, I in October 1943, Gerry in September 1946, and, last but by no means least in his mother's eyes, Hugh Maguire in May 1954.

Although always blessed with household help, including governesses charged with the messier aspects of childcare, mother was a concerned and highly supportive parent. She wished the world for her children. Among her aspirations for me that I did not fulfill were an appointment to the Naval Academy, a Rhodes scholarship, and presence as the first man on the moon.

A bright woman, mother emphasized reading. (Until recently I have assumed that whatever success I have enjoyed academically and professionally was owed to an endowment of grey matter inherited from my brilliant Smith grandfather and father. Recent research indicates that the best predictor of a child's IQ is the IQ of his or her mother.)[164] I recall her reading out loud to me when as a schoolchild I was occasionally felled by flu or other ailments. She made reading recommendations, which, as I now recall, reflected a strongly patriotic and "capitalist" outlook. The first was a famous 19th century short story, "The Man without a Country," about an individual condemned to spend the balance of his life aboard a ship and denied any information about the United States, after he criticized the United States during a trial for treason. The latter were Ayn Rand's novels *Atlas Shrugged* and the *Fountainhead*. I read these at age 14 and was not "infected" by their message of ruthless individualism and Darwinian capitalism, although mother, possibly due to respect for her father, may have intended me to take this message.

My father was happy to delegate "disciplinary" control of his four children to mother. I cannot recall a single chastisement directly from him. My mother could, however, convey his viewpoint. Once, at the age of 18, I arrived home after sunrise, somewhat disheveled, just as my father was leaving for work. Though the answer was self-evident, he simply asked "Are you just getting home?" A few hours later, my mother woke me up with the message, "Your father is very disappointed in you."

As with many others of her background and generation, mother smoked and drank rather freely. The smoking (unfiltered Chesterfields) ended with her breast cancer diagnosis in 1969, but she continued to imbibe freely. Liquor could bring out a feisty and argumentative side to her character, and family meals in the 1970s would not always go smoothly. Dad knew better than to enter sometimes preposterous arguments instigated by Mother. Often he would take recourse in a family game of "Ghost." Pursuant to this game, one goes around the table picking letters to spell a word with the objective of not having the word end on you. It is a game that aids in development of spelling and vocabulary and often, but not always, averts argument about more substantive matters.

We three older children all married by 1970. Mother felt some compulsion to retain power over her children and her in-laws. To this end, she occasionally engaged in graceless behavior toward her two daughters-in-law or her son-in-law. On at least one occasion, she reduced each of her daughters-in-law to tears. In this behavior, she did her children no favors.

Mother retained a network of fond friends, performed as a superb hostess and displayed a warm and lively sense of humor. She also delighted in provoking, even when the object of her attention was not a daughter-in-law. On one occasion in the early 1980s, she was seated at a dinner next to Bart Giamatti, President of Yale University. Among Mother's prejudices was facial hair. Giamatti sported a small medieval beard, perhaps in keeping with his career as a Renaissance scholar. Mother got right to the point by asking, "Why do you wear that silly little beard?" Taking no offense, Giamatti replied, "Because, Madam, I have a very weak chin." She enjoyed telling this story on herself.

Mother's sense of humor was not always available. At one memorable Sunday lunch around 1985 at Ratcliffe Manor, the wife of a guest of Sheila's (Congressman Chip Pashayan, who is now Sheila's husband) observing Hugh's daughter (and mother's granddaughter) Courtland, at the age of two or three, inquired of mother whether that was her "great-granddaughter." Mother's clenched teeth and corrective response to this inquiry cast somewhat of a pall on the balance of the luncheon party. Mother did delight in the presence of her grandchildren and, had she lived longer, would have been thrilled by her (presently) 17 great-grandchildren. She took her grandchildren to movies, played cards with them, and displayed toward them unfailing patience. Nine of 11 grandchildren had an opportunity to know her before her death in February 1987. Benjamin Tydings Smith was not born until nearly two months later, followed by his cousin Margaret the next autumn.

During her final weeks, mother requested a private visit from family friend and former CIA Director, Richard Helms. This visit led sister Sheila to speculate that mother and Helms had romantic ties. When quizzed on this score years later by Sheila, Helms, after consulting his glorious wife, Cynthia, reported that no romance was at issue. Mother, fearing her pain would worsen, had asked Helms whether, if necessary, he could secure for her the type of death capsule given secret agents. Of course he neither could nor would. In any event mother suffered her pain bravely with the help of acupuncture and opiates.

In her final illness, mother no longer felt like taking a drink, and either this fact or the strong intimation of mortality from cancer made her admirably wise and sensible. Her courage through considerable pain, as well as the continued love and sympathy shown all of us, gave bittersweet ratification to all that we loved and respected in her.

In the diary that my father created beside my mother's death bed, he states:

> Bernice made me whatever a man I became . . . nudging me out of playboy inclinations. . . . Bernice had wonderful healthy, handsome children, not too spoiled. . . . Bee was an essential partner in State, AEC, and ACDA. Work, entertainment and travels. She was ever elegant, stylish but modest, not puffed up, but withal "one tough lady" as the doctors recently found out.

In keeping with the tradition of her New Year's celebration of her birthday, one month before her death, mother hosted an elegant reception at Tracy Place that gave family, friends, and neighbors a final chance to pay respects and to relish her hospitality.

Shortly before mother's death, my father made a diary entry entitled, "Thoughts on Dying." Notwithstanding my mother's relatively young age, he took consolation that both he and mother had had "good, pretty long lives." He speculated that, "More likely than not, there is more to come. Either it will be like before we were born or paradise." He expressed gratitude that death with all faculties "intact" was much preferred to Alzheimer's. He again alluded to mother having made a man of him and apparently quotes mother as having said, "We've seen the world and many of its people." Indeed, they had.

After a funeral mass at St. Matthew's Cathedral, Mother's ashes were interred in Arlington Cemetery in a gravesite that would be Dad's when his turn came seven years later.

16

Two Divorces and Three Weddings

During the first half of the 1980s, while my father, as a private citizen, continued his quest for nuclear sanity, members of my generation were distracted by marital turmoil. To his credit, Hugh, in July 1982, married Chata Robinson, with whom he had enjoyed a 10-year relationship, and they have now celebrated their 30th wedding anniversary. In this same timeframe, Gerry and I both were divorced and remarried, Gerry to Isabel de Rancoyne in October 1984, and I to Mary Tydings in October 1985.

* * * * *

Reflection—A Digression on Divorce

In my parents' generation, divorce was relatively exceptional and carried with it a significant social stigma. Moreover, the Catholic Church condemns divorce and denies full participation in the life of the Church to any Catholic who divorces and then remarries. In my generation, however, divorce became more a rule than an exception. Of my rooming group of eight men at Yale, five of us divorced. Of the 14 surviving members of my "delegation," in Wolf's Head, half underwent divorce. At the time of my 25th Reunion at Yale College in 1989, a class poll revealed of the members of my class who had married, 50 percent had been divorced. The latest data show that this extraordinary rate of marital breakup has abated somewhat in the next generation, especially among educated couples. Nevertheless, it is worth reflecting on the factors that caused my generation to experience such a high degree of failure in first marriages.

In my parents' generation, as in previous generations, there was a relatively clear set of expectations regarding the respective roles of the husband and the wife. The husband was to be the breadwinner, and the wife was to manage the children and household. Wives with professional careers outside the home were the exception. The expectations of many in my generation were framed by the model of prior generations. Nonetheless, society's thinking advanced admirably and encouraged women to pursue employment and professional opportunities. It is possible that males of my generation were insufficiently sensitive to the implications of this changing set of expectations and were tardy in sharing the burdens of home and family with their newly liberated spouses. Lifelong marriage is not an easy matter for most, even in the best of circumstances. The abrasion added by the laggard response to changed circumstances by men of my generation compounded the normal stresses. Added to this change of role and expectation were significant liberalization of divorce laws; liberalized attitudes toward sexual adventures; increased temptations resulting from long hours with attractive co-workers; and a generally lessening hold of religious principle on conscience.

So much for generalization, especially as it relates to trends evident in retrospect. I had never imagined that I would be divorced. It was a shock, therefore, when Linda took the occasion of our 11th anniversary in April 1981, to inform me that she was seriously unhappy and wanted to consider separating. Soon, she presented me with her lawyer's draft of a separation agreement. There ensued an excruciating two-year period, where we continued to live unhappily under the same roof, unsuccessfully sought counseling, and negotiated terms of separation. During this period, I often reflected that I had been wrenched from a relatively normal and placid life, and was suddenly living within the pages of a novel. It struck me as more interesting to read about drama in other people's lives than to have it visit mine. Tolstoy begins his novel of adultery, *Anna Karenina*, with the famous observation, "Each happy family is happy in the same way, each unhappy family is unhappy in its own way." Silly me; I had thought I was living in a happy family.

During this two-year period, we kept our impending separation a secret from the children and from our friends and family. The thought was, if there was any chance of reconciling, public knowledge of our troubles would help accelerate our troubles. Linda and I did not formally separate until the end of July 1983, nearly 28 months after Linda's expression of unhappiness with our marriage. Whether the news of our separation came as a shock to friends, I can't tell. It was a shock to John and Will, ages 10 and 8. Linda's and my meeting with the two of them to tell them that we were separating remains the unhappiest moment of my life.

We did agree not to disparage one another to our children and to continually collaborate with respect to their welfare. The result, I hope, is that neither John nor Will was unduly scarred by his parents' divorce. Both are thriving in their 30s, and both enjoy sound and happy marriages. I devoutly wish that neither will experience divorce. I recognize that my generation has set a bad example in this respect. I hope that this example will not be seen as an acceptable or desirable "generational reflection."

* * * * *

A New Start

Immediately upon separation from Linda, I began to date Mary Tydings. I had first met Mary at Phil Nuttle's wedding in June 1981, two months after Linda had apprised me of her desire to separate, but two years before actual separation. During 1981–1983, I would occasionally encounter Mary jogging in Georgetown and when she was a house guest of my brother Hugh during his annual birthday celebration on the Eastern Shore. However, consistent with my sense of propriety, and my commitment to Linda to keep our troubles private, I did not go out with Mary until our separation. However, we began dating immediately upon my separation, possibly giving the impression that my relationship with a "younger blonde" had something to do with my separation from Linda. In fact, Mary had almost no part in my separation. That said, the pleasure of the company of a bright, self-assured, and accomplished young woman, who was evidently attracted to me, was a welcome compensation for 28 months of severe strain and unhappiness.

Both before and after our marriage in October 1985, Mary proved to be exceptionally adept in extending John and Will sympathy, affection, and friendship. Her own parents had separated and divorced when she was in her teens. Both had remarried, and Mary was "expert" on the relationships between children and stepparents.

Benjamin Tydings Smith arrived at the end of March 1987. Friends sagely advised me that becoming a father again at the age of 43 would "help keep me young." Certainly, Mary and Ben have done their best in this difficult task. It is a credit to all, in addition, that Ben and his two older half-brothers enjoy a warm and supportive relationship.

17

My Father's Final Years

My father was deeply affected by my mother's death. Family and friends sought to keep him occupied to divert him from his sorrows, and, indeed, his schedule filled rapidly. He readily acceded to a recommendation that the family charter a large sailboat in the Caribbean. There my father spent the last week of February and the first week of March 1987, accompanied by various children and grandchildren, reliving prior sailing ventures in warm seas. (It was during this cruise that my father remarked that one needed to believe in the resurrection of the body after death or all was lost.)

Upon return to Washington, my father renewed his involvement with Consultants' Group International, the Arms Control Association and writing for *Foreign Affairs*. In the spring of 1988, my father received a diagnosis of bladder cancer. The doctors thought that the detection had been relatively early and the prognosis good—and, Dad lived more than six years after this initial diagnosis before finally succumbing. Dad had always assumed that he would likely die from heart disease, having been diagnosed as a young man as having heart irregularities. While walking to work in the spring of 1989, shortly before his 75th birthday, Dad experienced chest pains. Sheila drove him to the Washington Hospital Center, where it was determined that he needed coronary bypass surgery. The operation was a success, but Dad ended up spending his 75th birthday in the hospital. This rather significant inconvenience required cancellation of a birthday dinner that we had planned centering upon the publication and distribution of the *Festschrift*,[165] put together by friends and colleagues at the suggestion of Henry Owen.

My memories of my father during the seven years he lived after my mother's death remain the most acute. While my mother lived, my father's attentions were primarily and appropriately directed to her. Moreover, she was in charge of arranging family activities. Upon her death, my father became much more directly involved with my generation enabling more frequent and more intimate contact, which all of us warmly welcomed. Such contacts became especially close when Dad decided to leave Washington and live full time at Ratcliffe Manor in 1989.

The extent to which my mother (as well as household staff) had sheltered and cosseted my father became amusingly evident. One day I encountered my father on one of his frequent walks down the Ratcliffe Manor lane, which extends a mile and a half from the manor house to the public road. I was on my way to the supermarket. My father inquired as to where I was headed. I told him I was on my way to buy groceries. He volunteered to join me. When we arrived at the supermarket, it became apparent that he had never in 75 years of life been inside a supermarket. He was impressed, even dazzled, by the array of goods displayed—even though Easton's Acme was a relatively modest facility as modern supermarkets go. A more consequential shopping trip occurred a year or so later at Christmas time, when Barbara Ayers, his Easton housekeeper, took Dad on a visit to Easton's relatively new Wal-Mart. There, he was truly astounded, and he embarked upon a shopping spree, obtaining for his children and grandchildren various inexpensive items of clothing, and the like. Dad had always believed in a "big" Christmas and, with mother's help, would lavish fine presents upon members of the family. We all remember the "Wal-Mart Christmas" with affectionate good humor—although, at the time, teenaged grandchildren were somewhat nonplussed by the receipt of oddly colored, poorly constructed Korean jogging outfits.

In August 1987, six months after mother's death, Dad joined me in a charter of a 63-foot sailboat in New England crewed by an Irish captain and his girlfriend. Dad, Mary, John, Will, and I sailed from Newport to Martha's Vineyard, then Nantucket, Block Island, and back to Newport. In Nantucket and Block Island, we were covering ground visited by Dad and Mother on their honeymoon cruise in August 1941. Appropriately, in Nantucket, we anchored off the White Elephant, where Dad had been scandalized 46 years earlier by a quoted room rate of $7 per night. This cruise gave John, aged 14, and Will, aged 12, an opportunity to spend time in close quarters with their grandfather, who, for his part, visibly relaxed and enjoyed himself. In Martha's Vineyard, I invited a woman friend, Dagney

Corcoran, aboard for a drink. She was accompanied by an attractive woman friend from Los Angeles. That evening, I knew from the sparkle in my 73-year old father's eye that he was making real progress in working through his sorrow at my mother's death.

Among my father's many admirable traits was his appeal to women. This appeal rested not only on his relatively good looks but also on his ability to convey his respect and admiration for women. Indeed, it was my sense that he preferred the friendship and company of intelligent, attractive women to that of men. I share this predilection.

In the last years of his life, my father formed a strong friendship with Andy Stewart, the widow of former Supreme Court Justice Potter Stewart. A woman of sympathetic intelligence and remarkable energies, Andy would spend weekends at Ratcliffe Manor and brighten up the place. She would come over to my house and play tennis while in her 70s. Another woman who brightened Dad's life was Peggy Sikes, whom Dad had known growing up in Long Island. Peggy had become a pioneering woman doctor and well-regarded oncologist. She helped Dad understand his symptoms and prospects after his diagnosis with bladder cancer. More importantly, she reinforced my advice to Dad that he undertake a memoir.

A friend of my parents, a charming Czech CIA agent, Jan Leibich, once commented in my presence, when he was in his 70s, that he was "still young enough to like older women." This was an attribute that my father, as a deep admirer of women, shared in full. Among Dad's female friends in his last years were the handsome, accomplished widow of Dean Acheson, Eleanor Acheson, and her friend, Luvie Pearson, widow of the columnist, Drew Pearson. The day after my 50th birthday, I attended my father's annual "oyster roast" at Ratcliffe Manor. I was wearing a button given me the night before that had the large initials "CRS" and in smaller print below said "I have just turned 50, can't remember shit." I was somewhat embarrassed when Mrs. Acheson noticed the button and asked me what the "CRS" stood for. I explained, and she laughed with appreciation. She then related a story about a revered senior partner of Covington & Burling, John Lord O'Brian. When he was a 90-year-old widower, he would attend cocktail parties populated by other elderly people. O'Brian would introduce himself to strangers by sticking out his hand and stating "My name is John Lord O'Brian. Can you remember yours?"

My father's final years of residence at Ratcliffe Manor were greatly enhanced by the fact that my brother Hugh had built a house on Ratcliffe Manor in 1987, a short distance from my father's house. He and Chata and their three children provided my father with relatively constant company and companionship. Other, older grandchildren liked to visit. Dad derived special pleasure from discussions of Greek and Latin roots of words with Sheila's daughter Louisa, a student at St. John's College. In addition, Dad's brother Gregory, moved to Easton around 1991 and would frequently enliven lunches and dinners with a large store of family lore and elaborate anecdotes told in a variety of foreign accents. Uncle Gregory had long been a patron of the arts and an aesthete with a series of residences extending from Manhattan up to Maine. I have the sense that my mother found some of his mannerisms irritating, but after her death, Uncle Gregory was "free to be Uncle Gregory" and provided Dad welcome companionship in his last years.

As is a family trait, Uncle Gregory was always prompt to social engagements. One Saturday evening in 1992 he was expected at Ratcliffe for dinner at 7 o'clock. At 7:10, when Gregory had not appeared, my father dispatched Hugh to see what could be amiss. Hugh entered Uncle Gregory's house in Easton and found him dressed for dinner but felled by a heart attack, lifeless in the front hall.

Even as his illness intensified, Dad stayed thoughtfully engaged as a student of history and international affairs and worked diligently on his memoir. His diary entries show constant reflections about world trends. And, as he went through old records to stimulate memories for his memoir, he encountered some causes for satisfaction. For instance, in the fall of 1993, nine months before his death, Dad wrote me to say that he had come across a copy of a letter he had written me in 1968. In it he had stated,

> When the Czechs start traveling by the hundreds of thousands in Western Europe, the stresses on Eastern Europe should be great, including the USSR. . . . My guess is that the USSR should look to its internal security and I expect some shocks before you are fifty. The earth is moving under its feet and perhaps under ours.

By the time I turned 50, a month after Dad had written me to remind of his 1968 prediction, the Soviet Union and the Iron Curtain no longer existed.

When not working on his memoir, walking on the lane, or entertaining friends or family, Dad continued a lifelong habit of reading. He was not a fast, but rather a deliberate and thoughtful reader. In his lifetime he made his way through the comprehensive multivolume world history by Will and

Ariel Durant, some volumes more than once. (The prodigious scholar, Will Durant, should not to be confused with my grandfather J.T.'s friend and founder of General Motors, William C. Durant.)

He focused on religious, philosophical, historical and biographical works. He had little time for fiction. An exception, however, was the British nautical series by Patrick O'Brian regarding Captain Jack Aubrey and Stephen Maturin, read with delight by practically every member of the family.

Reflection: A Digression on Reading

All four Smiths of my generation are keen readers. This fact stands to reason given the example of parents and grandparents. This habit carries through to many, if not all, of the next generation, but its perpetuation seems fragile in a distracting and digital age. I wonder, indeed, whether members of the next generation, much less their children, will even make it through this small volume of biographical musings, not to mention any of the sources cited in it. I cannot stress too strenuously the importance of reading, the benefits of which are so widely recognized and so widely discussed, that it is difficult to address them without resorting to cliché. In my case, reading was vitally important to expanding horizons of geography and imagination, developing of vocabulary, and presenting models for effective writing. Reading has provided a constructive escape when family or other troubles raised risk of depression. Reading can stimulate thought and yield new understandings regarding family, friends, politics, history, art, and science (and sex).

In his later years, my father took great pleasure from a subscription to the *New York Review of Books*. He gave me one, and I continue to subscribe. The late historian, Tony Judt, was once asked to name America's three strongest assets. He replied, "Thomas Jefferson, Chuck Berry (a rock and roll pioneer) and the *New York Review* of Books."[166] The pages of this journal contain consistently stimulating discussion of worthwhile books and a rich menu of reading choices.

Shared reading experience such as by book clubs or simply between friends and spouses can be a rich incentive to fruitful discussion and exchange of perspective. For the past seven years I have been attending a monthly seminar organized by St. John's College. There, participants in their 60s and 70s read and discuss short selections from the great works of literature and philosophy, such as Socratic dialogues, Shakespearean plays, Jane Austen novels, and essays of Montaigne, Spinoza, Hume, and Descartes. I previously had exposure to most of these materials in school and college. But I readily recognize that their full understanding and appreciation is possible, if at all, only after substantial life experience, unavailable to the typical college student. So, it is necessary to learn, live, and then learn again. The richest and best way to learn again is by reading.

Montaigne recommended the widest possible reading, while advising the reader not to worry about remembering what was read.[167] Possibly, he was anticipating the perception of a later Frenchman, Marcel Proust, who observed that:

> In reality every reader is, while he is reading, the reader of his own self. The writer's work is merely a kind of optical instrument which he offers to the reader to enable him to discern what, without the book, he would perhaps never have perceived in himself.[168]

Life is necessarily a process of self-discovery. In my opinion, reading is one of the principal means to this end.

18

Private Practice

This short book is not the place for any detailed recounting of my career at Covington & Burling. A year after I returned in 1977 from my second, short stint in government service, I was fortunate to be made partner, and I remained in this position until retirement in 2005. As already shown, I never intended to spend the bulk of my career in the private practice of law. Rather, in emulation of my father, I planned a career of public service. The fact that I ended up in private practice reflects the force of circumstances— the good fortune of working for Elliot Richardson, coupled with the bad luck of a premature and dramatic end due to the Saturday Night Massacre. Though I had started life as a Republican, beginning with the Reagan election in 1980, I became disaffected from the Republican Party, but had no real ties to Democrats. Accordingly, my prospects for senior government service in a politically appointed role declined to nil. In addition, the forces of inflation, cost of tuition, and the like, led me to a change of perspective. In the 1970s, I had felt "independently wealthy." By the mid-1980s, I appeared to need every dollar I could earn in the private practice. I touch upon the substance of my private practice involvements principally to illuminate reflections from the careers of my grandparents and father.

My grandfather, John Thomas Smith, was one of the great lawyers of his generation. I can make no such claim for myself. I had neither his brains nor his ambition, and his large success granted me a degree of economic security that abated zeal to be a "top earner" in the practice. Nevertheless, I was fortunate to spend my career at a firm of exceptional quality, an excellence recognized by John Thomas himself who had selected it as tax counsel for General Motors.

Putting aside my apprenticeship in 1974–1976, my legal career was divided into two halves. The first extended from 1977 until 1990, when I was dispatched by the firm to open an office in Brussels, Belgium. The second half extended from my return from Brussels in the fall of 1991 until my retirement 14 years later.

The First Half

Beginning in 1979, I assisted the firm's client, the Chemical Manufacturers Association, in analysis and advocacy regarding regulations issued by the Environmental Protection Agency under the Resource Conservation and Recovery Act (RCRA) addressing management and cleanup of solid and hazardous wastes. This rather unglamorous endeavor had its rewards. I worked with committees of highly competent company representatives, who educated me to enable me to write comments and briefs on their behalf. I obtained an invaluable education and emerged as one of the country's experts on this branch of environmental law. When, as General Counsel to the Commerce Department in 1976, I had signed a letter recommending President Ford's signature of RCRA, I had no inkling that a few years later it would become a central focus of my legal practice.

I also assumed responsibility as outside counsel to a trade association of the machine tool industry, comprising a large number of smaller companies that design and build the essential manufacturing equipment used in a wide range of industrial applications. Here I was immersed in a variety of legal issues of the sort that might be encountered by an actual general counsel such as my grandfather, albeit on a much smaller scale. On behalf of the industry, I also became involved in advocacy regarding issues of international trade at a time when Japanese manufacturers appeared to be quickly outstripping American competitors, with the aid of various interventions by the Government of Japan.

I also helped represent a large architectural and engineering firm (with offices at the top of the World Trade Center destroyed on September 11, 2001) that was being sued because estimates that it had made of the cost of construction of some nuclear power plants turned out to be inaccurate as costs burgeoned as a result of new regulations responding to a partial meltdown at the Three Mile Island nuclear facility in Pennsylvania in 1979. This latter assignment took me deeply into issues surrounding construction and regulation of nuclear power plants—with nuclear power having been a lifelong interest and concern of my father extending to his days as a young staff assistant at the Atomic Energy Commission. Finally, during this period I assisted my partner, Ed Bruce, in fascinating and fast-moving litigation regarding legal challenges to off-shore exploration for oil, principally in the Beaufort Sea off the North Slope of Alaska. These assignments took me to argue preliminary motions in federal district court in Alaska and necessitated an immersion in a wide range of federal statutes including Outer Continental Shelf Lands Act, the Coastal Zone Management Act, the Endangered Species Act, the National Environmental Policy Act, and the Marine Mammal Protection Act.

Following the catastrophic *Exxon Valdez* oil spill in April 1989, Exxon engaged Covington & Burling to represent it in negotiation of its potential criminal and civil liabilities to the U.S. government under the Clean Water Act. When Ed Bruce was notified he was under consideration for appointment as a federal judge, he had to step aside from direct representation of Exxon in these negotiations, and he tapped me to try to fill his shoes. For an eight-week period in the winter of 1990, I worked seven days a week in these high-stakes negotiations—aided immeasurably by Ed's wisdom (offered behind the scenes).

This engagement gave me insights into the deep contrast in negotiating style of leadership of a giant oil company, on the one hand, and that of the U.S. Department of Justice, on the other. The oil company executives addressed the matter much as they would a negotiation for an oil concession in a Third World country—with fearless, hardnosed bargaining and bluff. The Justice Department appeared to expect a greater measure of humility from Exxon in that the United States held an exceedingly strong hand, given draconian penalties prescribed in the Clean Water Act. As a former Justice Department official and as a believer in reasonable bargaining approaches, I was not altogether comfortable with Exxon's approach. But, to Exxon's credit, the company's tactics ultimately resulted in a relatively fair bargain—after I had left for Europe.

Brussels Interlude

In October 1989, the firm asked if I would be willing to move with my family to Brussels, Belgium, to open, with the help of a Belgian colleague, Henriette Tielemans, a new office. Covington had opened a London office in order to represent our clients with respect to activities in the emerging European Union. We had subsequently determined that, in addition to London, we needed an office in Brussels, the "federal capital" of Europe.

Mary jumped at the chance to move to Europe. Ben was not yet three years of age, and there would be no issue about pulling him out of school and giving up friends. John was away at boarding school, and Will resided with his mother while happily attending St. Albans School. I was less keen at the prospect than Mary, recognizing that I would be putting a long distance between myself and my father and two older sons. The latter had their whole lives in front of them, but the former was ill with cancer and a widower. Nonetheless, urged on by Mary's enthusiasm and a desire to be a good Covington & Burling citizen, I consented to go to Brussels.

In the fall of 1989, I made a series of trips to identify office space, to recruit Belgian lawyers, and find a house in which to live. Various visa and related issues delayed my actual move to Brussels until April 1990. But the winter of 1990 passed rapidly with the excitement of the *Exxon Valdez* negotiations.

Brussels proved somewhat frustrating from a professional standpoint in that there was little demand for environmental lawyers, and legislative and regulatory advocacy in Brussels was the province of non-lawyer government relations experts. The latter had little interest in sharing their turf with newly arrived American lawyers. However, Mary was delighted by her life in Brussels, where under the terms of our visas she could not work. Instead, she enjoyed the role of "traditional spouse," as mother, hostess and household manager. Her leisure, aided by a young Danish au pair, gave her opportunities to attend museums, take ski trips, and go horseback riding in the Ardennes. John and Will visited in the summer of 1990 for a two-week vacation in Portugal, and again in March 1991 for a week of skiing in France.

A highlight of our Brussels sojourn was cementing of new friendships. I had known Michael Pakenham, a British foreign servant and his American wife, Mimi, when Michael served in Washington a decade earlier. His presence in Brussels and Mimi's great social skills expanded our Brussels horizons immeasurably. Mary and Ben travelled with Michael and Mimi for a weekend visit to Michael's remarkable parents in Suffolk, England. There Ben was read to at bedtime by Michael's mother, Lady Elizabeth Longford, a renowned author. (Lady Longford had appeared in Brussels on the 175th anniversary of the Battle of Waterloo in June 1990. A noted historian who had chronicled the battle in her biography of her ancestor, the Duke of Wellington, Michael's mother, at the age of 80, delivered a lucid and stirring lecture—dressed in bullet riddled red jacket worn by a relative at Gallipoli in World War I.) The Smiths and the Pakenhams remain vital friends.

Mary Carpenter and her husband, *Time* magazine correspondent, Adam Zagorin, likewise provided fresh and sophisticated friendship, which continued to thrive after they took up residence in D.C. in 1992. Mary and I have a bond of ancestry. Her grandfather, Walter Carpenter, and John Thomas Smith worked closely together when the former was a senior executive of DuPont.

In February 1991, Mary and I attended a weekend "hunting party" in Westphalia, Germany. The invitation resulted from friendship of the host with Mary's mother and stepfather. The party took place at a magnificent "schloss" and an adjoining spa hotel. Although Germany proscribes use of "titles" in political and professional life, Germans with titles use them in social context. The weekend's published guest list included two princes and princesses, several dukes and duchesses, and numerous counts and countesses. Amidst the splendid roster of guests appeared good-old "John and Mary Smith."

We were treated with great courtesy by this refined group of Germans who gave lie to American stereotypes of our World War opponents. Due to stringent German licensing rules, we weren't allowed to hunt but were given a chance to stand in the cold forest with individual hunters waiting the approach of wild boar. When our host's son, Graf Marcus, who accompanied Mary, wandered off to track a deer, Mary had a close, unarmed, and memorable encounter with a wild boar.

In the spring of 1991, I learned that my father's health had taken a turn for the worse and his prospects were not good. In addition, John and Will's mother, now married to her law partner, Victor Ferrall, was moving to Beloit, Wisconsin, where Vic was to become President of Beloit College. Will, especially, wanted me to return to Washington so that he could finish his education at St. Albans. Given my father's failing prospects and a chance to have my older sons primarily resident with me, I informed the firm of my desire to return to the United States, which was readily accommodated by the fall of 1991.

Second Half of Covington & Burling Career

The second half of my Covington & Burling career focused on representing energy and natural resource companies in disputes with state and federal governments about cleanup of historical contamination. Some of these cases took me to sites of historic mining operations, including one in the Sierra Nevada range, where John Thomas had been involved with the Argonaut Mine. Others involved contamination from manufacturing operations that had directly supported the nuclear weapons programs that had been the subject of my father's endeavors. One involved contamination of a community adjacent to a thorium mill where thorium had been extracted from ores for use in the nuclear weapons program. Another involved massive contamination of ground water and surface water at a site in Nevada that had manufactured an essential ingredient of solid rocket fuel for intercontinental ballistic missiles. Still another involved an oil refinery in New Mexico.

Many of these cases presented broad issues as to how to allocate the economic burdens of the contamination that had been a necessary consequence of the nation's industrial development and, in some cases, its national security. In addition, there were related questions as to how much remediation of historical contamination was really necessary and justified to protect human health and the environment.

When my grandfathers were helping launch automobile and natural gas companies in the first half of the 20th century, environmental consequences were out of mind. The modern environmental movement began in the 1960s, and, by the early 1970s, broad environmental statutes (enacted at the behest of Republican Presidents Nixon and Ford) enjoyed consensus support. These statutes commanded that public utilities and industrial plants remove contaminants from their air and water discharges. A consequence was that toxic materials that had been widely dispersed into the air and surface water became concentrated in pollution control residues or "sludges." The management of these concentrated residues in landfills and surface impoundments resulted in the escape of these toxins to groundwater, a major source of the nation's drinking water supply.

The country then prescribed, at ever-increasing costs, measures to treat and manage these pollution control residues in a manner that would protect groundwater, and commanded costly measures to treat large quantities of groundwater to remove the contaminants. In 1980, Congress enacted "Superfund" legislation, which fixed liability for cleanup of soil, surface water and groundwater contamination on all past, present and future owners or operators of industrial sites and waste management facilities, as well as all industrial companies that had sent wastes to third party disposal facilities. The result was a vast amount of litigation between and among companies and with the government, entailing huge legal costs and achieving only halting and protracted steps to actually ameliorate the environment.

Supreme Court Justice, Stephen Breyer, while Chief Judge of the U.S. Court of Appeals for the First Circuit, cogently surveyed federal efforts to regulate environmental and human health risks in 1993.[169] He described a system badly out of kilter in which federal regulation of environmental and health risks were imposing costs grossly disproportionate to perceived benefits. He noted that the public perception of risk often differed radically from the view of experts, and this public perception was driving Congress to pass increasingly prescriptive statutes. These statutes in turn launched a regulatory process in which scientific uncertainty would be addressed by adoption of the most cautious and stringent standards possible. He noted the tendency of regulators to address the "last 10 percent" of risk and, in so doing, to drive costs of regulation to unsustainable peaks. His book contains a table of federal regulations and an analysis of their cost-effectiveness in terms of "cost per premature death averted."[170] In this table, three of the five most expensive regulations were ones central to my legal specialty—solid and hazardous waste management.

Breyer proposed creation of a new bureaucratic entity that would de-politicize risk decisions by entrusting them to a panel of scientific experts. Suffice it to say, Breyer's recommendation has not been adopted, but his concern about excessive mitigation of marginal health risks remains sound. And, as the political pendulum has swung in the direction of conservatives concerned about the power and cost of the federal government, the Environmental Protection Agency and its costly regulations have come under fire. Republicans routinely call all such regulations "job killing." Doubtless, some federal regulations are too stringent, seeking over cautious outcomes. However, it is not clear that most such environmental standards are "job killing." The promulgation and maintenance of sensible and uniform regulatory standards can stimulate economic activity by reassuring the public that industrial activities can be conducted without unreasonable risks and by guaranteeing industry a relatively uniform regulatory standard instead of a "patchwork quilt" of differing standards among 50 states.

Indeed, this antiregulatory backlash is occurring at a time when sound federal environmental intervention is more necessary than ever to address problems such as climate change, degradation of major estuaries, such as the Chesapeake Bay, sound regulation of safety of nuclear power plants, and other vital energy-related activities. The lack of sophistication of our political process, the shortage of financial resources, and our current hostility to international cooperation suggest severe challenges for future generations.

As previously mentioned, I was involved for a brief, but intense period in legal disputes arising from the *Exxon Valdez* oil spill. One of the major issues presented was how, if at all, to compensate for damages caused by the oil spill to ecological and natural resources for which there is no conventional market. For instance, there is no market for estuarine wetlands even though such areas provide significant "ecological services," filtering contaminated surface runoff, and serving as "nurseries" for juvenile aquatic species. This issue again looms large as a consequence of the massive BP blow-out in the Gulf of Mexico in 2010. This topic, of abiding economic and even philosophical interest, is beyond the scope of this short book, but it is one that remains a major societal challenge. Indeed, as we continue to weigh the costs and benefits of regulation, the costs are easy to measure. The benefits, while real, are more difficult to gauge with standard economic tools.[171]

As in the case of *Exxon Valdez*, the nation's voracious appetite for energy provides the context for some of our most interesting ongoing environmental debates. Some legislators believe that the nation's dependence on imported oil could be miraculously eliminated if we only expanded off-shore drilling on our continental shelf. Environmentalists, and the affected coastal communities are much less certain of the appropriateness of this course of action —which cannot, in any event, secure us "energy independence." Similarly, although fracturing or "fracking" of deep shale deposits promises vast new quantities of natural gas, opposition is growing to this practice based upon a concern that fluids used in this process may escape and contaminate valuable underground sources of drinking water. A recent book by Michael Graetz, succinctly but comprehensively outlines the four-decade long failure of our country to come up with economically and environmentally sensible energy policies.[172] An even more thorough treatment of this important subject, together with an analysis of future prospects, is Daniel Yergin's remarkable book, *The Quest*.[173]

19

Final Days and Reflections

Death

These generational reflections have necessarily touched upon the topic of death. They have also touched upon the mystery of whether there is life of any sort after death and, if so, what its nature might be. John Thomas Smith died suddenly in his sleep in a San Francisco hotel. Uncle Gregory died instantaneously on his way to dinner at Ratcliffe Manor. Elliot Richardson was felled by a stroke on New Year's Eve 1999, the last day of the 20th century. College friends, Bruce Warner and Dick Pershing, died in battle in Vietnam. Chuck Goldmark and Russell Byers were murdered. Jack Heinz died in a plane wreck. Dick Griffin, my brother-in-law, Coleman Hicks, my good friend and law partner, Dick Darman, Phil Nuttle, and, most importantly, my mother and father, died more slowly from cancer—all excepting my parents, unfairly young.

With my retirement and relatively good health, I have time to reflect both philosophically and practically on death. Its prelude may be protracted illness. I am, therefore, an interested student of our ongoing debate as a nation about the economic feasibility of prolonging human life. It is increasingly recognized that the single largest "driver" of costs to the government is health care under Medicare for growing numbers of "senior citizens," such as the author, especially during the last years of life. According to doctor-journalist, Atul Gawande, 25 percent of all Medicare expenditures are for patients in their final year of life, most of it for care of dubious benefit in the last couple of months of life.[174]

From my own study, and from my involvement on the board of the local Hospice, I am acutely conscious of ongoing debate as to the relative merits of alternative health strategies. The first spares no expense in efforts to prolong the lives of terminally ill patients, with medical and technical interventions. The alternative accepts the inevitability of death and seeks to give patients the greatest comfort and dignity in their final months or days through application of palliative care. The second approach is relatively inexpensive. Pursuit of the first approach is consuming an increasing share of scarce national resources.

Americans have always been "problem solvers." We have indulged the illusion that cancer and other terminal diseases may admit of a cure. As described in the acclaimed book about medical efforts to address cancer, *The Emperor of All Maladies*,[175] the effort to restore sanity and sanctity to the care of "end-of-life cancer patients" emerged not from "cure-all obsessed" America, but from Europe, where Dr. Cecily Saunders invented palliative medicine. She founded the first hospice in the UK in 1967. The first American hospice was launched at Yale in 1974.

There remains a tension between the hospice/palliative-care approach and the American conquer-the-problem approach. American medicine has made remarkable progress in improving and refining cures for breast cancer and establishing cures for childhood leukemia and testicular cancer in young men. Nevertheless, we still lavish extraordinary medical attention upon elderly individuals with incurable cancer and other terminal diseases, unwilling to admit as individuals, families or as a society that a greater quality and duration of life, as well as dignity, may be achieved at much lower cost through palliative medicine.[176]

Presently, doctors receive reimbursement under Medicare for the costs of medical interventions as well as the time recommending and describing these interventions. Medicare does not reimburse doctors for time spent counseling patients and their families regarding the alternative of hospice and palliative care. When an effort to provide cost reimbursement for end-of-life alternatives counseling was undertaken in recent health-care reform legislation, demagogues attacked it, claiming falsely that it would establish "death panels" of bureaucrats who would decide who would live and who would die. This was a shabby, reprehensible episode, and it points to the difficulty we have as a nation in making fundamental choices regarding the future of our society.

By the time my death approaches, society may have better resolved these issues, if only due to other economic pressures. In any event, it is, and will be, my direction to family and doctors that I pursue the palliative medicine approach—assuming I don't receive the "benefit" of a sudden death like that of John Thomas Smith or Uncle Gregory.

Dad's Death

The only death I have actually witnessed was that of my father in Easton Memorial Hospital on July 4, 1994. In contrast to that of my mother, his terminal illness did not entail great pain. He was not conscious, but made a final struggle to cling to life, breathing heavily with a "death rattle," as Sheila and I held him. Dad had been failing, and had been in and out of the hospital during the previous six months. He was aware that the end of his life was close. He had an opportunity to finish his memoir, dictating ideas to me in May 1994, which I then incorporated into a draft of the "Final Reflections" chapter of *Disarming Diplomat*. These reflections addressed nuclear weapons and proliferation risks, the profoundly important focus of Dad's life's work. (Dad died before he had an opportunity to review the actual text of this chapter. I turned to his friend and colleague, Robert Bowie, for critical review. In his mid-80s at the time, Bowie offered invaluable substantive and editorial suggestions, evidencing his high intelligence.) Dad had a chance to receive the final sacraments of the Catholic Church and to impart to me a polite "God bless you," while I sat by his bedside during his final full day of life.

Others more skilled than I have attempted to imagine what goes on in human consciousness as death approaches. The great American poet, Emily Dickinson, wrote profound, somewhat minimalist poetry that often touched on the topic of death, very much in the air during the Civil War in the mid-19th century. In a poem entitled "Dying," she brutally demythologizes death. She imagines a prosaic death as she lies in bed surrounded by family:

> There interposed a fly,
> With blue, uncertain, stumbling buzz,
> Between the light and me;
> And then the windows failed,
> And then I could not see to see.[177]

A nobler recounting of death appears in the masterful novel, *The Leopard*, about a Sicilian prince at the time of the passing of the Old Order in

19th-century Italy. The prince receives sacraments of the Church. He then listens to cheering gossip from his beloved nephew, while "making up a general balance sheet of his whole life," weighing "golden flecks of happy moments" against immense liabilities. The happy moments include his marriage and honeymoon, hours spent observing the stars, memories of his various pets, recollection of successful hunts, the occasional erotic passion, the receipt of a medal for a scientific discovery, and the "voluptuous air of a few women passed in the street." He then suffers a final stroke, and in the room he hears the sound of a "faint hiss," which he doesn't know is his own death rattle. He is near the seaside, and he hears the crashing of the sea, and then the sound disappears.[178]

In his recent book, *The Social Animal*, David Brooks applies the latest findings of science and sociology to the outlines of the lives of an imaginary couple—a professor and a successful business woman. In a manner that parallels that of the prince in *The Leopard*, as he dies, the professor loses consciousness but not life. Images flow into his head as they do in the seconds before one falls asleep. He regards these images in a way that is beyond words while "somehow feeling everything at once." These images include riding a bicycle as a boy, doing homework with his mother, participating in high school sports, speeches he had given, sex he had enjoyed, books he had read, and the epiphanies of realizing new ideas.[179]

If Dad's final moments paralleled the imaginings of these authors (other than Emily Dickinson), his final consciousness may have embraced: bright summer days on the Atlantic coast, as a child in New Jersey and as an adult in Southampton; the *Welkin* under full sail on a July afternoon; the arc of a hole-in-one; the thrill of hooking marlin; meeting and marrying mother; the blinding light and mushroom cloud of atmospheric nuclear explosions in the Pacific; moments of deep worship in Catholic churches and cathedrals around the world; long negotiating sessions with Russian counterparts in cold climates; the receipt of numerous honorary degrees and the Medal of Freedom; Ratcliffe Manor filled with children and grandchildren; and the old trees and boxwoods in long green twilight on Ratcliffe's back lawn.

Certainly, he had a good life and strove with intelligence, generosity, and discipline to make the world better and to nurture his family. Whatever mysterious and good may await after death surely is his.

He stipulated that children and grandchildren were not to participate directly in his funeral service. He was celebrated by two extraordinary Catholic priests who were his friends: Paul Mohan, a professor at Catholic University and Bryan Hehir, author of the Bishop's letter on nuclear weapons. At the close of his Funeral Mass, at Dad's request, Henry Owen delivered a eulogy. It was intelligent, affectionate, and relatively short—the model of what a eulogy should be. Dad is buried, with Mother, at Arlington National Cemetery.

* * * * *

Reflection: A Final Digression on War and Death and American "Exceptionalism"

The individuals chronicled in this short, reflective memoir all came of age and lived most of their lives in 20th-century America. Each contributed in measure to the nation's welfare. My two grandfathers played significant roles in developing the country's economic well-being. My father contributed measurably to its national security, broadly defined. The author, without making a comparable contribution, has nonetheless enjoyed a professional career including involvement with major issues affecting the nation's well-being.

The three generations described in this book were hugely lucky to be Americans at a time when our country emerged as the wealthiest, most secure and powerful country in the world. Generations of our family have benefited from America's provision of social and economic opportunity to immigrants and their children, irrespective of religion or national origin. We have all known a large measure of economic and political freedom, and we have witnessed the flourishing of an extraordinarily stable political system. And, within this context, we have enjoyed the privileges of personal wealth.

Our nation's good fortune is in part a reflection of the wisdom of the Founders and artfulness of our Constitution. It is in large part also a result of our geographic situation, surrounded by two oceans and peaceful neighbors, as well as the immense agricultural and mineral resources with which our North American continent is endowed. But we sometimes fail to recognize that our emergence as the most powerful nation in the world also resulted from the tremendous harms done by other potentially great nations to one another in the two World Wars of the first half of the 20th century. For instance, by the end of the First World War in 1918, nearly 50 percent of British men between the ages of 18 and 32 when the war began in 1914 had been killed or wounded, and France suffered a combat death toll almost twice as large.[180]

Our family has been fortunate to avoid war's harm—as has our nation when compared to others. Grandpa Maguire and John Thomas Smith were both too old to serve when the United States sent 2 million troops to the exhausted battlefields of Western Europe in the last year of World War I. Dad was physically disqualified from combat duty in World War II. Gerry and I both served during the Vietnam War but were not in harm's way.

Images of conventional war—as well as mushroom clouds—permeated my generation's childhood culture. We purchased and wore Army surplus clothing. We read comic books that focused upon the bravery of American soldiers fighting Chinese Communists in Korea. Toy guns were everywhere. The only television show we were allowed to watch on school nights in elementary school was a documentary regarding the U.S. Navy in World War II, "Victory at Sea." A general, Dwight D. Eisenhower, was our President. In the first decade of the 21st century the United States was again at war, in Iraq and Afghanistan. But most children are no longer encouraged to play with guns or do military role playing. Our military forces are all volunteers, increasingly unrepresentative of society at large. Moreover, the country has enjoyed tax cuts rather than any call to sacrifice to support our foreign military endeavors.

Osama Bin Laden, the instigator of the terrorist attacks on U.S. soil that occurred on September 11, 2001, received harsh criticism from Americans as a coward, butcher of innocents, and terrorist. In a little noticed rejoinder, the late leader of Al Qaeda remarked that the United States lacked moral standing to criticize him for the loss of 3,000 civilian lives, when our World War II bombing activities, including the use of nuclear weapons on Hiroshima and Nagasaki had killed orders of magnitude more innocent civilians than the activities of Al Qaeda on "9/11." There are obvious distinctions to be drawn between causing civilian casualties as part of strategic bombing in a war provoked by another country, on the one hand, and on the other, unprovoked peacetime attack, the sole consequence of which could be taking of innocent lives. Nonetheless, Osama Bin Laden's rejoinder is one reason to think hard about war and its consequences.

My father concluded that nuclear weapons had no moral purpose because they could not be used without risk of completely unacceptable harm to innocents. I never had a chance to discuss with him the provocative Bin Laden rejoinder. Dad's generation took it as a given that the bombing by the United States and its allies of Germany and Japan was justified in the context of a world war. I would have liked to have had an opportunity to discuss with Dad a recent book by the British philosopher, A. C. Grayling, who, while acknowledging the greater evil done by our opponents, makes the case that allied bombing in both Europe and Japan was a deliberate and unjustified attack on civilians.[181]

If the United States and its allies are retrospectively culpable for using excess force as part of bombing campaigns in the Second World War (Grayling estimates eight hundred thousand innocent civilian deaths), the Western Allies' activities pale in relation to the slaughter of civilians by Russia and Germany through starvation and genocide (including but not limited to the Jewish Holocaust) that occurred in 1933–1945 in Poland, the Ukraine and Belarus, in which 14 million civilians perished.[182] Similarly, it has been estimated that Mao Tse Tung, during his reign over the People's Republic of China, executed or starved as many as 70 million citizens.[183]

I recite these figures to reinforce the premise that 20th-century Americans were hugely fortunate when compared to citizens of the other major countries in the world. This good fortune has led to renewed talk about American "exceptionalism." Some appear to believe that our good fortune is a mark of blessing by Deity. They embrace it as an excuse—since we are "exceptional," we can do no wrong. This is pernicious nonsense. Our hubris has been manifested recently by political leaders who endorse "waterboarding" in interrogation of terrorists, a practice for which we prosecuted Japanese officers as war criminals after World War II. If the United States is exceptional for reasons other than geographic and historical good fortune, it is because of our openness and our nurturing of opportunity and equality. Modern political trends toward intolerance of immigrants, Islam, and even the national government, threaten one basis of our supposed exceptional status. So do our growing intolerance of international engagement and disregard for international law and precedent.

Epilogue

There is no way to end a book of this sort that is not abrupt. As a narrative about and meditation upon generations, it necessarily tells a story that continues. And the continuation of the story is now the privilege of the next and succeeding further generations. It is my hope that the children and grandchildren who may someday read this book will grow up with rational pride in their background and their nation, as well as a humble sense of how lucky they are to be part of America. That said, they should have a consciousness that their good fortune carries with it reciprocal obligations to lead worthy lives. If they do so, they will be acting consistent with the examples of my father and grandfathers.

Attributes of prior generations already are apparent in one or more of each of the 11 members of the next generation of my family. They include entrepreneurship, self-discipline, adherence to Catholic faith, appreciation of and involvement in education, generosity of spirit, excellence in parenthood, intrinsic kindness, love of sport (including golf and tennis), wide appetite and interest in reading, scholarly accomplishment and broad interest in the world of which they are part.

Especially gratifying is the respectful and supportive friendships that they maintain within their ranks. It is my hope that this small book will illuminate for them and their children the legacies and values that they inherit. Some of the more energetic of them may wish to review some of the sources that I have cited regarding the range of topics that preoccupied prior generations, including nuclear diplomacy, the continuing dialog regarding faith and reason, and means to find appropriate resolution of complex tensions arising from our energy and environmental aspirations.

At present the nation is suffering significant economic difficulties and resulting political tensions. Nonetheless, these difficulties are not insoluble, or even historically unique. I remain optimistic that future generations of this family will be able to live productive and constructive lives, capitalizing upon and reflecting the values and accomplishments of their predecessors.

Notes

1. Davies wrote a memoir of his time in Moscow, see Joseph E. Davies, *Mission to Moscow* (Simon & Schuster, New York, 1941); a biography of Millard Tydings was published in 1991, *see* Caroline Keith, *For Hell and a Brown Mule*, (Madison Books, Lanham, MD, 1991). The extraordinary Eleanor Ditzen authored an autobiography at the age of 93, *My Golden Spoon* (Madison Books, Lanham, MD, 1998).

2. Gerard C. Smith, *Disarming Diplomat* (Madison Books, Lanham, MD, 1995), preface.

3. "Natural Gas—Whoosh!," *Fortune*, Dec. 1949, p. 109.

4. In preparation of this chapter on Will Maguire, I draw heavily on a monograph entitled "William G. Maguire, Pipeline Pioneer, 1886–1965," prepared and published by Panhandle Eastern Pipeline Company in my grandfather's memory after his death in 1965.

5. *Gas Pipelines and the Emergence of America's Regulatory State: A History of Panhandle Eastern Corporation, 1928–1993* (Cambridge University Press, 1996) (hereinafter Castaneda and Smith).

6. *Id.*, p. 32.

7. *Id.,* p. 17.

8. Will Maguire knew Gossler. In 1929, he had successfully brokered the sale of natural gas holdings to Columbia and purportedly earned a commission of "several million dollars." *Id.*, pp. 39–40.

9. *Id.*, p. 71, *et seq.*

10. Initially Panhandle was a wholly owned subsidiary of Mo-Kan. In the course of a decade of litigation and financial tumult, Panhandle emerged as the surviving entity.

11. *Id.* The authors describe the two men as an "unlikely pair." Will Maguire later derided Parish as a "bumptious, unpleasant type of person." Maguire's insight into business matters commanded respect and Parish "had an ambition that overran his expertise." But both wanted more wealth and prestige. *Castaneda and Smith*, p. 40.

12. As was normal practice, Panhandle was formed as a controlled subsidiary of Mo-Kan to be the actual vehicle for constructing the proposed pipeline.

13. *See* www.measuringworth.com.

14. *Castaneda and Smith*, pp. 67–68.

15. *Id.*, p. 69.

16. *Id.*, p. 105.

17. *Id*, p. 79.

18. *Id.*, pp. 80–105.

19. *Id.*, pp. 101–103.

20. *Id.*, p. 128.

21. *New York Times* (October 11, 1965), p. 61.

22. *Newsweek*, October 1, 2007.

23. "America's Natural Gas Revolution," Daniel Yergin and Robert Ineson, *Wall Street Journal*, Nov. 3, 2009, p. A21.

24. Robert A. Nitschke, *The General Motors Legal Staff, 1920–1947* (1989).

25. See footnote 13, *supra*.

26. Nitschke, *op. cit.*, pp. 3–6.

27. *Id.*, pp. 13–15.

28. J.T.'s decision to remain at GM was encouraged by Durant, and these events did not diminish the friendship of the two men.

29. Bernard Weisberger, *William C. Durant, the Dream Maker* (Little Brown, Boston, 1979), pp. 214–15.

30. General Motors moved its corporate headquarters to Detroit in 1941, but J.T. received approval to keep the Counsel's office in New York.

31. Alfred P. Sloan Jr., *My Years With General Motors* (Currency/Doubleday, New York, 1963), p. 98.

32. "GM Throws Opel Deal into Reverse," *Wall Street Journal*, Nov. 4, 2009, p. 1.

33. *American Heritage Magazine*, April/May 1982 (Vol. 33, No. 3).

34. *See* Nitschke, *op. cit.*, p. 116.

35. *Id.*, p. 105.

36. *Id.*, p. 108.

37. A follow-on plan, the so-called General Motors Management Corporation, required a tax ruling from the Internal Revenue Service. Since J.T. was to be one of the substantial beneficiaries of this bonus plan, he retained Covington & Burling to handle the matter and, thereafter, Paul Shorb of Covington provided tax assistance to General Motors. Mr. Shorb wrote a letter of condolence to my father upon receiving news of J.T.'s death in October 1947, adverting to the "splendid character and many remarkable achievements" of J.T. Mr. Shorb's former secretary furnished a copy of this letter to me at Covington forty years later, a testament to long institutional memory (and possibly deficient records retention practices).

38. This recounting of the *Winkelman* suit is based upon a much fuller description of the matter that appears in the Nitschke book, pp. 63–79.

39. The issue in this case was delightfully complex involving important principles of both federal jurisdiction and so-called conflicts of law. Under the decision in *Erie v. Tompkins*, 304 U.S. 64 (1938), federal courts exercising jurisdiction in matters involving diverse parties (i.e., litigants from differing states) and potentially involving issues of state law are to use federal rules of procedure but state substantive law. In *Klaxon* the question arose whether rules governing choice of substantive law where citizens of two states were litigants were "procedural" or "substantive" under *Erie*. If such "choice of law" principles were "substantive," a federal court would have to apply the choice of law provision of the state in which the federal court was located, in this case Delaware. J.T. argued that conflicts of law principles were substantive and that the court should apply Delaware law to absolve GM from having to pay interest. He prevailed.

40. Nitschke, *op. cit.*, p. 132.

41. Dad's middle name honored a then close friend of J.T.'s, William Coad. Later the two men had a falling out (over an apparently trivial matter) and hence my younger brother Gerard, is

Gerard Lawrence Smith. Coad reappears in the middle name of my nephew, Gerard Coad Smith II, son of my youngest brother, Hugh. Others of the family bear the name, Gerard, testament to my father's example. Thus my second son is William Gerard Smith and Sheila's oldest son is Gerard Francis Griffin.

42. See Scott Stossel, *Sarge: The Life and Times of Sarge Shriver* (Smithsonian Books, Washington, D.C., 2004), p. 45.

43. See Gary Lawrance and Anne Surchin, *Houses of the Hamptons, 1880–1930* (Acanthus Press, New York, 2007), pp. 136–45. Interestingly, the house had been rented for several summers in the late 1920s by Marjorie Merriweather Post and her then husband, E. F. Hutton. Subsequently, Marjorie married Joseph Davies, my wife's great-grandfather.

44. Stossel, *op. cit.*, p. 88.

45. Nitschke, *op. cit.*, p. 118.

46. O. Henry Mace, *47 Down: The 1922 Argonaut Gold Mine Disaster* (John Wiley, New York, 2004).

47. *Id.*, p. 74.

48. See Canterbury School Alumni Magazine, *Pallium* Vol. 27, No. 1, Winter 2011, p. 47.

49. See *New York Times*, Sunday, September 29, 1996, for an article detailing the background of the construction of this building and J.T.'s role therein.

50. Obituary, *Time Magazine* (October 6, 1961). Misquote notwithstanding, many would have agreed that, in the 20th century the fortunes of General Motors and of the United States were closely linked.

51. See Will Durant, *The Life of Greece* (Simon & Schuster, New York, 1966), p. 533.

52. *Disarming Diplomat: The Memoirs of Ambassador Gerard C. Smith, Arms Control Negotiator* (Madison Books, Lanham, MD, 1996).

53. *Doubletalk: The Story of SALT I* (Doubleday & Co., Garden City, NY, 1980).

54. Henry Owen and John Thomas Smith II, eds., *Gerard C. Smith: A Career in Progress* (University Press of America, Lanham, MD, 1989).

55. Gerard C. Smith, *All at Sea* (William E. Rudge's Sons, New York, 1939).

56. Nitschke, *op. cit.*, p. 30.

57. See *Higgins v. Smith*, 308 U.S. 473 (1940).

58. *A Career in Progress*, p. 4.

59. John Corry, *Golden Clan: The Murrays, The McDonnells and The Irish American Aristocracy* (Houghton Mifflin & Co., Boston, 1977).

60. A superb recounting of the years in which the United States briefly (four years) enjoyed a monopoly of nuclear weapons is Michael D. Gordin, *Red Cloud at Dawn: Truman, Stalin and the End of the Atomic Monopoly* (Farrar, Straus and Giroux, New York, 2009).

61. *Id.*, pp. 49–52.

62. *Id.*, pp. 262–68.

63. Nicholas Thompson, *The Hawk and The Dove: Paul Nitze, George Kennan and The History of the Cold War* (Henry Holt, New York, 2009).

64. These extraordinary events are detailed in Priscilla J. McMillan, *The Ruin of J. Robert Oppenheimer and the Birth of the Modern Arms Race* (Viking, New York, 2005). See also, Kai Bird and Martin J. Sherwin, *The Triumph and Tragedy of J. Robert Oppenheimer* (Alfred A. Knopf, New York, 2005), pp. 487–550.

65. Gerard C. Smith, *Disarming Diplomat* (Madison Books, Lanham, MD, 1996), pp. 28–29.

66. For an exceptionally accurate, thorough, and evocative description of a Catholic childhood and education, see Joseph A. Califano Jr., *Inside: A Public and Private Life* (Public Affairs, New York, 2004), pp. 11, 21–44.

67. Richard John Neuhaus, *As I Lay Dying Meditations on Returning* (Basic Books, New York, 2002), pp. 74, 132–33.

68. See *Disarming Diplomat*, pp. 214–15.

69. *Newsweek*, February 22, 2010, pp. 43–45.

70. Sam Harris, *The End of Faith* (W.W. Norton, New York, 2004).

71. Christopher Hitchens, *God Is Not Great: How Religion Poisons Everything* (Twelve, Hatchette, New York, 2007), p. 266.

72. Robert Wright, *The Evolution of God* (Little Brown & Co., New York, 2009).

73. Hitchens, *op. cit.*, 262 (Spinoza was excommunicated from the Jewish community in Holland and, for good measure, was also condemned by the Catholic Church).

74. Walter Isaacson, *Einstein: His Life and Universe* (Simon & Schuster, New York, 2007), pp. 388–89.

75. Harris, *op. cit.*, 221.

76. Paul F. Knitter, *Without Buddha I Could Not Be a Christian* (One World Publication, Oxford, Eng. 2009), pp. 29–31.

77. *Id.*, pp. 38–39.

78. *Id.*, p. 89.

79. *Id.*, p. 77.

80. *Id.*, p. 91.

81. James P. Carse, *The Religious Case against Belief* (Penguin Press, New York, 2008), p. 209.

82. James Carroll, *Constantine's Sword: The Church and the Jews* (Houghton Mifflin Co., New York, 2001), pp. 249–53.

83. Freeman Dyson, Book Review, *The New York Review of Books*, March 10, 2011, pp. 8, 10.

84. Karen Armstrong, *The Case for God* (Alfred A. Knopf, New York, 2009).

85. *Id.*, p. 329.

86. *Id.*, p. 330.

87. *Id.*, p. 328.

88. WSJ.com, Friday, September 19, 2008. "David Foster Wallace on Life and Work." http://online.wsj.com/article/sb122178211966454607.html.

89. Plato, *Apology: Five Dialogues*, 2d ed. (Hackett Publishing Co., Indianapolis, 2002), p. 43.

90. A detailed recounting of my father's professional endeavors in this period can be found in *Disarming Diplomat*, pp. 31–109. A broader study of the Eisenhower Administration's nuclear policies, including insights into the constructive role played by my father, is Richard Hewlett and Jack Hall, *Atoms for Peace and War, 1953–1961: Eisenhower and the Atomic Energy Commission* (University of California Press, 1989).

91. Memorandum for the File, March 16, 1955, G.C. Smith.

92. *Disarming Diplomat*, pp. 75–77.

93. Memorandum from Gerard C. Smith to Mr. Herter, August 13, 1958. See www.gwu.edu/nsarchiv/nsa/DOCUMENT /DOC-PIC/950809.

94. *Disarming Diplomat*, p. 106.

95. An excellent recounting of the ensuing visit by Krushchev is Peter Carlson, *K. Blows Top* (Public Affairs, New York, 2009).

96. Here I use the term "establishment" broadly to denote those exercising political, religious, academic, and cultural authority consistent with "norms" that evolved in the United States during the 20th century. As such, I give it relatively broad sweep in distinction to "The Establishment," a phrase coined by British journalist, Henry Fairlie in 1955. Fairlie meant a relatively small number of individuals comprising an elite in the United Kingdom who exercised disproportionate influence

over that nation's affairs. In the United States, during the 1960s, Fairlies' term was applied to a circle of men who, through some combination of advantages of birth, elite education, and/or intelligence, presided informally over conduct of a "liberal internationalist" U.S. foreign and defense policy. Its goal was to prevent the spread of Communism by providing moral and political leadership to the world. See Godfrey Hodgson, *The Colonel: The Life and Times of Henry Stimson* (Knopf, New York, 1990), pp. 382–87. My father became a junior member of this U.S. establishment by the 1960s, but never sought or achieved the leadership stature of such mandarins as the two Dulleses, Averell Harriman, Dean Acheson, and John McCloy.

97. See *Disarming Diplomat*, pp. 111–47.

98. See "A Maritime Deterrent to the Communist Threat," *New York Times*, November 21, 1961, p. 38.

99. *Disarming Diplomat*, p. 118.

100. Personal conversation with Michael Krepon, Spring 2010.

101. See *Disarming Diplomat*, p. 245.

102. Chace contributed a short description of *Interplay* to Dad's festschrift. See *A Career in Progress*, pp. 129–31.

103. In preparing this book, I have noticed for the first time that Dad and his father were both quite young when they entered college. John Thomas Smith was 16 when he entered Creighton. Dad turned 17 in May of the year he entered Yale. When I received my "Classbook" in my final year at Yale, I undertook the prideful task of reviewing the birthdates of each of my 1,000 classmates to see how many were younger than me. I made it halfway through the class by which time I had identified 12 men who were younger. Of these, 11 were of evident Asian ancestry—an early indicator of the exceptional intelligence and capacities of this segment of our society.

104. Buckley, a Conservative/Libertarian had large influence in my times, founding the *National Review*, and having a say in a wide range of national debates. In 1965 he "ran" for Mayor of New York. When asked what he would do if elected, he quipped that he would "demand a recount." I recall watching a televised "debate" during the 1965 mayoral race. The debate included more than fifteen candidates of various bizarre political affiliations. I was amused when Buckley in patrician tones distinguished his viewpoint from those of the "zoo" surrounding him.

105. *Time*, July 20, 1962.

106. See discussion, p. 48.

107. See discussion, p. 29.

108. See Part II of Justice Breyer's dissent in that case, 551 U.S. 98 (2000).

109. See, Hodgson, *op cit.*, 312–41. Notwithstanding his compunction regarding reading others' communications, he was a key participant in the decision to use nuclear weapons in Japan.

110. Giuseppe di Lampedusa, *The Leopard* (Revised Paperback Edition, Pantheon, New York 2007), pp. 250–54.

111. Plato, *Symposium* (Hackett Publishing Company, 1989), pp. 58–60.

112. *Foreign Relations of the United States, 1969–1976*, Volume XXXII, SALT I, 1969–72 (Department of State, Washington, D.C., 2010). Hereinafter, *For. Rel. of U.S. Doc.*

113. Henry Kissinger, *White House Years* (Little Brown, Boston, 1979), p. 147.

114. See, for example, *id.*, p. 814.

115. See *For. Rel. of U.S. Doc.*, pp. 404, 477, 799, 800–801.

116. *Disarming Diplomat*, p. 159.

117. *For. Rel. of U.S.*, pp. 795–801.

118. Kissinger, *op. cit.*, p. 1243.

119. See, for example, *For. Rel. of U.S.*, p. 403.

120. Seymour M. Hersh, *The Price of Power: Kissinger in the Nixon White House* (Simon & Schuster, New York, 1983), p. 530n.

121. Kissinger, *op. cit.*, p. 1245.

122. *Doubletalk*, p. 444.

123. *New York Times*, Jan. 8, 1986.

124. Gerard C. Smith and Helena Cobban, "A Blind Eye to Nuclear Proliferation" *Foreign Affairs* 68, No. 3 (1989), pp. 53–70.

125. Obama Speech, April 5, 2009, Prague, Czech Republic.

126. Philip Taubman, *The Partnership: Five Cold Warriors and Their Quest to Ban the Bomb* (HarperCollins, New York, 2012).

127. *Disarming Diplomat*, p. 209.

128. In addition to my father's memoirs, I would direct future generations to Richard Rhodes's two books: *The Making of the Atom Bomb* (Simon & Schuster, New York, 1986) and *Dark Sun, The Making of the Hydrogen Bomb* (Simon & Schuster, New York, 1995), as well as John Newhouse, *War in Peace in the Nuclear Age* (Alfred A. Knopf, New York, 1988).

129. See Thompson, *The Hawk and the Dove* (Henry Holt & Co., New York, 2009), pp. 5, 515–16.

130. The price of the SALT I interim agreement on offensive systems was a commitment by President Nixon to seek funding for high capacity SLBM systems. See *Doubletalk,* pp. 339–40.

131. Freeman Dyson, *Infinite in All Directions* (Harper & Row, New York, 1988), pp. 214–15.

132. For a lucid, succinct summary of the promise and peril of nuclear power generation, *see* Daniel Yergin, *The Quest: Energy Security and the Remaking of the Modern World* (Penguin Press, New York, 2011), pp. 361–78.

133. See Ken Gormley, *Archibald Cox: Conscience of a Nation* (Addison-Wesley, Reading, MA, 1997), pp. 87–88.

134. Richard M. Cohen and Jules Witcover, *A Heartbeat Away: The Investigation and Resignation of Vice President Spiro T. Agnew* (The Viking Press, New York, 1974).

135. Gormley, *op. cit.*, pp. 318–377.

136. The most thorough recounting of these wiretaps can be found at www.historycommons .org./timeline.gsp?timeline= nixon_and_watergate_(___ nixon_tmin_illegal wiretapping.

137. *Id.*

138. This information eventually appeared in Woodward & Bernstein, *The Final Days* (Simon & Schuster, New York, 1976), pp. 51–53.

139. When first confronted by reporters in May 1973 regarding his role in the wiretapping, Kissinger tried to pass blame for the wiretaps to Bob Haldeman, White House Chief of Staff. Then he tried to limit his responsibility saying that he "almost never" requested such tapes. He escalated the matter to top management of the *Washington Post*, stating that it was "almost inconceivable" that he had sought such wiretaps. See Woodward and Bernstein, *All the President's Men* (Simon & Schuster, New York, 1974), pp. 313–16. The matter would haunt him. The issue arose again in 1974 and Kissinger threatened to resign unless the media ceased plaguing him with allegations about illegal surveillance. He also wrote to Senator Fulbright, Chairman of the Senate Foreign Relations Committee, asserting that innuendos of "new information" were false. In the letter he stated that his meeting with Senators Sparkman and Case "was conducted in the presence of Attorney General Richardson and Deputy Attorney General Ruckelshaus." See Kissinger, *Years of Upheaval* (Little Brown, Boston, 1982), pp. 1115–23. In fact the only Justice Department official present at the meeting with Sparkman and Case was the author. (Ruckelshaus wasn't confirmed as Deputy Attorney General until two months later.)

140. See *United States v. U.S. District Court*, 407 U.S. 297 (1972) (the "Keith" case). Kissinger and Nixon emphasized the fact that the wiretaps were discontinued before this Supreme Court decision and had the approval of Attorney General John Mitchell, former Nixon campaign manager. The FBI's "nervousness" about these taps reflected the fact that a 1967 Supreme Court decision found that wiretapping was a form of "search" subject to Fourth Amendment protections. It left open the question not presented in the earlier case whether the Fourth Amendment could require a warrant for electronic surveillance of U.S. organizations and citizens in national security cases. See *Katz v. United States*, 389 U.S. 347 (1967).

141. Cohen and Witcover, *op. cit.,* 348.

142. And in the record of hearings held in Congress during November 1973.

143. Elliot L. Richardson, *The Creative Balance* (Holt, Rinehart and Winston, New York, 1976), pp. 39–47.

144. Thomas Mallon, *Watergate* (Pantheon Books, New York, 2012).

145. See *Disarming Diplomat*, pp. 196–97.

146. Weekly Compilation of Presidential Documents, Vol. 17, No. 3, p. 2928 (Jan. 20, 1981).

147. Some flavor of this extraordinary man can be gleaned from a history of Covington & Burling that he wrote during his retirement. See Howard C. Westwood, *Covington & Burling, 1919–1984* (Washington, D.C., 1986).

148. *Washington Post*, March 24, 2011, p. A14.

149. The conference was in session on July 7, 1977, a date (7/7/77) that a G-77 spokesman greeted as auspicious.

150. Ann Hollick, *U.S. Foreign Policy and the Law of the Sea* (Princeton University Press, Princeton, NJ, 1981). William Westenbaker, "The Law of the Sea, Parts I & II," *The New Yorker*, Aug. 1 and Aug. 8, 1983.

151. The Seabed Negotiation and the Law of the Sea Conference . . . Ready for a Divorce? 18 *Va. J. of Int. Law* 43 (1977).

152. Scott G. Borgerson, *The National Interest and the Law of the Sea: Council and Foreign Relations* (May 2009).

153. "Global Bargains Better left UNCED," International Economic Insights (1992).

154. Richard G. Darman, *Who's In Control* (Simon & Schuster, New York, 1996).

155. The most thorough exposition of the Reagan "Star Wars" initiative can be found in Frances Fitzgerald, *Way Out There In The Blue* (Simon & Schuster, New York, 2000).

156. See S. Stossel, *op. cit.*, 647–48.

157. McGeorge Bundy, George F. Kennan, Robert S. McNamara, and Gerard Smith, "Nuclear Weapons and the Atlantic Alliance," *Foreign Affairs*, Vol. 60, No. 4 (Spring 1982), pp. 753–68.

158. Stossel, *op. cit.*, p. 651.

159. *Id.*, pp. 655–56.

160. *Disarming Diplomat*, pp. 214–15.

161. Fitzgerald, *op. cit.*, pp. 290–91.

162. *Id.*, p. 298.

163. See discussion in Fitzgerald, *op. cit.*, pp. 409–11.

164. David Brooks, *The Social Animal* (Random House, New York, 2011), p. 163.

165. Gerard C. Smith, *A Career in Progress*.

166. Tony Judt, *The Memory Chalet* (Penguin Press, New York, 2010), p. 198.

167. Sarah Bakewell, *How to Live or a Life of Montaigne* (Other Press, New York, 1910), p. 64.

168. Fred R. Shapiro, Editor, *Yale Book of Quotations* (Yale U. Press, New Haven, 2006), p. 607.

169. Stephen Breyer, *Breaking the Vicious Circle: Toward Effective Risk Regulation* (Harvard University Press, Cambridge, MA, 1993).

170. *Id.,* Table 5, pp. 24–27.

171. Drawing upon my Exxon-Valdez experience, I published a law review article on this topic in 1994. See *Natural Resource Damages Under CERCLA and OPA: Some Basics for Maritime Operators*, 18 Tul. Mar. L.J. 1 (1994).

172. Michael Graetz, *The End of Energy: The Unmaking of America's Environment, Security, and Independence* (MIT Press, Cambridge, MA, 2011).

173. Daniel Yergin, *The Quest, Energy Security, and the Remaking of the Modern World* (Penguin Press, New York, 2011).

174. Atul Gawande, "Letting Go," *New Yorker Magazine*, August 2, 2010.

175. Siddhartha Mukherjee, *The Emperor of All Maladies* (Scribner, New York, 2010), pp. 224–25.

176. Gawande, *op cit.*

177. Emily Dickinson, *Selected Poems* (Dover Publications, New York, 1990), p. 21.

178. Di Lampedusa, *op. cit.,* pp. 250–54.

179. David Brooks, *op. cit.*, 375–76.

180. Adam Hochschild, *To End All Wars* (Houghton Mifflin Harcourt, New York, 2011), p. 348.

181. A. C. Grayling, *Among the Dead Cities* (Walker & Co., New York, 2006).

182. See Timothy Snyder, *Bloodlands: Europe Between Hitler and Stalin* (Basic Books, New York, 2000).

183. See Jung Chang and John Halliday, *Mao the Unknown Story* (Alfred A. Knopf, New York, 2005). Of the 70 million at least 30 million occurred due to a famine induced by Mao as he exported grain to earn capital with which to finance acquisition of nuclear weapons.

Bibliography

Armstrong, Karen, *The Case for God* (Alfred A. Knopf, New York, 2009).

Aristotle, Nicomachean Ethics, Book VIII.

Bakewell, Sarah, *How to Live or a Life of Montaigne* (Other Press, New York, 1910).

Bernstein, Carl, and Woodward, Bob, *All the President's Men* (Simon & Schuster, New York, 1974).

———, *The Final Days* (Simon & Schuster, New York, 1976).

Bird, Kai and Sherwin, Martin J., *The Triumph and Tragedy of J. Robert Oppenheimer* (Alfred A. Knopf, New York, 2005).

Borgerson, Scott G., *The National Interest and the Law of the Sea: Council and Foreign Relations* (May 2009).

Breyer, Stephen, *Breaking the Vicious Circle: Toward Effective Risk Regulation* (Harvard University Press, Cambridge, MA, 1993).

Brooks, David, *The Social Animal* (Random House, New York, 2011).

Califano, Jr., Joseph A. Inside, *A Public and Private Life* (Public Affairs, New York, 2004).

Carlson, Peter, K. *Blows Top* (Public Affairs, New York, 2009).

Carroll, James, *Constantine's Sword: The Church and the Jews* (Houghton Mifflin Co., New York 2001).

Carse, James P., *The Religious Case against Belief* (Penguin Press New York, 2008).

Castaneda, Christopher J. and Smith, Clarance M., *Gas Pipelines and the Emergence of America's Regulatory State: A History of Panhandle Eastern Corporation, 1928–1993* (Cambridge University Press, New York, 1996).

Chang, Jung, and Halliday, John, *Mao: The Unknown Story* (Alfred A. Knopf, New York, 2005).

Cohen, Richard M., and Witcover, Jules, *A Heartbeat Away: The Investigation and Resignation of Vice President Spiro T. Agnew* (The Viking Press, New York, 1974).

Corry, John, *Golden Clan: The Murrays, The McDonnells & The Irish American Aristocracy* (Houghton, Mifflin & Co., Boston, 1977).

Darman, Richard G., *Who's in Control* (Simon & Schuster, New York, 1996).

Dickinson, Emily, *Selected Poems* (Dover Publications, New York, 1990).

Di Lampedusa, Giuseppe, *The Leopard* (Revised Paperback Edition, Pantheon, New York, 2007).

Ditzen, Eleanor, *My Golden Spoon* (Madison Books, Lanham, MD, 1998).

Durant, Will, *The Life of Greece* (Simon & Schuster, New York, 1966).

Dyson, Freeman, *Infinite in All Directions* (Harper & Row, New York, 1988).

Fitzgerald, Frances, *Way Out There in the Blue* (Simon & Schuster, New York, 2000).

Gordin, Michael D., *Red Cloud at Dawn: Truman, Stalin and the End of the Atomic Monopoly* (Farrar, Straus and Giroux, New York, 2009).

Gormley, Ken, *Archibald Cox: Conscience of a Nation* (Addison-Wesley, Reading, MA, 1997).

Graetz, Michael, *The End of Energy: The Unmaking of America's Environment, Security, and Independence* (MIT Press, Cambridge, MA, 2011).

Grayling, A. C., *Among the Dead Cities* (Walker & Co., New York, 2006).

Harris, Sam, *The End of Faith* (W.W. Norton, New York, 2004).

Hersh, Seymour M., *The Price of Power: Kissinger in the Nixon White House* (Simon & Schuster, New York, 1983).

Hewlett, Richard G. and Hall, Jack M., *Atoms for Peace and War, 1953–1961, Eisenhower and the Atomic Energy Commission* (University of California Press, Berkeley, 1989).

Hitchens, Christopher, *God Is Not Great: How Religion Poisons Everything* (Twelve/Warner Books, Hatchette, 2007).

Hochschild, Adam, *To End All Wars* (Houghton Mifflin Harcourt, New York, 2011).

Hodgson, Godfrey, *The Colonel: The Life and Times of Henry Stimson* (Knopf, New York, 1990).

Hollick, Ann, *U.S. Foreign Policy and the Law of the Sea* (Princeton University Press, Princeton, NJ, 1981).

Isaacson, Walter, *Einstein: His Life and Universe* (Simon & Schuster, New York, 2007).

Judt, Tony, *The Memory Chalet* (Penguin Press, New York, 2010).

Keith, Caroline, *For Hell and a Brown Mule* (Madison Books, Lanham, MD, 1991).

Kissinger, Henry, *White House Years* (Little Brown, Boston, 1979).

———, *Years of Upheaval* (Little Brown, Boston, 1982).

Knitter, Paul F., *Without Buddha I Could Not Be a Christian* (One World Publication, Oxford, UK, 2009).

Lawrance, Gary and Surchin, Anne, *Houses of the Hamptons, 1880–1930* (Acanthus Press, New York, 2007).

McMillan, Priscilla J., *The Ruin of J. Robert Oppenheimer and the Birth of the Modern Arms Race* (Viking, New York, 2005).

Mace, O. Henry, *47 Down: The 1922 Argonaut Gold Mine Disaster* (John Wiley & Sons, 2004).

Maguire, William G., *Pipeline Pioneer, 1886–1965* (Panhandle Eastern Pipeline Company).

Mallon, Thomas, *Watergate* (Pantheon Books, New York, 2012).

Mukherjee, Siddhartha, *The Emperor of All Maladies* (Scribner, New York, 2010).

Neuhaus, Richard John, *As I Lay Dying Meditations on Returning* (Basic Books, New York, 2002).

Newhouse, John, *War in Peace in the Nuclear Age* (Alfred A. Knopf, New York, 1988).

———, *Cold Dawn: The Story of SALT* (Holt, Rinehart, Winston, New York, 1973).

Nitschke, Robert A., *The General Motors Legal Staff, 1920–1947* (1989).

Owen, Henry and Smith II, John Thomas, eds., *Gerard C. Smith: A Career in Progress* (University Press of America, Lanham, MD, 1989).

Plato, Apology, *Five Dialogues*, 2d ed. (Hackett Publishing Co., Indianapolis, 2002).

———, *Symposium* (Hackett Publishing Company, Indianapolis, 1989).

Reich, Charles A., *The Greening of America* (Random House, New York, 1970).

Rhodes, Richard, *The Making of the Atom Bomb* (Simon & Schuster, New York, 1986).

———, Dark Sun, *The Making of the Hydrogen Bomb* (Simon & Schuster, New York, 1995).

Richardson, Elliot L., *The Creative Balance* (Holt, Rinehart and Winston, New York, 1976).

Shapiro, Fred R., ed., *Yale Book of Quotations* (Yale University Press, New Haven, CT, 2006).

Sloan, Jr., Alfred P., *My Years with General Motors* (Currency/Doubleday, New York, 1963).

Smith, Gerard C., *All at Sea* (William E. Rudge's Sons, New York, 1939).

———, *Doubletalk: The Story of SALT I* (Doubleday & Co., Garden City, NY, 1980).

———, *Disarming Diplomat, The Memoirs of Ambassador Gerard C. Smith, Arms Control Negotiator* (Madison Books, Lanham, MD, 1996).

Snyder, Timothy, *Bloodlands, Europe between Hitler and Stalin* (Basic Books, New York, 2000).

Stossel, Scott, *Sarge, The Life and Times of Sarge Shriver* (Smithsonian Books, Washington, D.C., 2004).

Taubman, Philip, *The Partnership: Five Cold Warriors and their Quest to Ban the Bomb* (HarperCollins, New York, 2012).

Thompson, Nicholas, *The Hawk and The Dove, Paul Nitze, George Kennan and the History of the Cold War* (Henry Holt & Co., New York, 2009).

Weisberger, Bernard, *William C. Durant: The Dream Maker* (Little Brown, Boston, 1979).

Westwood, Howard C., *Covington & Burling, 1919–1984* (Washington, D.C., 1986).

Wright, Robert, *The Evolution of God* (Little Brown & Co., New York, 2009).

Yergin, Daniel, *The Quest, Energy Security, and the Remaking of the Modern World* (Penguin Press, New York, 2011).

Index

missile. *See* antiballistic missile; intercontinental ballistic missile; Peacekeeper missile; submarine launched ballistic missile
missile defense, 117
missile gap, 84, 91
MLF. *See* multilateral force
Mohan, Paul, 222
Mo-Kan, 6–8
Molotov, Vyacheslav, 81
money, changing value of, 7–8
Montaigne, Michel de, 210
Moore, Jonathan, 156
Moran, Alfred, 50
Moriarty, Marshall, 131–33
Morton, Billy, 96
Moscow, Soviet Union, 86
Moscow Summit Meeting, 120–22, *p11*
Moses, Al, 174–75
Moulton, Terry, 96
Moyer, Homer, 176
Mukherjee, Siddhartha, 220
multilateral force (MLF), 92–93
multiple independently targetable reentry vehicle (MIRV), 117, 143
Murphy, Dan, 134–35
Murray, Thomas, 55–56, 60–63
Myles, Jane, 5

Nantucket, 48, 206
national command authority, 139
National Conference of Catholic Bishops, 192–93
National Industrial Recovery Act of 1933, 24
National Labor Relations Act, 24
National Review, 233n104
National Security Council, 127
National Security Study Memorandum, 139
NATO. *See* North Atlantic Treaty Organization
natural gas, 6–7, 12–13, 13, 179–80
Navy, 49–50, 91
New Deal, 8
Newhouse, John, 121, 186
Newhouse, Symmie, 186
New Jersey, 137–38, *p6*
New York, 34, 43–44; Hamptons, 10, 31, 43, 52, *p8*; Manhattan, 34, 38–39, 51–54, 182
New York Review of Books, 209
New York Times, 91, 155, 193
Nichols, Dane, 186
Nicomachean Ethics (Aristotle), 189–90
Nitschke, Robert, 15, 23
Nitze, Paul, 57–58, 115, *p10*; ABM Treaty and support for Reagan's Strategic Defense Intiative, 143, 195; missile gap and, 84
Nitze, Phyllis, *p10*

Nixon, Richard, *p11*; Agnew corruption case and, 157; reelection of, 132–33; SALT and, 117–20; Watergate and, 148–53; wiretaps and, 153–55, 163
"no first use" policy, 192–93
Non-Proliferation Treaty of 1968, 141
North Atlantic Treaty Organization (NATO), 92–93
Northern Star, 45
nuclear power, 145, 212
nuclear umbrella, 192
nuclear weapons: Catholic Church and, 72–73, 192–93; development of, 55, 57; escalation scenarios with, 139–40; France and, 82–83; international trusteeship, 142; Iran and, 135; Israel and, 135; military view of, 142, 144; morality of, 224; Pakistan and, 135; proliferation of, 1, 81, 141, 168, 184; reduction/elimination of, 56–57, 141–45; in schoolboy awareness, 66; Smith, John Thomas II, and, 138–40; Soviet Union and, 57, 81, 141, 143; tactical, 60, 83, 144; tests of, 59, 82; United Kingdom and, 82–83; US and, 141–42; use of, 83–84, 145, 224; world cataclysm risk from, 139. *See also* Smith, Gerard; *specific weapon type*
Nuttle, Philip, 188
Nuttle, Philip III, 188

Obama, Barack, 189
O'Brian, John Lord, 207
ocean, mineral resources in, 180–81
Office of Strategic Services, 40
oil, off-shore drilling for, 213, 218
Olds, 19
Oldsmobile, 19
Opel, acquisition of, 24
Oppenheimer, Robert, 56, 60–63
Osprey, 185
Owen, Henry, 81, 86, 223

Pakenham, Michael, 214
Pakenham, Mimi, 214
Pakistan, 135
palliative care, 220
Panhandle Eastern Pipeline Company, 3, 6, 8–9, 229n10
Parish, Frank, 6–8, 21, 229n11
Pascal, Blaise, 79
Pashayan, Chip, 199
payments, questionable, 178–79
Pentagon, 135–36, 139
Pentagon Papers, 148
Perle, Richard, 59, 195
Pershing, Dick, 106

Persian Gulf, 136
Peters, Charlie, 186–87
Plato, 78, 112
Plumbers, 148
plutonium, 145, 168
Power Plant and Industrial Fuel Use Act, 13
Power Trust, 7–8
product liability litigation, 176
Proust, Marcel, 210
public transport, 35

Al Qaeda, 224
Quemoy, China, 83–84
The Quest (Yergin), 218
questionable payments, 178–79
Quito, Ecuador, 17–18

Rancoyne, Isabel de, 201
Rand, Ayn, 198
Rankin, Al, 104, 106,125
Rankin, Clara,104
Rankin, Viki Griffin, 104
Ratcliffe Manor, 50–54, *p16*; Smith, Gerard,
    at, 206–8; Smith, John Thomas II, at, 187;
    visitors to, 170–71; weekends at, 85
reading, 67, 209–10
Reagan, Ronald, 169, 189; arms control and,
    191–92; SDI and, 143–44, 194–95
Red Maples, 31
Reich, Charles, 103
religion, 68, 76; criticism of, 75–76; at Harvard
    University, 75; history of, 70; science and,
    77; Smith, John Thomas II, and, 69–71, 76;
    in US, 75
The Religious Case Against Belief (Carse), 77
Republicanism, 172, 189, 211
Resource Conservation and Recovery Act, 178,
    212
Richardson, Anne, 132,172
Richardson, Elliot, 60, 130–33, 160, 172,
    p14; Agnew corruption case and, 158–59;
    aircraft carrier naming and, 147, *p13*; as
    Attorney General, 134, 140, 147–48, 152;
    at Commerce Department, 173, 178–79; at
    DOD, 122, 133–41; drinking by,
    163–65; at HEW, 128; in Law of the Sea
    delegation, 180–82; as mentor, 131–35, 151;
    Saturday Night Massacre, 159–63; Watergate
    and, 103, 153, 160–63
Richardson, Henry, 132
Rickover, Hyman, 59, 92
Robinson, Chata, 201
Rockefeller, David, 94, 167
Rockefeller, Nelson, 81
Rodman, Peter, 121

Roosevelt, Eleanor, 96
Roosevelt, Franklin, 25
Ruckelshaus, William, 153, 162
Russian (language), 54

sailing, 32, 45, 49, 205–6
Sakharov, Andrei, 196
SALT. *See* Strategic Arms Limitation Talks
Saturday Night Massacre, 104, 151, 157, 159
Schmidt, Benno, 105
Schmidt, Mott, 34
Schwartz, Victor, 177
science, religion and, 77
Scranton, William, 167
SDI. *See* Strategic Defense Initiative
Second Vatican Council, 69
senior societies, 99
September 11, 2001, 224
sex, 110; Catholic Church and, 71, 111;
    literature and, 111–12
Shanley, Bernard, 45
Shanley, Maureen, 45
Shorb, Paul, 230n37
Shriver, Sarge, 32, 40, 101, 172, 192–93
Sikes, Peggy, 207
sit-down strike, 24–26
Skull and Bones, 99
SLBM. *See* submarine launched ballistic missile
Sloan, Alfred, 20, 24, 28, 47
Smith, Benjamin Tydings, 203
Smith, Bernice Latrobe, 6, 197–200, *p2*, *p14*;
    cancer and, 197, 200; death of, 200, 205;
    drinking by, 198; early life of, 197; humor of,
    199; intellect of, 198; marriage of, 47–48; as
    mother, 197–98; in SALT delegation, *p10*
Smith, Clarance, 6, 9
Smith, Gerard, 37–38, *p5–p6*; at AEC,
    55–63; as Ambassador at Large for Nuclear
    Nonproliferation, 168, 184; as Assistant
    Secretary of State, 85; books by, 38, 45,
    116, 169–70, 221; cancer and, 205; at
    Canterbury School, 39–42; career, early, of,
    47–48; Catholic faith of, 72–74; childhood
    of, 38–39; death of, 73–74, 221–23; diary of,
    4, 38, 42–43, 200, 208; final years of, 205–9;
    funeral of, 222–23; historical interests of, 44,
    208; international study by, 54–55; Kissinger
    on, 117–18; letters from, 43–44, 93, 116;
    marriage of, 47–48; moral ruminations of,
    58; National Medal of Freedom and, 171;
    Naval service of, 49–50; "no first use policy"
    and, 192–93; nuclear tests witnessed by, 59;
    professional life of, 2, 85; public advocacy
    by, 191; at Ratcliffe Manor, 206–8; SALT
    and, 115–16, 122–23, *p10–p11*; as sports

treaty: ABM Treaty, 191–92, 194–97; atmospheric nuclear test ban, 82; Non-Proliferation Treaty of 1968, 141
Trilateral Commission, 167–70
Trinder, Beatrice, 53
Truman, Harry, 57, 67
Tydings, Emlen, 69
Tydings, Joseph D.,ix
Tydings, Mary, 188, 201, 203, 213–14
Tydings, Millard, ix

U-2 spy plane, 84–85
UNCLOS. *See* UN Law of the Sea Conference
unionization, 24, 26
United Auto Workers, 24
United Kingdom, 82–83, 232n96
United Motors Company, 20
United Nations, 57, 182
United States: Berlin and, 90–91; greed in, 71; MLF and, 92–93; national interest of, 184; nuclear weapons and, 141–42; political impasse in, 144, 183–84; religion in, 75; Soviet Union relationship with, 191; 20th Century, 223; window of vulnerability in, 143
UN Law of the Sea Conference (UNCLOS), 180–82

values, clash of, 1–2
Vandenberg Air Force Base, 113
Veil (Woodward), 127
Vienna, Austria, 116
Vietnam War, 89–90, 100, 105–6

Walker, Diana, 186
Walker, Mallory, 186
Wallace, David Foster, 78
Walsh, James, 60
Warner, Bruce, 106
Warner, John, 135, 187
The Washington Monthly, 186–87
The Washington Post, 193, 234n139
Watergate, Nixon and, 148–53

Watergate scandal, 140, 147–51, 159–63; government-press relationship and, 156–57; Richardson and, 103, 153, 160–63
wealth, 211, 223
Welkin, 51–54, p8
Westwood, Howard, 175
W.G. Maguire and Company, 6
White Elephant, 48, 206
White House, 110
White House tapes, 150, 153, 160–63
With, Tim, 13, 187
Wirth, Wren, 187
Who's In Control (Darman), 189
Wilson, Charlie, 35
window of vulnerability, 143
Winkelman v. General Motors Corp., 26–28
wiretaps, 153–55, 234n139, 235n140
Witcover, Jules, 151
Without Buddha, I Could Not Be a Christian (Knitter), 76–77
Wolf's Head, 99
Woodward, Bob, 127, 157
World Crisis (Churchill), 44
World War I, 223–24
World War II, 49–50, 223–24, 225
Wright, Robert, 75

yachting. *See* sailing
Yale College: age and, 233n103; as cocoon, 100; co-ed, 133; fraternities at, 95, 98–99; history at, 96–97; senior societies at, 99; Smith, Gerard, at, 42–43; Smith, John Thomas II, at, 95–101; traditional era of, 95
Yale Law Journal, 16
Yale Law School: faculty of, 102–3; Smith, Gerard, at, 46–47; Smith, John Thomas, at, 16; Smith, John Thomas II, at, 101–7; Smith family ties to, 46
Yergin, Daniel, 218
Yoder, Forrest, 18
Yom Kippur War, 160

Zagorin, Adam, 215